HUNTERS
OF THE
ARCTIC

★

ROGER FRISON-ROCHE

Translated by
LEN ORTZEN

Photographs by PIERRE TAIRRAZ

J. M. DENT & SONS (CANADA) LIMITED

Contents

PART ONE

The Indians of the Bush

1

Prologue to the Adventure

OUR PLANE was chasing the sun.

We had left France only six hours earlier, and the Boeing jet of Air France was nearing the coast of Newfoundland. Below us, the sky was speckled with light white clouds indicating fine weather, and we could see our first icebergs, like seagulls among the foam. The ocean currents appeared as transparent watermarks beneath the ice-floes; the estuary of the St Lawrence was frozen over. To the south of the great river, the wide plain was a chequer-board of snow-covered fields, with strange conical hills standing out like places of worship. To the north, the river seemed gnawed by clumps of trees on the sparsely forested Laurentian Plateau, prefiguring the barren lands.

The landscape was slipping rapidly beneath us, leaving just a few details in the mind's eye. Montreal was in sight, with its three great bridges; ocean-going steamers were trapped in the ice. A stack of skyscrapers rivalled Mont Royal.

The airport was very close now—modern and functional. They are all alike, whether at Paris, Montreal or Cairo; you see the same faces of travellers hurrying towards their destinies along endless corridors, grumbling about the slowness of Customs and delays over luggage.

However, a surprise was waiting for us. Some journalists were there to meet us, from the press, radio and television; most of them represented French-language newspapers, but a few were English-speaking. Questions were fired at us: "What have you come to

Canada for?"—"Are you going to write about Quebec?"—"About Expo 67?"—"Have you come on a lecture tour?"

My answer came like a cold shower: "We're going to film the life of the last hunting tribes—Indians and Eskimos."

"What, again? That's very French! You get your ideas of Canada from romantic novels like *Chapdelaine* and folk-songs like *Alouette*. We've finished with that, mister. Quebec is developing fast. We've a tremendous building programme . . ."

"I know, gentlemen, but other people will write about that. Every man to his own last. Another time we shall come back to learn about your Canada, the cultivated, well-populated and industrialised Canada. But right now we're off to the Northwest Territories."

The press conference ended. My Canadian colleagues swallowed their disappointment and showed me the greatest kindness. If such was my plan, then they might as well give me all the help they could. Everyone had some advice to offer, knew someone who might prove useful.

So, hardly had we set foot in Canada than we had a dozen appointments in our diaries. I do not think there can be any other country where the welcome is so warm and friendly. Even for a Frenchman! For it should not be thought that the French are held in high esteem. Canadians, especially French Canadians, regard France (and Britain, too, for that matter) as a very small country—but which claims great influence in world affairs. Seen from Canada, France is indeed very small. Canada is the second-largest country in the world, smaller than Russia but larger than China and the United States. It is bigger than the whole of Europe. But size is one thing and the life of a country another. The climate across two-thirds of Canada's three-and-three-quarter-million square miles is too cold for crop cultivation; most of the agricultural land lies along the band of territory which borders the United States.

The Province of Quebec alone is three times the size of France, but has a population of only six million. If its density of population were as high as that of Belgium, it would have five hundred million inhabitants.

In the whole of Canada there are more than twenty million inhabitants—a third of the population of Great Britain.

These figures tell a story; and in order to understand Canada and her people, and the divisions between French-speaking and English-speaking sections, one must always bear in mind the great distances. Forests, lakes and rivers cover most of the territory of these immense plateaux, which were ground by ice-age glaciers. Montreal is on latitude 45—the same as Bordeaux and Venice; but it has the same climate as Stockholm. Little more than thirty miles to the north of Montreal the sub-arctic forest-lands begin. The northern point of Ellesmere Island, on latitude 83, is 435 miles from the North Pole and 3,100 miles from Montreal. The distance between Paris and Montreal is less than between Montreal and Vancouver.

Our confusion, doubts and bewilderment will be better understood if one realises what was ahead of us in the production of our film. We had to face journeys to the ends of the earth, it seemed, across vast empty spaces that have no equal. We wondered whether we should manage to pull it off. These great distances and the sparseness of northern communication facilities made me realise why most Canadians know almost nothing of their northern territories.

Montreal is a continually expanding city where new buildings are mushrooming and skyscrapers springing up. I must confess to my shame that this was the first time I had set foot on the North American continent, so that I had no real idea of what a big Canadian city was like. However much one reads about them, the real thing is beyond imagination. I was quite stunned at the sight of those huge avenues cutting across each other at right-angles, at the gigantic buildings around Place Ville Marie, which itself constitutes an air-conditioned centre which could house a small town. I have no desire to live in a city, however beautiful, and there is plenty of choice in Europe; and they are living places, with small shops, old houses and palaces, ancient monuments, all linked by centuries of history, welded by a thousand years of human presence. Whereas Montreal had chiefly its skyscrapers, towering over the very heart of the city.

At night, everything is transformed: the city sparkles and becomes alive; it is the American fairyland of neon signs, floodlighting and thousands of shining windows. The building-sites which appear so ugly by day become pools of darkness among the columns of lighted buildings.

Montreal should be seen at night, from the top of a skyscraper or better still from Mont Royal, on a soft evening in June.

Later, on our return journey, we visited the City of Quebec, the Upper Town of which is full of old-world charm, has streets that twist about, climb hills and cut across each other at odd angles, giving views of the St Lawrence and the landscape, one of the most beautiful in the world. This is the Canada of old, whereas Montreal seems more American. People in France who still think of Canada as a French country would be disappointed, even though the French language has been carefully kept alive. The Canadians of Quebec Province speak French but are by choice part of North America.

We were going to the Northwest Territories, and as the permits we required were issued by the N.W.T. Council in Ottawa, we went to the federal capital to obtain them.

The preparations and organisation of this private expedition had already lasted more than a year. What a correspondence it had entailed with Mr Trottier, the cultural attaché at the Canadian Embassy in Paris, and with "the right man in the right place"—Mr Hyslop, the chief assistant administrator of the Northwest Territories!

Both had thought at first that, like others before me, I intended to make a kind of journalistic tour of the Arctic, travelling by scheduled airlines and staying at the many comfortable bases that exist, where I would be able to indulge in my taste for folklore. In fact, our intention was quite different. We wanted to leave the bases and to live the life of the last hunting tribes in the world; that is to say, those who even now depend entirely on hunting to provide their food and clothing and generally to keep themselves alive.

In the Canadian Arctic, these people are the Indians and the Eskimos. Books and films have made the general public in Europe and America familiar with Eskimos, especially those in Greenland; but there are still some hunting Eskimos in the Far North of Canada who have practically no contact with modern civilisation.

We had been warned, however: "You'll see, there are hardly any left. The building of the American DEW Line along the 69th parallel has caused them to settle down, and they've been quite changed by discovering the benefits of our civilisation." The most pessimistic told me: "They've degenerated a lot."

As for the Indians, the usual reply was: "What, are there still some left? Do they still wear feathers and do the scalp dance?"

The scalp dance and the head-dresses of eagles' feathers are things of the past, and the Indians now dress like anyone else who lives in the North, but there are still plenty of them in the vast expanses of the sub-arctic bush country. This is the region bordered to the south by the prairies where once the buffalo roamed and which are now the great wheat belt, and it extends north to the limit of the Tree Line, which cuts diagonally across Canada without any regard to latitude, from the southern shores of Hudson Bay to the mouth of the Mackenzie River, on latitude 69.

In the forests and plains are the Indians. In the Barren Lands, frozen all the year round, are the mainland Eskimos, sometimes known as the Caribou Eskimos.

I had neither the time nor the money to travel all over a territory which is larger than Europe from the Atlantic to the Urals. I had to make a choice, and so my plans were all prepared when I arrived at the offices of the Northwest Territories Administration in Ottawa, on a bright, cold day in early March 1966. I was warmly received and, bearing in mind the lengthy preparation which had preceded my arrival, a wonderful surprise was awaiting me. That very same day a meeting was arranged for me with the heads of the departments concerned and the experts on the Far North, the administrators and officials in charge of hunting and the game reserves, and those responsible for Indian and Eskimo affairs. So that everything became very clear and precise.

Pierre Tairraz and I decided that the best way of using our resources was to divide our expedition into two parts. We would spend March and the first half of April with the Indians, and the second half of April and the whole of May with the Eskimos. In this way, on both expeditions, we should have the winter conditions we needed.

"You're choosing the most difficult season," I was told. 'Just now, it's still thirty-five below in the region of Great Slave Lake, and forty to fifty below[1] in the Arctic. Moreover, it's the season of blizzards, which are terrible enemies. In fact, hunting conditions aren't exactly ideal."

It would have been much easier for us to have visited the Arctic in the summer, certainly. Even if there are sharp cold snaps, they do not last. There is daylight during one period for all twenty-four hours, and in July, August and September the Canadian Arctic abounds with game. But we decided that in order to give a truthful and precise picture of the life of the hunting tribes, we had to go and live with them during one of the most difficult periods of the year, such as the one that we had chosen.

How can anyone know the Sahara by crossing it in winter?

Nevertheless, it was rather rash of us! Our great experience of the Alps, where we had endured the cold blast of the north wind on Mont Blanc when the temperature was forty below, seemed sufficient training. Pierre had on several occasions spent nights in an igloo at altitudes of more than thirteen thousand feet, and I knew he could stand up to conditions of severe cold. Moreover, we had brought with us the high-altitude clothing which had been so successful in the Himalayas and the Andes.

But we had to resist the temptation to stay at trading posts and

[1] Centigrade is used throughout.

settlements. What we wanted was to take part in hunting expeditions, to participate in the life of the Indians and the Eskimos, to join in with them in their nomadic existence if possible and really try to understand them.

"It won't be too easy with the Indians," we were warned. "They are versatile and impulsive. But you'll manage all right with the Eskimos; they laugh at everything."

We were to find that the truth was quite different.

After the conference in Ottawa, arrangements were made by telephone for us to stay at Snowdrift, an Indian village on the shores of Great Slave Lake, in the Indian Affairs Hut, and to prepare our expedition from there. The appropriate people everywhere were alerted concerning our journey. In the weeks that followed, many of our difficulties were smoothed out by them.

I had no fears or qualms when we set out. "You'll see," I said to Pierre, "it will all work out as it did in the Sahara. We've got all the necessary permits and letters of introduction, but the important thing is to win the confidence and friendship of the people on the spot. If they think we're all right, they'll do everything they can for us. But if they don't take to us, we shall get an official welcome—and nothing more."

And, indeed, the friendliness of people was to help solve many of our difficulties.

The choice had fallen on Snowdrift chiefly because it is a fairly new settlement, only six or seven years old. The Canadian government has built a school, and there is also a trading post of the Hudson's Bay Company and a Roman Catholic Mission. School, trading post and Mission are the familiar trilogy of the Canadian North. The aim is to establish the Indians and the Eskimos, those eternal migrants, in order to give them some schooling, medical attention, and gradually adapt them to a new way of life. Only fifty years ago these immense areas of the Northwest Territories were practically unknown; contact with the nomadic inhabitants of the woodlands or the icefields was almost solely through the scattered posts of the Royal Canadian Mounted Police (the legendary "Mounties") and, especially, the trading posts of the "Bay". But the post-war years, the "cold war" in particular, brought many changes; the United States began to build the DEW Line, the Arctic was explored in detail, and the discovery of important mineral deposits in the Northwest led, in the past decade, to a transformation of this territory—probably similar to that of the Siberian tundra.

The era of fur-traders, missionaries and red-coated Mounties is past. A complete upheaval is taking place. A world is coming to an end and a new way of life beginning. It was time to record what might prove to be the final spasms of the primitive life of men struggling against cold and hunger.

The 2,200 miles from Montreal to Edmonton, the capital of Alberta, took four hours by plane—four hours in which we went from one world to another.

Edmonton, with a population of nearly half a million, is the West's "Gateway to the North". The city stands on a high tableland overlooking the north bank of the Saskatchewan, which is as wide and as long as the Danube. It is a rapidly growing city, the home of immigrants and nonconformism. Here, anyone who is prepared to work hard can soon make a go of it, provided he has a trade—bricklayer, carpenter, plumber, engineer. It is important to have technical ability; but there is a bright future too for intellectuals. The main campus of the University of Alberta is located in the capital. Members of the working class are beginning to have time for things of the mind, though business fever increases every day. New buildings are going up, new streets being started or existing ones extended. The Alaska Highway, which crosses the Yukon Territory, starts from here, as does the road to the Arctic, which meets the great Mackenzie River at the Township of Hay River. This is the road to gold, to rare and precious minerals, along which roll hundreds of heavy trucks.

We arrived late in the evening at the Macdonald Hotel, a first-class inn, and feared we looked shabby figures in our anoraks, woollen jerseys and breeches, among the sumptuously furnished rooms in which we found ourselves as soon as we stepped through the entrance. But we little knew the West. "Welcome!" said the doorman, covered with gold braid like an admiral. We had dinner to the strains of a chamber orchestra and in a rich setting of tapestries and candles. The mixed and congenial crowd of diners in the restaurant included couples in dinner-jackets and long evening-gowns next to a table of outdoorsmen returning from the North—or leaving for it—who were dressed in cowboy shirts and corduroy trousers. But no one took any notice. It was quite normal here.

Outside, a fine snow was falling and a strong wind was blowing.

From Edmonton, we had to take a plane belonging to a small airline which runs services to all parts of the Northwest Territories. There are ten or a dozen companies in Canada which run scheduled air-passenger services or charter aircraft. It is normal practice for people to charter a plane, small or large, and we were often to have recourse to the system, for the one and only means of travelling quickly about the North is by private plane.

Our immediate destination was Fort Smith, the administrative centre of the Mackenzie District, on latitude 60, the southern limit of the Northwest Territories. The plane was a DC-4, and the airport was in the centre of the city. The passengers had to be there fifteen minutes before departure time. We were not kept waiting and there was a minimum of formalities, chiefly over luggage—but ours was an impressive weight.

Unfortunately the cloud ceiling was very low and there was a fierce wind sending the snow scurrying across the runways. It was announced that the flight would be held over until next day. Fort Smith was "Q.G.O.", which caused no surprise. The passengers returned to their hotels, taking it all very calmly; there was no grumbling or complaining.

"That's how it is in the North," a burly man wearing a trapper's fur-hat said to me philosophically. "Sometimes you have to wait a couple of weeks."

The human cargo was a mixed bunch. There were Indians, easily recognisable although dressed like everyone else, an Eskimo family returning to Aklavik, some bulkily dressed technicians, huddled into fur-lined parkas and wearing mocassins, on their way back to their stations. As soon as we entered Edmonton airport we seemed to be in the North.

Everyone was back there the following morning, with the weather as bad as ever. But after waiting three hours, and although the ceiling was even lower than the day before, the luggage was registered and our flight was announced. The plane would apparently be able to land at Fort Smith.

It was a difficult two-hour flight for the pilot, through low cloud for much of the time. There were occasional glimpses of snow-covered fields, then the plane went down through the cloud and flew at about 1,500 feet over the forest, which extends for three thousand miles, giving no variety of view—just forest and lakes, then lakes and forest.

Canada is said to have the largest area of fresh water in the world—about 300,000 square miles.

The airstrip at Fort Smith is no more than a clearing among the fir trees, along the bank of the Slave River. The plane landed, and we stepped out; and at once the cold bit, the dry, sharp cold of the North. A magnificent avenue through the trees led us right to the centre of the town site; its wooden, one-storey buildings are spread over a wide area. There is a cathedral with a trim steeple pointing towards the grey, snow-laden sky, two shops, a Mounted Police barracks, a large high school and one hotel.

Built in frontier style, with a wooden veranda, the hotel was comfortable and well heated. Silence reigned during the day, but when the bar opened at six o'clock, things livened up. It was the general meeting-place, and Indians and whites mixed together without any racial discrimination. Indian children hung about on the veranda, looking for a chance of earning a few cents, but none of them attempted to beg.

We paid a visit to Father Pochat, an Oblate Missionary and a Savoyard like ourselves, since he comes from La Clusaz in Haute Savoie. He is in charge of the Grandin College, the fine, modern high school for boys and girls, and he showed us through it. I doubt whether any school in France is as modern and well-equipped as this one, which has everything from a large games-room (closed because of the cold) to a library. The pupils live two or three to a room, and have complete freedom, apart from the general discipline. They do not abuse this freedom; they are eager to learn, and come from all over the Northwest, from the bush country of the fur-trappers, from the Barren Lands and the shores of the Arctic. Eskimos and Indians thus learn their lessons side by side at Fort Smith.

"In five or six years from now we shall see the results of our efforts," Father Pochat told us. "Then many of the senior pupils will be ready to go on to higher education, and become engineers, doctors, technicians. It will be up to them to take over from us eventually."

Even then, a young Indian nun was in charge of the girls' department. She was tall and slender in her plain grey and white habit, and her hood ringed a face of great nobility. She was twenty-two. Her capabilities and powers of discipline were unrivalled, apparently. But sometimes the severity of her features was relieved by a slight touch of humour.

"We'll soon be sending you away," she said to Father Pochat. "We shall be capable of running the place ourselves."

"I'm relying on that," he retorted.

I remembered something similar to this sally being written forty years ago by E. Gautier in his book on the civilisations of the Maghreb (French North Africa, as it was then): "A colonisation comes to an end when the colonised people send away their colonisers." Recent events have shown that sometimes a colonised people does not wait all that long.

Father Pochat knows the Indians particularly well; one might almost call it an hereditary knowledge, for Oblate Missionaries were among the first pioneers, with trappers and prospectors, in the frozen solitudes of the Arctic. He allowed us to benefit greatly from his knowledge, as did later his fellow-missionaries whom we met in the most desolate places of our journey. He knows the ways of the Indians and the very real qualities of these people who are proud of the term natives. The way to win their friendship is to discern those qualities.

We did not intend staying long in Fort Smith. Our reason for stopping there was to see the head of the game reserves, but he and all his assistants had gone to Ottawa for a conference, except Mr Olson, the superintendent of Wood Buffalo National Park. It is the largest animal reserve in the world, half the size of France, and cuts through the northern border of Alberta, bounded on the east by the Slave River.

Mr Olson is a Canadian of Icelandic origin, nearing retirement age but still passionately interested in his job. He has made a great success of the National Park; there are now twenty thousand bison in this huge area of forest, lakes and rivers. They are the original species, heavier and taller than the prairie bison, or buffalo, as they are generally called.

"When the white man first arrived here, there were twenty million buffalo in the forests and prairies," Mr Olson told us. "A few decades ago, there were only some hundreds of them left. But now, in this reserve alone, there are more than twenty thousand, living in complete freedom in their natural surroundings and in danger only from predatory enemies and disease. And the latter is what ravages. Last summer we had to slaughter more than seven hundred buffalo attacked by an epizootic disease and burn the carcasses to prevent the disease from spreading. It was the only way to save the rest of the herds."

He gave a gentle smile. "You're going to film my buffalo, aren't you? They're the pride of Canadian wildlife."

We shook our heads; we hadn't the time, the means.

But he interrupted us. "I'll hire a plane for you tomorrow, if you like, and you can film anything you wish. The pilot will land whenever he can, I'll give him his instructions myself. You'll see the most unusual sight in the world. No one ever comes here in winter."

So, the following morning, Pierre and I climbed into a Beaver, a small but powerful aircraft, heavily built but sturdy enough to be put through any aerobatics—as we were to discover. The pilot, Chris, was a Dutchman aged twenty-five who knew the National Park well. There was a break in the weather, and we were to be lucky in that the fine spell lasted all morning.

We flew very low and could see where the snow had been trodden down by a herd, the places where the animals had gathered to graze, to get at the frozen tufts under the snow.

"There are some."

It had taken scarcely fifteen minutes to find a herd. We swooped towards them, and at once the big bull with a dark tawny mane rounded up cows and calves, and all went at a mad gallop across the clearing for the shelter of the forest. Pressed together in the form of a triangle, the youngest in the middle, the herd left behind it a wide trench more than three feet deep, with the scattered, powdery snow sparkling in the air. What a strange and wonderful sight it was! This frantic charge inevitably called to mind the exciting tales I had read when a youngster. The fleeing herd reformed, was dislodged again from the forest and galloped across a great plain which was probably a swamp in summer. We did not pursue any farther.

"It's not right to tire them out too much," said our pilot. "We'll soon find some more. There's plenty of them."

The difficulty was to film them. I had given up my seat in the cockpit to Pierre; securely strapped in, he could use his cine-camera through the open window of the door. The seat in the back of the plane had been taken out to make room for parcels and luggage. A rifle and ammunition, a pair of snowshoes and some emergency rations were carefully stowed right at the back in case of a forced landing. All I had to sit on was my pack containing spare clothing. For the next four hours I was tossed about like a parcel during the most extraordinary display of aerobatics that I have ever been submitted to. Each time we sighted another herd of buffalo, it started all over again. The plane dived, made a wide sweep to make the herd turn in a circle, then flew over it several times, swooping, banking, looping the loop, making figures of eight and doing a roll or two. In order to assist Pierre, the pilot performed these aerobatics at the slowest possible speed, between 85 and 125 miles per hour. But it was still much too fast to take detailed photographs. However, Pierre was getting different shots each time we flew over a herd; and we had a better sight of the tawny manes, humps and steaming muzzles, the stamping hooves sending the snow flying in all directions.

"Can you land near a herd?" Pierre asked the pilot.

"Impossible," he cried. "The snow is soft and too deep, and then there are tree-stumps—I daren't risk it. You need a helicopter."

A great pity.

"Look—moose!" Chris exclaimed.

We caught sight of two of the largest grazing animals in the world in a small clearing. They stood more than six feet at the withers, had legs like stilts, huge heads, muzzles with drooping lips and flapping ears. Ugly animals, but endowed with incredible strength. We were seeing these at the worst possible moment, for they had shed the magnificent antlers which give balance to the massive body and make the moose the king of the Canadian forest.

Thus were the mysteries of the forest revealed to us. It stretched beyond the horizon on all sides, bristling with conifers; a few deciduous trees were clinging to the edges of the frozen ponds and lakes. Vehicle tracks appeared beneath our wings; we followed them and came upon a yellow snowmobile, one of the famous Bombardiers that are used for transportation in the northern snow. The men in it were probably forest rangers, on their daily tour of inspection. They waved to us, but we were already passing over another lake, another stretch of forest. We saw a pack of wolves, about a dozen, with a big grey one squatting on a snow-covered hillock, keeping watch. They scattered at the approach of our plane, making off in irregular bounds and sometimes disappearing for a moment in the deep layer of snow. But the big grey wolf stayed to keep guard over a dead buffalo. The pack had been gorging after its successful hunt.

Sometimes the wolves multiply to the point of becoming a nuisance. That winter, in fact, only fifty miles or so north of Montreal and Quebec, they had killed many head of deer. But in the forest, where there is so much game, the wolves play a useful role. Certainly, they kill, but they generally pull down old or worn-out animals that have strayed from the herd. And they clean up the bush, devouring the numerous carcasses which escape the human eye but not the wolves' sense of smell.

During the short time we were at Fort Smith a wolf came into the town every night and went through garbage cans. Parents were advised not to let their children play outside late in the evening, although dangerous encounters between man and wolf are extremely rare.

Pierre had filmed several herds of bison and a few moose, and we were returning to base with these wonderful sights still vivid in our minds.

"There's a herd in just the right formation," cried Pierre. "Make one more run, Chris, will you?"

The buffalo were resting in the middle of a large clearing; we were able to fly low over them several times before they reached the shelter of the forest. The aerobatics began again. Pierre leaned sideways with his camera, giving orders to the pilot, and the plane passed over the fleeing, compact mass of animals at a height of only a few score feet. It seemed as though one of the wings was scraping their backs. There came a jerk, the plane zoomed abruptly—there was a rush of cold air into the cabin and I found myself hanging half out of the plane, held by the legs, having luckily spread them wide in a quick reflex action. The door had swung open as I was thrown against it. I clung to the fuselage, yelling. The other two turned to look, and burst out laughing. Chris quickly banked the plane the other way, and I fell back into the cabin. It was all over in ten seconds, and after a moment of stupor I laughed like the others. There had been no time to feel frightened, and anyway how could one be frightened when two youngsters were laughing their heads off? It was a great joke!

I fastened the door with a length of string. This was the North. It was all in a day's work for the pilot, who flew in every kind of weather over this endless forest where one area is like any other, almost brushing the tops of the fir trees, landing on a frozen river or lake in an emergency, then shooting game for food and to pass the time while waiting for help to arrive. We were to meet several of these free-lance pilots during the next few weeks, all courageous young men fond of freedom and ever ready to take off on any kind of scientific or rescue mission: Good Samaritans of the North. A fine life for a flier with mechanical skill and versatility, daring, stamina and keenness—for there are very few days when flying conditions are good.

When we landed again at Fort Smith we felt we had made a step forward in our accumulation of knowledge. Some of the secrets of the great forest, its abundant game, herds of wild buffalo and packs of wolves, had been revealed to us from the air; and in a few days we should be penetrating it on foot, making contact with the Indians and trappers who lived by hunting, as others had done before them for centuries.

That evening an odd sort of man came to see us at the hotel. His age might have been sixty-five. He had an untidy beard and was wearing mocassins, thick canvas trousers, a sweater and fur-lined parka, and a cap made from the pelt of a muskrat. He walked into our room without knocking and looked at us with curiosity.

"I heard some Frenchmen had arrived at the hotel, so I've come to see you," he told us, speaking French, "Are you going prospecting?" He uttered the last word in English.

"Going what?"

"Prospecting—looking for minerals. Unless you're drilling for oil? But the oil is farther north, where the Eskimos live. Down here, it's gold, copper and rare metals."

He spoke with the rough accent of countrymen in south-east France.

"You're from the Dauphiné, aren't you?" I said.

"I come from near Vienne, in the Rhône valley."

"How long is it since you were last in France?"

"I went back a few years ago, then I returned here; but if I don't strike it lucky in a year or so, I'm leaving again."

We found out later that he is always talking of going back to France, but can never make up his mind. One of these days he will be found frozen to death at the foot of a tree, like the man in the tale he told us. For he had not come to question us but to tell us the story of his life, and we had to sit and listen while he went on and on with his slow recital in a voice as rough as mountain rapids, mixing so many English mining words with his French as to make almost a new language.

Gold was what he lived for. He had struck gold several times, but always the vein had soon given out. For thirty years he had travelled the bush with his sled and dogs and sticks of dynamite. Now it was not just nuggets that he was after, but a big strike, a deep vein which he would sell to an American company.

His eyes shone while he talked, and he was possessed by this passion for gold. Not so much for the wealth and life of ease that it would bring him, no; his joy was in finding the precious metal, in fondling a nugget and weighing it in his hand.

As he talked, I could see his domain through the misted window, that dark mass of forest which was all around us, right into the town site.

He enquired again as to what we had come to do.

"To film the Indians and live with them in the bush."

He roared with laughter. "And you think you'll make dollars with that?"

"That" was our mad project—coming here for nothing, without any ambition to make dollars. He looked at us pityingly, and stared at me. Obviously, I was getting on a bit, and his look seemed to say: *In any case, it's too late for you. You need to come out here when you're still young, as I did thirty years ago. You'll never last out. As for going among the Indians! To go out of curiosity, all right. But for Pierre, a strong and energetic young man, to lend himself to such a sorry business . . .*

He shook his head, and returned to his favourite subject. "Ah, when you really strike gold!"

He was silent for a moment, entranced. "When you find a deep vein—not one that's rich on the surface, for it soon gives out, but one that goes deep and gets bigger, and each drilling confirms that you've struck it real rich—then you have to hurry and stake your claim, so that the big companies can't swindle you. Then you've got gold, mister. And the dollars come flowing into your hands like a river—and you're one of the great of this earth."

"Do you know many who've succeeded like that?"

He mentioned some names; they had all been poor wretches like himself, having had a hundred narrow escapes from dying of hunger, or being frozen to death in a blizzard.

"There was Big Bill. For thirty years he had been roaming the bush, always hungry and poor. He was a skilful trapper, he'd married an Indian, and then one day when he was out hunting he made a lucky strike. All at once, he was rich, very rich. And it turned his head. He still lived in the bush, where he'd had a house built, but now and again he hired a plane on the spur of the moment and flew off to Providence or Yellowknife or Edmonton. For several days he'd never be sober. And then there were the women. Ah, he liked his women—that's what did him in the end. One day he took a plane to go to a dance down south; it was winter, and he was wearing thin shoes, a silk shirt and a fine new suit, but not even a parka. There was no point—he'd only be an hour in the plane, and the cabin was heated.

"Money had gone to his head, you see, and he'd forgotten all about the dangers of the forest. If he'd gone with his dogs . . . But just think, in a plane . . . Then it happened, some mechanical trouble, and the pilot made a forced landing on a frozen lake—right out in the middle, so that he could be spotted from a distance. It was seventy below; a blizzard got up. The pilot stayed in the cabin and shared out the emergency rations. But Bill wanted to take to the bush, to his old life. 'Come into the forest,' he said to the pilot. 'We'll make a fire, go hunting.' The pilot refused. 'If there's a break in the weather for only a quarter of an hour, that can be enough to save us,' he said. 'Please yourself,' replied Bill.

"And off he went, taking the axe. But he didn't get very far—about two miles. He had on his thin shoes and silk shirt. When he was found a couple of months later, he was lying half-naked and covered with snow, still clutching wads of bills that he'd been burning one by one—all high values, fifty and one hundred dollars. The charred bits were still scattered all round him. The pilot was rescued a few days after the accident."

There was silence in the room. We could hear the wind shrieking round the hotel, making the wood creak. The temperature had dropped to fifty below a week before.

The man's thoughts were still on his story. "Yes, he'd burnt his money as he lay dying. It was as if he'd wanted to tell us that all the gold in the world wasn't worth as much as a good fire and a juicy haunch of caribou."

"And you yourself—you must have had many adventures? The cold, the wolves . . ."

"You need to beware of wolves," he said. "But you'll be with Indians, and they know."

"There won't be any risk as we'll have dogs with us?"

He laughed. "Dogs all flee from the wolf. No animal in the

North attacks the wolf—not even the polar bear. Sometimes a wolf gets ripped open by a slashing horn or a kick from a hoof, but nearly always the wolf is the victor."

"Do they attack men?"

"No. At least, not unless they're starving—or because they get an idea in their heads. You never know. Ah, the wolf's an intelligent animal."

I could see another tale coming. We waited for him to gather his thoughts. He was reliving his past, the hours and days spent away from the industrial world. He had not stirred on his chair, just sat there smoking his pipe.

"About fifty miles from here," he began, "there was a woodcutter who lived alone with his dog, a fine, big dog. When he came into town on snowshoes, the dog often had a load on its back, forty pounds or so. The dog and its master got on well together. One day, the woodcutter struck gold, in a rocky gorge a few miles from his cabin. Every morning he went off with a pick and dynamite, and stayed there all day, digging to see how deep the vein went. He wanted to know if it was worth exploiting. This took him weeks and weeks, and every day at the same time he passed along the narrowest part of the gorge, where the bush was dense. The dog followed him along the trail, or went ahead, a few yards' distance. They never met anything dangerous.

"But one day the dog came into town alone, still with a load on its back and completely exhausted. Something had obviously happened to its master. The Mounties and the Fathers set out, the dog leading the way, and they found the poor fellow's body, half-eaten by a wolf. It was quite clear what had happened. The wolf had kept watch for days, hidden in the thick undergrowth, seeing the man and his dog go past regularly. It's full of low cunning, a wolf is. It knew the dog was easy meat; what it wanted was the man. When it knew the gold-prospector's route and habits, it jumped on him one morning from a rock where it was hiding. The man had just had time to hear his dog give a howl, to see it dart away with its

Bison in Wood Buffalo National Park

hair standing on end, but before he could get at his rifle he was knocked down by the wolf.

"It was rotten luck, but even the most knowing get caught like that."

"When are you going back to France?" I asked him.

"In the fall. I'm giving myself until then to know if my dig is a good one. Afterwards, I'm going back home."

He got up from the chair. "Well, it's been nice talking with Frenchmen again. It's done me good. *Adieu.*"

He left as he had come in, without shaking hands, shyly and warily.

"Poor wretch," I said. "For thirty years he's been living on dreams, the dreams of gold-miners. He'll never see France again."

"It might be better for him if he doesn't."

Later on, we heard the truth about him. He had been looking for gold for many years, but he was a lumberman too, and was still a crafty peasant type. He owned several trucks and tractors and had a good timber business. He was quite a rich man, in fact, yet his life was just as miserable as when he had first arrived in the backwoods. He will never return home to France because all he wants is to strike gold, the big vein—the one that would at once put him among the great of this earth. And all the profits from his timber business are poured into the bottomless drilling operations, without producing any result.

In the evening, in the bar—the saloon—I looked at the colourful crowd of customers, the trappers, prospectors and officials. Over a beer or a whisky, they talked of their ambitions, their dreams—of the vein they would find one day, the big strike; and they made the gesture of weighing a lump of yellow ore in the hand.

The gold-rush is not a thing of the past, but the form of it has changed. None of those poor fellows and their like will ever strike it rich—although there have been one or two amazing discoveries. The men who will profit are seated comfortably in leather chairs in offices of banks and financial companies at Edmonton or Calgary. From there, they organise the setting up of large base-camps, where engineers, geologists, physicists and technicians make united efforts to prospect over a wide area. Actually, they are more interested in copper and uranium and other indispensable ores than in gold.

But there will always be solitary men living in the forest and look-ing for the invisible rich vein of gold until the end of their days, in a lonely pine cabin when they no longer have the strength to set traps, shoot game and tend a fire.

The forest is the background to many strange adventures. Here is one that was told to me that same evening in the hotel bar.

For nearly twenty years a strange educated man had been living alone in the woods; he was said to be wealthy, and it became known afterwards that he belonged to an English titled family. He had first come to the Canadian North with an organised hunting expedition of the kind laid on for millionaires. But when the others had returned home he had stayed, tired of the futile social round and attracted by the simple life. He decided to spend the rest of his life in this bound-less forest where the solitude reigns, where one can hike for days on end and see nothing but lakes, rivers, trees, but where each step brings one into contact with wildlife, with animals which lead the freest existence on earth: moose, buffalo, caribou, bears and wolves. He became a trapper, and not just in name. His cabin was no different from those of the poor devils he sometimes met on the trail when out with his dogs and sled. His dogs were well trained, and he lived as poorly as his neighbours. Admittedly, he had some books, not a great number but a good selection; before withdrawing from the world he had probably decided on the books which made a "desert island choice". He remained a cultured man to his finger-tips; and, amazingly, the Indians and white trappers valued his knowledge, they who have always sought to probe the secrets of nature, of life and death. They respected his solitude.

And so the years went by and the mysterious "lord" was just a trapper like the others, occasionally going to the trading-post of the Bay to get supplies, exchanging his skins of muskrats, martens and foxes for flour, salt, gunpowder and cartridges, like any Chipewyan Indian. He had found peace of mind.

But a day came when he felt a drawback to his lonely state. Not that he was in any way dissatisfied himself; he was still determined to remain in the depths of the forest for the rest of his days. But he felt he ought to find someone to succeed him; someone who would continue to enjoy this great peace and serene happiness when he had departed. In short, he felt the need for an apprentice. So he made the journey to England and saw his family; one of his nephews, a young man of twenty, seemed to have the necessary qualities. He was idealistic and romantic, cultured and athletic—and so became the uncle's elected. Physical strength and a high moral code were equally necessary to live as he did. Loneliness is supportable only if one has a deep inner life; to live alone, one needs to be capable of meditating.

The nephew accompanied him back to Canada, and soon there were two living in the cabin. It was summer, fishing was good and there was plenty to eat. Then came winter, a terrible winter. The cold was intense, fog was continuous, and a howling wind swept over the forest, bending the trees in a tumult that seemed as if the Last Judgment had come.

The young man went out with his uncle, who showed him how to set traps, to keep off the wolverines that gobble everything up, and to fish for lake-trout by slipping a net under the ice. But the young man was awkward; perhaps he thought he would never make a good hunter and skilful woodsman. His uncle chopped wood every day, stocking up to keep the fire going continuously; he went out on snowshoes, visiting his traps, and was ever on the watch for game, for a moose that had strayed from the herd and whose dried and smoked meat would enable the two of them to keep famine at bay throughout the winter. Every other day he went fishing to feed his dogs. In fact, he never stopped but was active throughout the long arctic night, leading the same existence as the Indians with their trap lines thirty or forty miles away.

The tragic accident occurred in mid-winter.

The chief tool of the Indian and the trapper is the axe. It is used for everything, for breaking the ice, felling trees, cutting up carcasses and planting stakes. The Indian wields it with a skill that makes one tremble for him; standing on a felled tree, he slices at the trunk and cuts his logs. Sometimes he cuts himself too. The cold is so intense in winter, in this region between Lake Athabasca and the Great Slave Lake, that an axe can break on a tree, for the tree itself gets frozen to the heart.

One day when the trapper-lord was chopping wood he cut his leg badly. The nearest infirmary was a fortnight's journey by dog-sled. He could not be carried that far, in any case. With the cold, his wound soon became gangrenous, and a few days later he died in the presence of his nephew, who was probably still unaware of the full extent of the tragedy.

He placed his uncle's body on the shelf where the meat was put to dry, out of reach of animals, and then wondered what to do next. He knew he would get lost if he set out alone for the nearest post; the best thing was to stay and wait for an Indian or a trapper to pass by. There was still a stock of food in the cabin. He had half-watched his uncle making bannock, or flat cakes of buckwheat, and frying them over the stove. He tried, but merely obtained some unpleasant dough; however, he ate it.

Before long, the stock of dried meat and pemmican gave out. He had not gone hunting for a month. He had always been with his uncle, and everything had then seemed so easy. His uncle could read the signs like any Dog-Rib Indian and knew all the habits and tricks of the dwellers of the forest. The nephew set out to try his luck, but dared not go far from the cabin. He felt stifled, hemmed in, when alone in the forest; he was aware of the invisible presence of a thousand famished beasts seeking their prey. There were wolves roaming round the cabin, approaching nearer each day. He set traps, or tried to; all he caught were martens and weasels, excellent for their furs but no good as food. He tracked moose, but could not get near enough to them, as he had never learned to move silently through the forest.

Then his morale broke; he completely lost confidence, was stricken by fear and shut himself up in the cabin. Sunk in despair, he waited for death to overtake him, incapable as he was of keeping himself alive in the forest from which other men obtained their food. He was found by chance in the spring, stretched out in front of the dead hearth, frozen. His uncle's body was still on the shelf, looking peaceful and serene.

Thus did the young aristocrat die because he did not know how to live like the hunters of the forest.

The above is a true story, and it happened only a few years ago in the Upper Mackenzie district, where nature is so lovely in summer than one can imagine oneself in an earthly paradise. But it happened in winter, which is implacable.

In a few hours we should be leaving Fort Smith for Yellowknife.

"The plane will leave at three o'clock," Mr Olson told us.

"What, in all this cloud and with this wind?"

"Our pilots are used to worse. If they took off only when the weather was fine, they wouldn't do very much! Well, what did you think of my buffalo? Are you pleased?"

"Indeed! And most grateful to you. We've made a fascinating contact with the forest. Now we're eager to go into it on foot and live in it."

"I can understand that, and I envy you. But come back in the fall. Then you'll see leaves and flowers everywhere, and birds, masses of birds, and russet and golden foliage that makes a lovely setting and goes well with the tawny manes of the buffalo."

"You're not a poet, Mr Olson, are you?"

What a silly thing to say! Mr Olson comes from Iceland, the country of sagas, of poetic tales that give an epic quality to life.

He insisted on coming to the airstrip with us. Father Pochat was there to see us off, too; he gave us the names and addresses of friends and colleagues at Yellowknife.

"Your equipment seems good to me, but your footwear. . . ." he said in a bantering tone; "I shouldn't like to run behind my dogs in shoes like yours. Still, Father Marec will advise you."

Our shoes were our great pride. We had bought them at Chamonix; they were specially made for climbing in winter, were guaranteed at forty below, had thick rubber soles, and another light pair made of crylon and felt were fitted inside them—all quite perfect, and expensive. But when we had put them on at Fort Smith, everyone had looked at them askance.

"Can you really walk in those things? They're not too heavy?"

The Indians sniggered, the trappers laughed openly. They all went about silently and with supple tread in their deerskin mocassins, much lighter than town shoes.

"You see!" I said to Pierre. "We ought to fit ourselves out on the spot. When I was in Lapland I was as warm as anything in *skallers* made of reindeer skin."

"We'll see, we'll see."

Pierre is very methodical, which does not mean he is orderly, for he is always looking for the cover of his camera. Each time he finishes taking photographs he gives a yell: "The cover. Where have you put the cover?"

"It's in your hand."

"Oh, so it is."

He is as strong and tough as a mountain guide, as befits one whose father, grandfather and great-grandfather were mountain guides. He has made a name for himself in the realm of films and television, and learned his art from his father, Georges Tairraz, the great photographer of Alpine scenes.

Georges had been sad to see us leave without him, but he is now past the age for long expeditions; for forty years he took part in all the most difficult mountaineering photographic expeditions. I should certainly have liked him to accompany me again, as in the Sahara, where he took the illustrations for my book *Le Grand Désert* and made a film. But at least the team was not broken up; Pierre had been with us to help take the pictures for *Sur les traces de Premier de Cordée* and *Gens des Neiges et Vallées Blanches.* He was the cameraman for several television films, notably the climbing of the Eiffel Tower by mountaineers, and of the southern face of the Aiguille du Midi in a snowstorm. Another of his television successes was the filming of the descent into the subterranean caves at Pierre-Saint-Martin.

I look upon Pierre as a friend more than anything, a young friend of the same age as my children. He had not hesitated a moment when I asked him if he would like to accompany me on this expedition.

"How many shall we be?"

"Two—you and me."

He laughed. "The head and the legs."

"You'll be the head and legs combined, only too often. Would you like someone else to come along?"

"We'll do better with just the two of us. We make a good pair."

This mutual understanding between young and old was wonderful. It brightened the long journey we had come to make.

But to return to the plane waiting to fly us from Fort Smith to Yellowknife. . . .

A fine snow was falling, yet it was still very cold, about twenty below. The cloud ceiling was no more than three hundred feet, and the fir trees were sixty feet high; though as we flew north they would diminish in size.

The plane was an old, two-engined Beech-craft which could take eight passengers. It served the towns and settlements around Great Slave Lake, and would land at Fort Resolution and Hay River before taking us to Yellowknife. These place-names evoked the age of exploration and the opening up of the arctic regions; they conjured up gold-miners, fur-trappers, Indians.

We said goodbye to Father Pochat and Mr Olson as though leaving old friends. The plane took off, the fir trees slipped past to left and right, and then we banked to pass over the Slave River, a wide ribbon of ice containing many little islands bristling with spruce trees. The pilot was flying along a tunnel between tree-tops and low cloud, a turbulent wind-tunnel in which the plane was tossed about; but everyone in the cabin was quite calm. Besides ourselves, there were two young girls going to rejoin their parents at Yellow-knife, a forest ranger returning to his post, and two Indians travelling for the fun of it. The old man belonged to the Slave tribe and was curious about everything. He kept pointing to the forest which was speeding under us like rows of sharp, dangerous stakes, then suddenly giving way to a clearing with buffalo bounding across it. He noticed everything down there—the tracks of wolves, of moose, of a trapper on snowshoes. He sat smoking his pipe, estimating the distance.

"In the past," he said to me, "it took three days and nights on the trail with a dog-sled to cover the distance we're now doing in forty minutes."

We put down briefly at Resolution, which is little more than a trading post. The two Indians got out and two others got in. Then the plane flew westward, over the southern shore of Great Slave Lake. On one hand was the great stretch of ice, on the other the forest with large quadrilateral clearings here and there, showing the areas of claims.

There are new and prosperous mines at Pine Point. The ore is sent by boat to Hay River, and then transported by rail, by a new line specially built to serve this developing region. Hay River, built where the river of that name flows into the lake, is destined to become a strategic town in the Northwest Territories, being at once a port, a railway and highway terminus, and situated in the new mining region of the Mackenzie District. The town stands on the permafrost, ground frozen to a great depth and which thaws only a matter of inches on the surface during the short, warm Arctic summer. The buildings, as at Yellowknife, are little concerned to be absolutely upright and lean in all directions.

We took off again and flew over the port where large barges were hauled up on land or had been caught in the ice, and were now waiting for the thaw in order to sail again down the long Mackenzie River to the Arctic Ocean. The weather was not showing any improvement. Each time the plane landed we stepped outside for a few minutes, but the biting cold drove us quickly back to the heated cabin.

We flew across Great Slave Lake at its widest point. As with everything else in this country, when mentioning a Canadian lake one has to seek a comparison. This lake is larger than Belgium or Holland—a real inland sea, swept by storms of great violence in summer. There are numerous wooded islands scattered about its surface; boats sail on it in summer, sleds glide across the ice in winter. Fish abound in Great Slave Lake, but there is little fishing on a commercial scale.

We reached the northern shore in the calm of an evening which lingered on. The wind had dropped and the clouds were clearing from the sky as our plane landed at the fine airport a few miles from Yellowknife.

The landscape had changed; the beautiful arctic forest of vigorous firs—comparable to those of northern Finland, where the landscape is very similar—had come to an end on the southern shores of the great lake. On the northern side was a chaos of granite moraines and small rocky slopes separated by open spaces that were really small lakes; the forest had become the sub-boreal bush, and here consisted of spruce trees that grew as straight as a candle but had very short branches. The farther one travels north or west towards the barren lands, so the spruce diminish in size, becoming no more than straight poles sheathed in branches less than a foot in length.

North of Yellowknife the Arctic really begins—the land where little grows, except for a few stunted willows in sheltered hollows and the moss and lichens on reddish rocks, which are among the oldest on earth. In May and June a surprising array of arctic flowers colours the landscape.

"Yellowknife" was derived from the name of an Indian tribe, the Yellowknives, which was completely wiped out, crushed between the warring and more numerous Chipewyans to the east, Crees to the south and Dogribs to the west. Their name was due to the fact that they had worked the copper diggings in their area, to make tools and weapons. But there was gold among the copper, and now there are two mines exploiting the yellow ore; one of them is within a short distance of Yellowknife, the other is fifty miles to the north. To them is due the development and growth of Yellowknife, the gold capital of the Northwest, built round a sheltered cove.

The aeroplane has brought great changes to the Northwest Territories, abolishing distance. The waterways can be used only during the short summer season of from six to eight weeks. Frequent portages may be necessary and roads non-existent. In 1966, however, a highway was completed linking Yellowknife with Edmonton. The exploration and exploitation of these virgin regions, practically uninhabited, have been made possible on a wider scale. Their mineral wealth is a rich asset.

At the time we were there, the population of Yellowknife was about three thousand, of whom more than half were white men, employed by the mining companies or running the thriving trade of the town. There are two fine hotels, wooden buildings with large saloons and shops. They are always full. The bedrooms are functional, overheated, completely quiet, each with a bathroom and telephone. Such comfortable accommodation is unexpected in northern latitudes. The clientele is much more varied than at Fort Smith, which seems a small village by comparison.

Everyone and everything on the way to the Far North and the Canadian Arctic seems to go through Yellowknife; it is practically a compulsory stopover. Every day, groups of prospectors arrive or leave. Every evening the saloon is filled with a convivial gathering of mining engineers, geologists, pilots, army officers, officials, traders and dealers, with a sprinkling of old-timers, trappers and Indians and half-breeds. The talk is always of gold and copper and oil—oil from the flat islands in the extreme North of Canada.

One cannot help wondering what the cost must be, not just in salaries but for transport especially. Heavy equipment can be sent by barge down the Mackenzie River to the Arctic for only a few weeks of the year; the rest of the time, it has to go by plane.

Pierre and I were in the bar one evening, wearing our mountaineers' jerseys, when we noticed an alert young man looking at us from a neighbouring table where he was sitting with friends.

"Hello, you're French!" he exclaimed, seeing my tricolour badge. "And Savoyards too—that's the badge of mountain guides." His face glowed with surprise and pleasure. "What the devil are you doing here?"

We introduced ourselves.

His name was Thierriaz and he was a geophysicist with a big French company that was about to start drilling operations on Mackenzie King Island, near the North Pole. His home was at Passy —not the district in Paris but the town in Haute Savoie only a dozen miles from Chamonix—and his father was a mountain guide too.

How extraordinary these chance meetings sometimes were, more than six thousand miles from home! We had already met Father Pochat who came from La Clusaz and had been to school with Pierre at Thônes. And we were to have other meetings just as surprising.

Thierriaz and his companions had been stuck here for a week, waiting for a big freight plane to come from Resolute. But a blizzard was blowing up there, and the plane was grounded.

"It's still sixty below, up there," he told us.

We all talked about our hopes and plans, exchanged information and compared equipment.

"Be careful of static electricity," warned a young American cameraman with the polar expedition. "One little spark, and it can spoil a whole roll of film without you noticing."

The whole place was electrified. There was not only electricity in the air but in people's behaviour, in the way they lived and acted, going off on a three-thousand-mile journey on the spur of the moment, and with less thought than Londoners or New Yorkers who go to the coast for the day. However, the electricity was chiefly in the air. Our hotel was a reserve of static electricity. You put the key in the lock, and you got a shock; you switched on the light, and got another shock; you turned on the tap in the bathroom, and you leapt in the air. There was more swearing during the four days we stayed at this hotel than during the whole of our travels. The trick was always to have a key or some metal object with you; by giving it a sharp little tap, you could discharge the table, camera or washbasin. The hotel staff were used to it; but we needed more time.

The pride of the hotel was in the dining-room. One wall was covered with a huge white bear-skin quite twelve feet long—a record. As we were hoping to film live polar bears on the icefields, it made us think a bit.

"Must have been a size," murmured Pierre.

"Do you see its claws?"

"While it was making a meal of you, I'd have time to film it," he joked.

"There's nothing to laugh about," said Thierriaz. "Last summer, on Mackenzie King Island, we had a man dragged from his tent by a bear. Have you got firearms?"

We looked at each other and laughed. "Why should we need firearms?"

The others obviously thought we were crazy.

"We haven't come here to kill game but to film it," I said. "Besides, the Indians and the Eskimos will no doubt be armed and can protect us."

They were still not convinced. We must have been the first to arrive in the region without firearms.

However, all this conversation was very friendly and pleasant. Everyone here knew the backwoods, the Indians, the hard life in winter; and the fact that we had come simply to share this life readily earned us their friendship. They all wanted to help us.

And we greatly needed this help. Our expedition would really begin after leaving Yellowknife, and our only knowledge of the region came from a few books and the information given to us in Ottawa. The Northwest Territories Administration had asked Mr Murdoch to look after us. He was apparently a most charming man and very hospitable, and also knew the region and its climate, its fauna and its inhabitants better than anyone. Mr Murdoch was the Northern Affairs officer at Yellowknife; but he had been suddenly called to Ottawa for a conference on Indian Affairs. So we should not see him, though I was to hear his friendly voice over the telephone, wishing us a good trip, just before we left Yellowknife. Though he was not present himself, it was thanks to him that preparations had been made for us.

There are many Roman Catholic and Anglican missions all over the Northwest. The former are in the care of Oblate missionaries, most of whom are French—from France—and a few are German or Belgian. The Catholic mission at Yellowknife was in the charge of Father Le Moat, a Breton from Quimper, and Father Marec, another Breton, but from Morlaix, who was a specialist in Indian affairs and had lived for many years at Snowdrift, which was our next destination.

"In Murdoch's absence, go and see Marec," we had been advised at Fort Smith.

It is wonderful to find no hostility whatever between state officials and the missionaries. I should add that the work of the latter, whose predecessors were for many years the only white people in these parts, and their excellent knowledge of the Indian dialects

make them indispensable auxiliaries to the officials of the federal
government, who were later in arriving in the region.

I telephoned to Father Marec at the Mission, and had said only a
few words when he cut in with: "Right, I see what it's about. I'll
be over straight away."

Five minutes later, he was at our hotel.

Father Marec is an amazing person. One would never take him
for a priest, just to look at him. We saw before us an athletic man
of about forty with a face deeply lined by the cold and the wind.
With his muskrat cap, parka, and wearing embroidered Indian
mukluks on his feet, he looked just what I had imagined a Canadian
backwoodsman to be from reading Jack London, James Fenimore
Cooper, and our own Maurice Constantin-Weyer. Those books I
had read as a boy came vividly back to mind; what I was discovering
confirmed the accuracy of their descriptions of life here. Except for
the introduction of the aeroplane, nothing seems to have changed.
Men of the same frontier stamp are found, and their pursuits
are still unusual compared with those of men in the urban areas
far to the south. Of course, Father Marec and his colleagues
have not come and buried themselves in these northern wastes in
order to make dollars, but through love of their fellowmen. They
do not look for happiness in riches, but find it in teaching the true
sense of life to the Indians and Eskimos, to the hardy outdoor
people around them. What interests them is the effort to improve
the way of life of these people in the icy solitudes, to lead them
gradually to better conditions; but at the same time they honour the
respect of Indians and Eskimos for their own cultures. The missionaries are in no hurry; their idea is to proceed by stages. This is
one difference of opinion between them and the Canadian government administrators, who are equally concerned with the welfare
of the Indians and the Eskimos but who would like to proceed
somewhat faster.

The future will tell, and very soon, which of these two tendencies
is the better. By going too fast, there is a risk of turning the Indians

and even more so the Eskimos, into dependants. They are worthy of more than that; they should be educated to assist in the running of their own regional affairs. But this touches on a critical problem: paternalism—and this in a country which to all appearances is among the least colonialist in its attitude (Canada had some harsh things to say about France at the time of the war in Algeria). The missionaries I spoke to are not in agreement with this official paternalism, and some of them are the most forward-looking and enlightened people I have ever met. (It must be added that government programmes are being revised.)

Father Marec sized us up—myself, with my insufferable self-confidence, then Pierre, an athletic figure looking no more than a grown lad. Father Pochat's recommendation was probably good enough, but Father Marec wanted to hear from us just what our projects were.

I told him: "To live with the Indians, go hunting with them, try to get to know them directly, without all that guardedness on their part when dealing with people sent to them with official references. We want to break through that suspicious attitude."

"I see what you mean," he said. "It's a good idea. But do you realise what you're in for? Dog-sleds are fine in books"—he gave me an amused glance—"but not so fine in real life. You'll be very cold, terribly cold. Nobody who's travelled on one can say he's never been cold on a dog-sled, and just now it's thirty-five below. Look outside."

Through the frosted windows of our hotel bedroom we could see the blizzard sweeping across the wide, deserted streets. The very few passers-by were huddled in their furs and darted from the sheltered corner of one building to the next, trying to keep out of the wind. There were great black crows—the largest I have ever seen, larger than African crows—perched on the telephone wires, waiting for night to fall to search the garbage cans. Yellowknife seemed a gloomy, mournful place; yet I had a view of the undulating white hillside festooned with stunted conifers, around which the

ARCTIC OC

ALASKA

VICTO
ISLA

Mackenzie River

INDIANS

PACIFIC OCEAN

Yellowknife
Ba
Snowdri
Ft.Smith

Edmonton

Vancouver

KEY
───── Tree line
------ By Indian sled
·········· By Eskimo sled
───→ By air

Route taken by the expedition

NORTH POLE

80°

0   200   400   600 miles

ARCTIC CIRCLE

GREENLAND

Eureka

ELLESMERE ISLAND

105 Resolute

BAFFIN LAND

Iglöölik

Frobisher Bay

ake

HUDSON
BAY

Fort Chimo

ATLANTIC OCEAN

Montreal

snow was swirling madly. The sky was very clear and the sun was shining, though there was no warmth in it. No, this was not a gloomy land; hard and cruel, yes, but one can become attached to it.

"I realise that you know the Sahara and Lapland very well," Father Marec said, "and I've heard of your young companion, of course. All the same, you must be very careful. The cold here can be fatal. Is your equipment good?"

We got out our sleeping-bags, quilted jackets, top-clothes made of nylon, our gloves, and showed them to him with enthusiasm. He has always worn thick cloth and furs, heavy clothing but most suitable for these northern climates. He was sceptical about our equipment; it seemed much too light. "And you think that will do?" he said.

"I've bivouacked several times on the summit of Mont Blanc when it was forty below," said Pierre, "and I slept out in the open, on the snow, in this sleeping-bag."

"In that case . . ." Father Marec did not insist. But he suddenly said: "Show me your footwear."

We produced, though with some misgivings this time, our splendid shoes for climbing in winter. He turned them over several times, admiring the skill and talent of the craftsman, then shook his head.

"You'll never manage to walk on snowshoes or run behind the dogs with these on your feet. Take my advice and buy some mukluks."

These are light mocassins made of canvas or caribou skin with soles of moose-leather.

"It's too late to do anything about it this evening," he said. "Tomorrow is Sunday, I shall be too busy. I'll come and see you on Monday, and we'll get all the things you still need. But where are you going to stay at Snowdrift?"

"Mr Murdoch must have seen to that."

A telephone call to the Northern Affairs office confirmed that Mr Murdoch had seen to everything before leaving for Ottawa.

"He's an amazing fellow, Peter Murdoch," said Father Marec. "You've been given the Indian Affairs Hut; it's available just now. As for your cooking, I'll see Father Helcoat—another Breton," he added with a smile. "Well, I'll see you on Monday. I must go to the Indian village now. An old woman is dying."

He filled his pipe, put on his fur cap, and went down the corridor with the springy step of an outdoorsman.

That evening we made the acquaintance of Dr Tenner, a young zoologist whose special study is the musk-ox. Thirty years ago there were only five hundred in all the immense Canadian mainland. No one has ever taken a census of those inhabiting the Arctic archipelago, for obvious reasons; but they are not easy prey, although the Polar expeditions of the nineteenth century, in search of the Northwest Passage, depleted their numbers. The musk-ox inhabits the most inaccessible regions of Canada and Greenland. Some were removed to Iceland, and did not survive; others to Spitzbergen, where they are in their element, and to Norway, where breeding has been satisfactory. The Americans have put some on an island off Alaska and are studying the possibilities of domesticating them. The musk-ox first appeared on earth during the quaternary period, and is one of the most ancient mammals to have retained its original physical appearance.

Dr Tenner had with him a colleague who was studying the prairie wolf (coyote), the wolf of the forest (timber wolf), and the big white wolf of the Arctic. These men were devoting themselves to obscure but useful scientific research, which led them to spend many long and perilous periods in the most inhospitable parts of the globe. They are devoted to research. Their university salaries will never equal what even mechanics or electricians can earn at the new stations in the Arctic.

Our ambition was to include the musk-ox in our photographic bag, and Tenner gave us some very useful information. He spread a large-scale map of the Barren Lands on the table, showing all the mainland territory between the Mackenzie River and Hudson Bay.

"You'll find a few here, and there, all along the Thelon River, and in the reserve between the Thelon and the Back River. But it's doubtful if a plane can land there at this time of year."

Later in the evening we made a note of all his advice—how to approach a herd, and what to do if they charged. It would be useful later on.

We had nothing to do on Sunday, so we went for a walk. We had dressed as we should have done for going skiing in the Alps in December. And at once we were aware of the cold. A blizzard was blowing, it was thirty-five below, and when I faced the wind its sting was unbearable and I felt my skin shrink as though about to crack. The wind went straight through my woollen bonnet and even through my special jacket.

"This will take some getting used to," said Pierre.

When we had been walking for fifteen minutes, I suggested returning to the hotel and putting on more clothes, especially headgear. He was bareheaded but did not want to give up. I insisted. "Let's go back and dress as if bivouacking."

When we went out again, well wrapped up in quilted jackets with fur-lined hoods, the cold was more bearable—provided we did not walk against the wind for too long.

We were soon out of the town, away from the buildings spaced out over a rectangular plateau. The wooden houses have no particular style. The striking feature is the great number of gaunt telegraph poles along the wide streets of frozen earth. The chief feature, in fact, of Canadian towns and cities would appear to be these unsightly telegraph poles and their criss-cross of wires—the great despair of photographers. There is some justification for it at Yellowknife and such places, but at Edmonton and Ottawa! Yet one must add that many miles of wires have been taken down and laid underground.

We took the road out to the mine, and walked for a few miles through a pretty landscape of woods of stunted trees, rocks and frozen lakes. Now and again a vehicle filled with a miner's family

passed us, slowing down. The passengers looked at us with curiosity
—no one walks here—but as no one ever asks indiscreet questions
either, they drove on and left us to our icy walk. The exercise gave
us a certain feeling of well-being; it was a long time since we had
been physically active. When the wind blew too strongly into our
faces, we turned our backs to it until the gust had passed.

Every dip in the ground had a stretch of water, frozen over, and
even the smallest of them was too large to be called a pond. An
Indian was driving his team of dogs across one of these lakes, standing on the back of his sled, and we saw him disappear into the forest.

We returned to the hotel very pleased and reassured. The cold
already seemed to have lost a little of its cruel bite.

"You'll see, we'll soon get used to it," said Pierre.

We had reduced our luggage to the absolute minimum. I knew from
experience that the best way is to equip oneself on the spot, that one
never finds in Paris the things that are of use in the Sahara. The
traders at Yellowknife are accustomed to people buying all their
equipment on arrival. There are several well-stocked shops and
stores, but the largest is the branch of the Hudson's Bay Company.
The Bay, as it is generally called, is a national institution. For almost
two centuries it was a great commercial empire. In 1670, Charles II
bestowed a royal charter upon "The Merchant Adventurers of
England trading into Hudson Bay". This Company was given
the monopoly of trade in the Hudson Bay basin and full ownership
of all lands reached through Hudson Strait. The company was
expected to administer this vast territory and to maintain law and
order within it. In 1869 the Company agreed to surrender its lands
to the British government in return for compensation, and the
territory became the property of Canada.

Although law and order is now maintained by the red-coated
Mounted Police, whose mode of transport is more often by plane or
motor-launch or snow-mobile than horseback, the Bay still has
trading posts all over the vast territory. If they were all to shut up

shop suddenly, daily life would become impossible for residents of the neighbouring areas. In the early days, the trading posts were simply places of barter where Indians and Eskimos exchanged their furs for firearms and ammunition and basic needs such as salt and flour. This is still the main business of the Bay's trading posts, the most northerly of which is at Arctic Bay, on latitude 75.

The one at Yellowknife has little connection with the fur trade. It is a large self-service store, a supermarket which supplies all the needs of people living in the North, from clothing and footwear to tools such as axes and electric-saws, and even tractors, trucks and aircraft. There is a wide range of food, both fresh and canned, chiefly the latter; but it is all very good, and the instructions on the tins are so detailed that any trapper can soon become a *cordon-bleu*. You could easily forget you were in the North until coming to the firearms department, one of the largest, where the racks hold all kinds of modern rifles, of all calibres and at all prices, for the shooting of small game or the large animals, the bear and the elk. There are no restrictions on the sale of firearms.

We bought everything we needed at this store, including the valuable mukluks made of caribou skin, with soles of moose-hide, to replace our luxury footwear for going up the mountains in winter.

Father Marec's advice was also extremely useful in the matter of hiring a plane. There are two airports at Yellowknife, a large one for the regular and long-distance services of a few big airlines, and a small one on a little lake near the Indian village; the latter is used by private planes for hire, small planes on skis and which make flights of three or four hundred miles at most, carrying three or four passengers. They can be hired as readily as one would hire a car anywhere else. We should have no difficulty in flying to Snowdrift; a Stinson could take us there in an hour, whenever we wished, for one hundred and fifty dollars. But there was the second part of our expedition to consider, when our base would be Igloolik, on an island between Melville Peninsula and Baffin Island. The distance from Snowdrift to Igloolik is about fifteen hundred miles, flying over the most desolate region on earth, and this part of our journey had to be given close attention.

The hut which served as office and warehouse for the owners of the charter planes was empty except for an elderly mechanic. He listened to our request without batting an eye. Nothing surprised him, apparently. But he was a little taken aback, nevertheless; the direction of flights from Yellowknife to the Arctic was usually directly north. The settlements and posts along the Mackenzie valley ensure a succession of landing-strips and fuel supplies, and a plane is always in touch with one radio station or another; but our route would take us diagonally across the Arctic, from Great Slave Lake to northwest of Baffin Island. There would have been no difficulty if we had been able to charter a big plane such as an Otter or even a Beaver. But the charge for one of them was one hundred and sixty dollars—nearly sixty pounds—an hour. It would have cost us a small fortune.

The mechanic scratched his head. Both the pilots had gone off on flights, and he was the sole representative of Ptarmigan Airways.

"Fifteen hundred miles: need to refuel somewhere," he said, going across to the large wall-map of the Northwest Territories and measuring with a slide-rule. "It's not beyond the bounds of possibility. We can land at Baker Lake, in the Keewatin district, refuel there and reach Igloolik next day. We've just taken delivery of a new small plane, a Cessna 180. Good opportunity to try it out, if Bill agrees."

"Ptarmigan Bill" was a typical free-lance pilot, like Chris, whom we had met at Fort Smith. Bill was older, and flew all over the Northwest in winter and summer alike; he knew the Mackenzie District as one knows one's own garden.

We discussed the charter price; it would obviously be less for the Cessna, which does not drink up fuel like a Beaver or an Otter. The point was whether the Cessna could take off with all the weight aboard—the pilot, Pierre and me, our luggage and full fuel-tanks.

"Bill will fly you to Snowdrift tomorrow," said Father Marec. "You'll have time to fix it all up with him."

The following morning this kind man brought his Land-Rover round to our hotel, helped us load our luggage and equipment into it, and drove us out to the small airport. We were about to say our farewells when he smiled and told us:

"I'm coming with you. Bill will bring me back. It's better if I come to see you fixed up. My successor has been there only a few months, and he doesn't know my Indians very well yet."

Dear Father Marec! I realise, now, that we should have made a good many blunders if it had not been for you. In the first place, you gave us some very useful insights into the Indians' way of thinking. We should have soon lost face with them otherwise. But above all, it was due to you that we had such a marvellous team of Indians to conduct us, and that I cherish the memory of our journey over the tundra by dog-sled.

Father Marec had thought of everything: "Look, I've got one!" he exclaimed, producing a mouth-organ.

I had told him that I could play one, and apparently the Indians love listening to music, so he had gone round all the stores at Yellowknife until he found one.

"You'll soon win them over with that."

There was a comparatively gentle wind blowing across the lake; the hard drifted snow had been flattened for about three hundred yards to facilitate take-off.

Bill looked at our pile of luggage and asked how much it all weighed. "Will you have the same amount when you fly to Igloo-lik?"

"Yes, just a few pounds more or less."

"That's okay then; we'll use the Cessna for that trip. It's a fine plane, faster than the Stinson, with a cruising speed of about one hundred and fifty."

And with that, the whole thing was laid on.

"Give me a few days' warning when you want to leave Snowdrift for Igloolik, because of waiting for favourable weather conditions. We'll be flying across an empty wasteland and, with the weather so changeable, we must take all precautions."

"We'd like to see and film some musk-oxen."

"I know where they are. I saw them recently, when flying to Baker Lake. Well, let's go."

We were making only a short hop this time, across Great Slave Lake to Snowdrift. There was no other means of getting there in winter, except by plane.

The engine had been warming up for more than an hour. Bill took off, flew low over Yellowknife and turned on an easterly course.

The woods, lakes and moraines slipped past. I saw a clearing with an Indian's cabin in the middle, a wisp of smoke coming from it— the only cabin we saw during the one-hundred-mile flight. The plane left land behind and flew across the eastern end of the great lake, where it is almost divided by a peninsula more than sixty miles in length.

Bill had remained silent during the flight, but suddenly pointed to something ahead. "There's Snowdrift," he said.

I looked, but could not see anything at first. Then, on a small headland jutting out into the lake, I picked out a little white chapel, right on the edge, and some cabins spaced regularly in lines, looking like sugar-cubes, with the larger buildings of the Mission, the school and "the Bay".

"Put us down in front of the Mission," said Father Marec.

Bill usually landed in a small creek by the school, which is also the administrative centre. But to avoid carrying our luggage some distance, he put the plane down on the rough surface of the frozen lake, and we bounced from one hard snowbank to the next like a motor-launch speeding over the waves. These planes must have amazing shock-absorbers. Pierre, who flies himself, fully appreciated the manoeuvre.

We slid to a stop by the jetty used in summer, and the icy wind of the wide open spaces greeted us as we stepped from the plane. A small man with a white beard came forward to welcome us.

"I'm Father Helcoat," he said, all smiles. "Welcome to Snowdrift!"

Some Indians were already busy taking our luggage, with great care, to the cabin which was to be our base. So here we were at Snowdrift at last. The adventure was about to begin. Pierre and I looked at one another with a smile and some surprise.

Father Marec was going to stay only for an hour or two, just to see us settled in and, especially, to choose the Indians to be our guides on the expedition. He has a great reputation among the Chipewyan Indians and speaks their language fluently. Father Helcoat, his successor at Snowdrift and a much older man, had spent all his years as a missionary among the Dogribs, many miles to the west; they speak a different dialect, and he was having to start afresh.

Father Marec was stumping about, making decisions and arranging everything.

"You'll be eating with Father Helcoat. There'll be no time for slacking while you're here. Let's go and pay our respects."

Our first call was on the one white woman, Mrs Jackson, from Aberdeen, the wife of the manager of the Bay. She had given birth during the arctic winter twilight when the temperature outside was sixty below. Her baby was now five months old, and she was waiting for the thaw and the fine weather to take the child out into the open for the first time. The family had a comfortable house, well heated and easy to run, like all the homes we visited in settlements in the North. We were given the inevitable cup of white coffee, which is drunk here at all times of the day, and we met the schoolmaster, Mr Douglas, who is also the government representative. Then we went with Father Marec to the Mission, which is contained in the one building. When the chapel is not being used as a place of worship it serves as a recreation-room or for meetings.

Father Marec had told a few Indians to come and meet us, for the news of our arrival in Snowdrift had soon spread. The settlement had been established about seven years previously. When the Mission, school and trading post were ready, the Indians who had been living scattered along the shores of the lake and in the bush, came to live together as a community, thirty households in all, consisting of about one hundred adults and children. Most of the cost of building their cabins was met by the government. The Indians were comfortably housed, and built kennels and sheds round their cabins; but the important advantage was that parents received their monthly family allowance cheques from the Federal Government. The Indians receive them only on condition that the children are sent to school; at least, this stipulation seemed to apply in this community.

Since our arrival at Fort Smith, it had become a daily, normal occurrence for us to see Indians. They were usually found in hotel lobbies and the Bay's stores, engaged in endless palaver between themselves in low voices, smoking their pipes and generally passing the time. Some hoped to find a job to earn some money, though the job had to be something they liked doing.

There are few Indians working in the mines around Yellowknife. Many miners are Italians, Spaniards, or Eastern Europeans uprooted by the war. The Indians are not interested in this type of work. I asked Joe Mitchell, one of the Indians who became our guides, what he would do after we had left. "I'll go and work at the mine," he replied.

"You see, they do go, after all," Pierre remarked.

But on further questioning it emerged that Joe was not referring to working in a mine but to helping at a prospectors' camp. When the fine weather comes, prospecting parties of geophysicists and geologists set up camps, as far north as the Barren Lands; and the Indians readily take on jobs as drivers of sleds or snow-mobiles, as guides, hunters or cooks. This camp life is what they are used to. But they turn a deaf ear to some of the less adventurous occupations.

Those who joined us in the small room which was Father Helcoat's office and kitchen combined were all big, healthy-looking fellows of few words. There was nothing in their dress or appearance to distinguish them from men of European stock, except for their slightly slanting, narrow Mongolian eyes. They could otherwise have been taken for gipsies, with their swarthy skin.

There were half-a-dozen of them, all invited individually by Father Marec. A few young women came to join them—wives, sisters or daughters, all tall and really beautiful; but a beauty with a touch of haughtiness and disdain. After all, these people were not slaves or inferiors. They discussed the matter with us as between equals. And why not? We should be entirely dependent upon them when out in the bush, for with our lack of experience we should not last very long by ourselves. When one remembers that there are not many white trappers in the whole of the Northwest Territories, trappers who live solely by hunting and lead an existence similar to that of the ancient Indians, then one quite realises that such a primitive way of living is not within everyone's capabilities.

Father Marec told the assembled Indians about us, speaking in the Chipewyan dialect, a harsh-sounding tongue in which the slightest change of intonation gives a different meaning to words. The Indians listened, sitting stiff and erect on their chairs.

"These two Frenchmen," he began, "friends and compatriots of mine, wish to make a film of your life in the bush, to hunt the caribou with you, go with you when you set your traps and fish in the lake. You should not regard them as ordinary tourists; they will eat and sleep as you do. They want to go off on a trip lasting several weeks. Do you know where the caribou are now?"

"There was a herd about ten miles from here," said one of the men. "But not now."

"Gone farther afield?"

"No. All killed."

"Well, where must you go to find a herd? This is the period when the caribou move north and east, towards the Barren Lands."

"There are some on the other side of the lake, a lot of them."

"Are you sure?"

"I've just come back from there."

"There will be just these two Frenchmen and they will have about two hundred pounds of equipment and stores to take with them. How many teams will be needed?"

The Indians thought it over, taking their time. Cups of coffee were handed round. The men questioned each other, and the women gave their opinions in a decided manner, while the children played freely around our legs. Father Helcoat smiled gently upon all these people who had invaded his office and showed the patience of a saint.

"Three teams might be enough," someone finally suggested.

But the others did not agree.

"If you're not too restricted in your budget," Father Marec said to me, "take four teams. That won't be too many, not by any means. There's been a lot of snow this year. Usually, we have about two feet of snow during the winter, but this year there's more than three feet of it."

"We'll take as many dogs and men as you consider necessary," I told him.

"Then have four teams." (The word team is always used, not dog-sled.)

"Agreed."

"Good. Now let's select the men. Henri, are you free?"

The Indian thus addressed was smoking a cigarette with obvious enjoyment. He nodded slowly; he was available.

"His name is Henri Catholique," Father Marec told me. "Oh, yes. They've nearly all got French names. That dates from a long way back, and some thousands of miles to the south. Henri is unmarried. He speaks English, and he's a good trapper."

"Have you got some dogs, Henri?" Father Marec asked him.

He had five in good condition—a fine team.

"Now let's see. Who else? Joe Mitchell—would you like to go?"

Joe Mitchell was older, in his forties; he had a thin face and looked a bundle of bones and nerves, but probably had plenty of muscle too. He hesitated. He belonged to the Dry Geese tribe. No one laughs here when people talk of the Dogribs, the Dry Geese or the Yellowknives.

"You've got some fine dogs, Joe," said Father Marec.

The Indian smiled. His team was one of the best in Snowdrift. But Joe had his nets to pull up, then he wanted to visit his trap line, and it would soon be the time for trapping muskrat, and that paid well. He needed to think the matter over, but in the meantime— there was his brother Nap.

Nap—Napoleon Mitchell—was the youngest of those present, a tall, handsome man in his early twenties. Carefree, always running after women, he was a most inconstant fellow. One day he would be at home; the next he would take it into his head to set off to cover three hundred miles with his dogs. When he had earned fifty dollars he spent it at once on useless things like beauty-cream, sun-glasses that got broken a few hours later, or he lost it all on gambling. He was reputed to be an excellent shot, like his elder brothers.

Nap had no hesitation. To go off with these two foreigners meant earning some dollars, but first and foremost it meant going hunting. "I'll go," he called.

Father Marec had the final word. "My friends will naturally supply the ammunition and all the game you shoot will be yours. In fact, all you'll have to do is to conduct them."

"Just a moment," said Pierre. "They can have what they kill, yes. But they must leave me time to photograph the animals before they shoot them."

A shadow passed. No Indian sighted a caribou without firing the instant range and aim were right.

"Don't ask everything of them all at once," Father Marec advised us. "Once you've won their confidence, they'll make it a point to find as much game as possible for you. Just be patient. There's an absolute rule in the North—be patient and always smile. Even in the most difficult circumstances, smile."

I bore this in mind. It came in very useful later on, in the Far North, where our smiles sometimes changed to grimaces of pain.

Joe Mitchell had finally agreed to come along. That made three teams. Then a young woman murmured something to Nap, and he stood up.

"I'll go and see if Augustin would like to come."

"That would be splendid," Father Marec said to me. "Augustin is a young man very much like Nap, but a fine hunter with amazing stamina. Nice chap too."

Ten minutes later Nap was back with his friend Augustin, who was very like him in appearance, with the same tall, lean figure and striking looks.

"Augustin will come with us."

"Bravo!" exclaimed Father Marec. "Make a note of their names," he said, turning to me. "Henri, who'll be their leader; Joe Mitchell, who could have been but did not want the responsibility; and the two young ones, Napoleon and Augustin. And now it might be as well to discuss terms."

This was true; we had not said a word on the subject. And here we touched upon one of the chief characteristics of the Indians. They are not interested in money. Dollars slip between their fingers; they seem, on first acquaintance, to be most improvident people. These four had agreed to go with us because they were enticed by the hunting expedition; they would have plenty of cartridges and their food provided, the rest would be so much pleasure. Nevertheless, the terms had to be agreed beforehand and in front of witnesses. Father Marec's presence was most necessary to settle these details. The agreement would be a verbal one.

I knew the official scale of fees—fifteen dollars a day (about £6.) for each guide, which included his sled and dogs. So four men would cost me sixty dollars (£24) a day. As a comparison, the fee for a mountain guide at Chamonix is eighty francs a day—almost £7 or about seventeen dollars.

"Do you agree? Are you satisfied with that?" Father Marec asked the Indians. "Fifteen dollars a day per man, with food and ammunition in addition. You will supply your own tents."

There was a little hesitation at this. Henri Catholique said something in Chipewyan to Father Marec, who cut him short. "Don't worry about that. Two tents will be enough. You can share them." He turned to Pierre and me. "They're very surprised that you should wish to sleep in the same tent as they, to eat and drink with them. They're not used to that."

We laughed. And this set them all at ease. They laughed too— even the children, who stopped their play and laughed as loud as anyone.

We had won them over.

"When do we leave?" asked Henri.

It was our turn to hesitate. Pierre said he would like to take some village scenes, to become friendly with the Indians, get used to the light. But Father Marec interrupted him.

"You'll leave tomorrow morning. You've plenty of time to buy your provisions at the trading post. If you delay, they'll change their minds. Believe me—Indians are so impulsive that you never know if you can trust them to do a thing. They keep their word, though. But they've no idea of time. If you don't leave tomorrow, these four will very likely go off somewhere and not be back for a fortnight. And it would never occur to them that they had failed to keep their word to you. No—you leave tomorrow."

"I fully agree. We'll leave tomorrow morning at ten," I said.

We got up to go, but the Indians had something to ask. They put their request slowly and gravely: the trading post closed at five o'clock, they had some purchases to make and would like an advance.

I was used to this kind of transaction. The same thing had happened when travelling across the Sahara. I gave my answer without asking anyone's advice. "You'll receive straight away half of your salary for six days, that's to say forty-five dollars. This sum

Our teams on Whitefish Lake

Leaving Snowdrift to cross Great Slave Lake

Great Slave Lake

will be placed to your and your family's credit at the Bay. The balance will be paid to you in cash when we get back here."

This was the only way of ensuring that their families were provided for during their absence.

Father Marec interpreted, then smiled at me. "You're used to this kind of thing."

"You know, Father, whether they're Indians, Touaregs or Lapps, they're all nomads. I understand them and get along very well with them."

"Don't forget to be jovial, to sing and play the mouth-organ."

And so the arrangements were completed for this expedition, which came under the sign of heartiness from the very start.

We accompanied Father Marec to the plane. While all the arrangements were being made, Bill had sat quietly in a corner of the room reading his paper.

"I hope I haven't kept you waiting too long, Bill?"

"That's okay, Father. Let's go."

The small Stinson took off with a roar which shattered the deep silence of the North. It circled the settlement, then turned west and sped away over the forest. We would never see Father Marec again. But in this land where the traveller never stops in one place for long, he often leaves behind him friendships that are more solid than any made during a long sojourn in Europe.

The great day came at last. We just had time to go over our luggage and equipment, check the food supplies and especially the film. We were taking our whole stock—more than sixteen thousand feet of 16 mm. Ektachrome—for we should not be going south again, to Montreal, until the end of the whole expedition. To use that term may seem presumptuous; yet expedition it was. I can think of no better comparison with our situation than the time when I was crossing the Sahara and used to leave a comfortable desert post to press on with my guides and camels into the empty yellow wastes. One had to provide for any eventuality. And here, in the North, the tundra can be as savage and cruel as the desert. One has to know its rules and laws, and never make mistakes; for that purpose we had our Indians, with whom I at once felt confident and in accord.

The cabin we had been given at Snowdrift was so much what we had hoped for that each of us kept humming *Ma cabane au Canada*. There was a big oil-burning stove that gave out a good heat, camp-beds and a well-equipped kitchen. But as we should be leaving in the morning, we had accepted Father Helcoat's invitation to eat with him.

Night fell at eight o'clock and the cold was intense. We had to remember not to go outside without putting on a parka and gloves, for as soon as one stepped out the wind sweeping across the great open spaces seemed to cut one in two. But the pure sky was magnificent and everything around had an unearthly appearance.

The silence of the icy expanses was broken by the concerted barking of the dogs. It was the time of evening when they were fed; each was tied to a stake in the frozen ground, and from all quarters came their yelps and snarls and whimpers. The twilight blurred everything that would have marred the scene—rubbish and odd planks and dirty snow.

A glimmer of light came from the windows of the Mission, and reflections of the stars glistened on the frozen lake. Some children came out to fetch water, going to a hole dug in the ice on the lake which was kept open by daily use. Each urging on his dogs, pulling a small sled, the children went and filled their buckets, then returned to the mission.

The bell started to ring: a familiar sound, calling the people to prayers. One or two old Indian women, bent low by the weight of years, slowly made their way to the chapel, using a twisted stick for support.

A little later the missionary came out with a bucket in each hand and went towards the lake. He knelt on the ice at the edge of the hole, and then the regular movement of his arm and body could be seen as he dipped a long-handled saucepan, drew it up full and poured the contents into one of his buckets. When both had been filled he rose painfully to his feet, said a few words to a child, then made his way back to the Mission. He did all this twice a day, and had made a narrow path across the hard snow. The door closed behind him. The dogs had fallen silent, and the solitude was again complete.

It was my turn to fetch water. Wrapping myself up well—the temperature was thirty below—I went down to the lake, broke the thin film of ice which had already formed over the hole, and drew up water as though performing a rite. These gestures were soothing to the mind and seemed quite natural. The modern world was a long way off. Snowdrift is not a post, but a tiny agglomeration of Indians in the immensity of the sub-Arctic.

Pierre was standing outside the cabin and looking up at the sky, despite the cold and the wind which had risen again. Vapour clouds had formed and were racing across the sky; then they fused together to make a kind of luminous veil which streaked away like a comet. This disappeared altogether for a few moments, then reformed only to burst into a mass of luminous sparklets which whirled upwards out of sight and came plunging down again to sweep low across the dark bristling forest. Three, four times the phenomenon crossed the sky before fading away.

"Whatever is that?" asked Pierre.

"The aurora borealis, the northern lights: one of the last of the season. It's a sign of blizzards and rough weather for tomorrow. Let's go in, we've a lot to do."

But we stood listening to the night for a few more moments. The dogs began barking again: calls of the wild had sounded faintly in the forest—perhaps wolves on the prowl.

A few children, heedless of the cold and the night, were playing with a ball on the snow-covered shore, among the boats caught in the ice.

There was still a light showing in the big white building of the Bay; Mrs Jackson was probably giving her baby a last feed, while her husband read the papers that Bill had brought.

In the school building, hidden from sight by the spur of the head-land, studious Mr Douglas was perhaps preparing tomorrow's lessons.

Sounds of singing suddenly came from two or three cabins. Parties were being given for those going off in the morning; there was much eating and drinking, for our coming was a godsend from which everyone would benefit. Tomorrow there would not be a cent left, it would all have gone on food and drink—but tomorrow we should be off.

2

The Chipewyans' Great Caribou Hunt

THE WIND, that eternal sculptor, whistled as it dawdled over the apparently deserted settlement of Snowdrift, and with the touch of a magician's wand left a spiral of hard snow round a post, covered a sleeping dog with a thick blanket, swept away a pile of snow from outside an open door and scattered it over the streetless settlement. A few Indians were up and about in the biting morning cold, backs bent and the hoods of their parkas over their heads. Suddenly, a prolonged moaning came from somewhere in the upper part of the settlement, and at once other sounds broke out, sullen whines then howls of rage. All the dogs in Snowdrift were voicing their protests at the departure of the teams.

"There they are!" I exclaimed.

Above the din of the howling, the sharp barking and whining of Snowdrift's one hundred and seventy-five dogs, could be heard a faint tinkling of bells, so faint that it seemed like a descant to the canine cacophony, the tones of each bell distinct in the clear, cold air. Each sound seemed to break through some solid but transparent matter in order to reach us.

The first team came dashing down the slope, and the long galloping line went snaking between the cabins, just avoiding the fences, and then stopped dead in front of our cabin on a command from the driver. Napoleon Mitchell was the first to arrive, dressed for hunting. Not in a feathered head-dress and leather trousers, though! He was in black from head to foot—black fur-lined jacket, black parka, tight-fitting trousers of coarse black canvas, and mocassins of caribou-skin. His headgear was the usual cap with ear-flaps, commonly known as a Norwegian cap. Attached to the steering-handles of his sled was a pair of large muskrat gloves complete with gauntlets, most necessary for driving. The advantage of muskrat is that it never gets frozen and retains its suppleness, whatever the temperature.

Another team came bounding towards our cabin, skilfully driven by Joe Mitchell. It drew up alongside the first and the two brothers offered each other cigarettes. Then Augustin Enzio's team was seen approaching from the west; the dogs climbed the hillock on which the Mission stood and trotted along the frozen shore to the meeting-place. Only the leader, Henri Catholique, was missing; but he, it seemed, was always late. Some children were sent to see if he was on the way, for his cabin was at the far end of the settlement. They came back shouting and waving, and at last we saw Henri coming down the slope and urging on his dogs.

The party was complete.

Dog-teams are harnessed in two different ways in the Arctic, according to the region. The Eskimos hitch their teams in fan-shape, the Indians in single-file.

In the bare and treeless regions of the Eskimos, the sleds have to glide over icefields. The Indians' sleds have to slide through the bush, over the tundra with its stunted spruce trees, and along rocky gorges between two lakes.

The Eskimo sled of the Canadian Arctic is a light chassis on two wide runners about twenty-five feet long which are connected by transverse bars lashed with thongs. The driver controls his huskies, eight or more of them, each attached by a long leather trace to the common tow-line. The larger Eskimo sleds can carry loads of more than a ton.

The Indian sled, on the other hand, is extremely light. It has no runners, and is little more than single maple plank about a foot wide, curving upwards at the front, like a toboggan. Its chief characteristic is its suppleness. But canvas sides are lashed to the plank, giving the whole thing the appearance of a flat-bottomed boat. The driver stands on a little platform at the back of the sled and guides it by means of two handles set like those of a plough. In this flat but rocky and uneven region such a sled never carries more than seven or eight hundred pounds. The dogs are hitched in single file and the team is joined up with double traces; their harness consists of a padded collar and girth-band. The driver guides his team by commands and uses his short whip to call the dogs to order.

The team has a leader, a highly intelligent dog who picks out the trail, recognising where the snow is hard or crusty and avoiding the deep and powdery. This lead-dog does very little pulling, except when setting off; but by keeping the traces taut it obliges the others to pull. An Indian will usually have two lead-dogs in the team, so that when one is tired he can give the other a turn, putting the first into third place. Then there is the last dog in the line, hitched directly to the sled. This is the martyr of the team. It has considerable weight to pull when the sled is getting under way; and when running downhill the sled often catches up with this dog, bumping into it.

The dogs of the Chipewyan Indians, like those used in the sub-Arctic, are neither as strong nor as big as the Eskimos' huskies. They are of a finer breed, and their pointed head has something of the fox about it. Their coats vary from white to deep black, ranging through all shades and markings, tawny, grey or brown. They are lovely dogs to look at, and one is tempted to pat them. But anyone unwise enough to go near a team may well get bitten. There are, of course, exceptions, and Napoleon Mitchell's team was one. But during our journey we saw dogs being beaten with a cruelty that would have horrified dog-lovers. Being accustomed to blows, the dogs may snap at anyone who moves a hand towards them, even to stroke them. After a few days, Pierre and I had to fall in with the practice;

we would threaten a dog first with our fist or a stick, then stroke the animal when it was curbed by fear. It was a bad method, and we never had the fun of playing with the dogs. And yet, how faithful they were to their masters! A dog that had been beaten, its head bloody, would lick the hand of its master when he brought the meat a few minutes later.

It was at the end of the day's run that the dogs were particularly dangerous, when they dropped in their tracks, worn out and famished after a long hard pull and longing for rest. We had to be very careful when passing near them. However, after a few days we had a somewhat similar smell to that of their masters, so they adopted us; but a couple of bites that I had received in the first day or two checked my affectionate impulse towards these faithful companions of man.

The cruelty of some of the Indians is revolting to a sensitive person. But in order to understand it—for it was in continual evidence throughout our expedition—one should remember that the Indians must hunt for their food; that they have different attitudes to suffering and death, and that in spite of many years' contact with white people some of them still have the feelings of prehistoric hunters.

When we were deep in the bush, after the first day's run, the behaviour and attitude of our Indians quickly reverted to that of primitive man. They ceased to be the so-called civilised beings we had known at Snowdrift. Henri became a cruel woodsman, hard and brutal, displaying superhuman strength in all he did, laughing as he hamstrung a caribou to prevent its escaping, and beheading animals with a single blow of his axe. He killed all the game he could, even when he was no longer hungry, even when he already had more meat than could be carried.

Throughout the journey I was given a station that I could well have done without—the privilege of age. Out of deference I was given the sled with the finest team—a leader's team—the one belonging to Nap.

He had eight dogs, which was unusual; six or seven are generally the maximum needed in the bush country. To hitch on more is a touch of vanity, a showing-off. A sign of power.

The children were running about and playing with the dogs, straightening out the harness and cracking the whips. They were envious of the men who were going into the bush and who would come back with sleds laden with meat. We had shared out the supplies and equipment as well as possible. Pierre was to ride on Augustin Enzio's seven-dog sled; Joe Mitchell and Henri Catholique, with their five and six dogs respectively, were taking the camping material and supplies. There was no question of Pierre or me driving a team; that was something which could not be learned in a day, and the dogs would only obey those who had trained them. However, later on, when the going was hard and difficult, we did take the place of the Indian drivers while they went ahead on snowshoes to pick out the trail. At the beginning we were just live bundles heaped on the light sleds, letting ourselves be pulled along, tossed about and thrown off at times.

"We shall have a long and tiring day," Henri warned us before the start. "Forty miles across the lake. It's going to be very cold."

I had a Fahrenheit thermometer, and as I am used to Centigrade I had to do a little sum each time I read it. When we set off the temperature was thirty-two below.

"Ready?" Henri called.

He gave a shake at the traces; all four teams streaked off across the lake, the dogs exciting each other with much barking. The suddenness of it took me by surprise. There was no impression of a solemn setting forth on a long journey of several weeks; it was more like taking part in a race. Very different from the slow, majestic starts in the Sahara.

I wanted to say something of the sort to Pierre, but he was several hundred yards away. I could just see his head and shoulders; he was clinging to the sled and clutching his cine-camera, being shaken up as I was. The thought crossed my mind that making a film in these conditions was going to be no joke. However, the speed soon slackened and the dogs dropped into a steady trot which they would keep up hour after hour.

When we returned south at the end of the whole expedition we added up the miles we had covered each day, both with the Indians and then the Eskimos, and the total came to 1,250 miles—the distance between Paris and Bucharest. We checked the figures and added them up again, so astonished were we; at the time, we had had no impression of covering such a long distance. It had taken about forty days by sled. The daily mileage covered naturally depended upon the nature of the country and the snow conditions. The Eskimo teams were generally the faster, and we sometimes covered seventy-five miles in a day on the icefields. The Indians, travelling through the bush, had many short but difficult slopes to negotiate, and there were frozen rapids which called for much care when crossing them, or else long detours had to be made. But on the many lakes we crossed, the Indian teams easily covered ten miles in an hour. The only way to warm up was to run alongside the dogs, but it was difficult to keep up with them for more than a few hundred yards.

In any case, walking is almost impossible in winter, except on the frozen lakes, as one sinks to the waist in the soft snow. Snowshoes are as necessary as skis are for Lapps. But the Eskimos we met never needed such equipment in their windswept regions which had much less snow.

We had to get used to this new form of transport. It would be far from the truth to say that sled-riding is comfortable. Much depends on the surface conditions. Skimming over the level, unbroken ice of a lake is an exhilarating experience when not too cold. But remaining wedged among the load for hours on end, with only the telescopic leg of a camera as a blanket, is no joke.

Yet there was plenty of variety, and the novelty of it all soon made us forget the hardships. Snowdrift was disappearing from view.

The Indians' cabins could just be seen between the white building of the Mission with its belfry, and that of the Bay, but this picture grew smaller and was absorbed into the landscape.

We were in an empty world.

The wide bay stretched into the distance to a line of rugged hills. Wherever one looked, there were islands and banks of bristling pines, bays and inlets changing in shape and then giving way to others as we progressed across the lake. The eastern end of Great Slave Lake is almost divided by a rocky peninsula more than sixty miles in length. The blurred outline of these shores could just be made out through the fall of snow heralding a blizzard. Our four teams were trotting steadily along at a good distance from one another, the lead-dogs heading towards some point which they alone seemed to recognise. The drivers, thin silhouettes at the rear of each sled, guided and urged on their teams. The dogs were fresh and had been well fed with fish just before the start. They knew that their masters were after meat, and they were already entering into the spirit of the chase by giving sharp, joyful barks.

Long trailing clouds were veiling the sun. Although we were heading due north, the wind was bearable as we were in the lee of the islands. This journey was more like a sea voyage than a land expedition. We might have been sailing.

Everything was novel—the unaccustomed motion of the sled, the line of dogs with their gaily bobbing pompoms and tinkling bells. Stuck into each dog's collar was a little black-and-white tuft from a wolverine's tail; and some had the brush of a fox or a wolf attached to their girth-bands. These furry trophies swayed on the dogs' backs like wind-blown decorations for some festivity. And we were indeed being bidden to some festive occasion. Napoleon, standing behind me, was humming to himself as he kept his eyes on the dogs. It was probably a hymn set to an Indian tune, and he kept singing it over and over again, breaking off only to give sharp commands to his dogs. For there is a special dog-language, and unless it is used the team will not obey.

Three commands are used by the Chipewyan Indians to direct their dogs. Keep straight on—*He-tet*; bear right—*Cha-cha-cha*; bear left—*Yee! Yee! Yee!* These are usually enough; the dogs have keen hearing, and the leader is always on the alert, often turning to catch his master's commands, usually when coming to difficult places where instinct is of little help, such as among rocks or deep gullies piled with snow.

It was fascinating to watch the dogs at their task; they certainly communicated with each other. Their different characters became apparent—there was always the lazy one who let itself be carried along by the traces and did not pull at all. This slacking did not escape the driver's notice for long; he would leave his little platform, whip in hand and stride towards the culprit to punish it. Knowing what to expect, the dog would curl up in the snow, whine, and sometimes try to bite; but it would get such a beating as to leave it lying with its nose in the snow, whimpering. If the punishment was deserved, the other dogs just stood around; but if they considered it too severe, they bounded about excitedly, howling and barking (Indians' dogs howl far more than they bark), jumping up at their master as if to say: "No! You're going too far. It's not his fault." This fracas caused the traces to get tangled, the middle dogs were caught up, and it all had to be sorted out. The master grasped the dogs by their legs and turned them on their backs as though tossing pancakes. The crisis was over, and we could set off again. Napoleon went back to his place, giving the runner a kick to free it. The dogs knew the sound, leapt forward yapping joyously, and streaked off to catch the other sleds which were far distant, no more than little boats tacking on the horizon.

During this time the passenger, chilled to the marrow, tried to move an arm or a leg to change position, but for the most part clung to the canvas sides of the sled to avoid being tipped out. Even on a lake the ice is far from smooth; the wind has formed ridges, it all looks like a sea that has been frozen over, and the sled rides the crests of these waves, pitching and rolling like a trawler in rough water. The dogs usually take the ridges of this hummock ice at right-angles, so that the sled points towards the sky, then plunges down the other side. It tends to overturn when this ice is very hard. The driver tries to forestall the action by gripping hard on the steering handles, but the passenger is often tipped out.

Driving an Indian sled for twelve hours on end is hard and laborious, and so is hunting on snowshoes in the bitter cold and over deep snow. And yet the Indians are said to be lazy. They are when it is a matter of doing some daily routine task which does not interest them; they would not readily take to ploughing and planting, nor even to watching over herds of reindeer like the Lapps. The Indians we knew had remained hunters, in preference at least; their constant struggle against nature had kept them natural. They hunted in order to live, and with such an outburst of free vitality that it was easy to understand why they would rather have uncertain contests with an elusive prey than a high standard of urban social security.

When we had been travelling for three hours we came to the head of a long low island covered with dark woods, and beyond was a very wide arm of the lake where the currents had caused a small ice-pack. Blocks of ice were piled upon each other, and here and there spikes as sharp as daggers were sticking up dangerously.

Now we could see a great open expanse of lake, with the far shore quite visible twenty miles away; our guides said we were going to cross diagonally to reach it.

But first they intended to light a fire. And what a fire!

The place chosen for our halt was a rocky islet a few hundred yards square which was covered with branches torn by the wind from the small spruce trees. The farther north one goes, the smaller the spruce trees become, till finally they peter out on the edge of the Barren Lands. That was as far as our Indians had decided to go; for beyond that was a bad land, they said: there was nothing for making a fire.

It was difficult to get on the islet. The drifted snow had piled up along the bank, and we and the dogs sank deeply into it. Henri and Joe put on snowshoes and went ahead, making a deep track which the dogs could follow. In this way we scrambled up the steep rocky bank and came to rest in a sheltered spot among spruce trees. The dogs were not unhitched; they dropped in their tracks, worn out by the long, hard pull, and eagerly lapped at the snow. The Indians quickly got to work with their axes.

Ah, the Indian's axe! What a terrible instrument it is in his hands! He uses it for everything, but first and foremost for cutting wood.

This was our first halt and we looked with great interest at everything that was going on. The Indians took no notice of us, busying themselves in chopping down spruce.

"But it's a massacre!" I exclaimed to Pierre. "Look, they've already cut down about a dozen. Why all those?"

This was the natural thought of a Savoyard, to whom timber is very valuable.

We soon saw what they were going to do with all the piles of wood—build a great fire to make a pot of tea. But a fire to warm ourselves by, too. They quickly and skilfully chopped off the branches and spread them thickly on the snow, which they had flattened and beaten down with their snowshoes. On one side of this green carpet the wood had been placed in a great heap; some lighter-fuel was poured over it, ignited, and it blazed up at once. Spruce burns very easily; the wood was old and dry. The flames leapt up to a height of five or six feet, and we were soon roasting ourselves. When our faces were burning, our backs were frozen, but by turning round frequently and keeping at a few yards' distance from the flames we soon felt comfortable.

The snow in the pot had melted and Henri Catholique was getting a meal ready. He was inclined to be wasteful. If I had not kept a close eye on our food supplies—at least until we obtained some meat from hunting—our four Indians would cheerfully have eaten the whole lot at one meal, and then been perfectly prepared to fast for a week. But Henri was very good at getting out the cooking and eating utensils, at finding the bread—which had come from Yellowknife—and toasting it over the fire. We all had hearty appetites and the tea was excellent. It was a moment to be enjoyed to the full; the sun was at its height, shedding light but no warmth. Pierre was busy with his camera, taking shots of everything—the blazing fire, the lake and the hummock ice, the wind-tanned Indians, the dogs cradled in the snow, the jagged trees, mocassins, everything.

"Pierre, come and eat."

"That's all right. I've tried the cameras and they seem to be in good order—but what a blinding light!"

The northern light is indeed very strong. In the past, the Indians and the Eskimos used to protect their eyes by wearing wooden or bone eyeshades with a narrow slit in them. Now they all sport dark glasses; they prefer large ones with imitation tortoiseshell rims, and they are always breaking them. However, the Indians do not seem to take care of anything, they are constantly breaking or losing things. The one exception is their firearms. These they really value and take great care of; an Indian's rifle is taken from its caribou-skin case only to fire at game, and is given the best place on the sled. I had the breech of one cutting into my side all the way, but it could not be helped; the rifle had to be there, so that at a sign from its owner I could hand it to him at once.

We had left the islet on frozen Great Slave Lake and could see the fire we had lit dying down behind us. It was a strange sight—the flames and smoke apparently rising from the ice. During the short rest we had all got to know each other better. Pierre and I had made no fuss over the bleakness of the halt; we had eaten as the Indians did and shared the same food, not insisting on something different and better, as was often the case with white travellers whom they conducted; and perhaps for these reasons the Indians seemed to have a more friendly attitude towards us. They still took little notice of us, and spoke between themselves in their own dialect;

Henri only said something to us in English when absolutely necessary. However, he now decided to keep us informed.

"It will be hard now, and very cold. We're going right across the lake. It will take about four hours to reach the other side." He pointed it out to me, and I could see what looked like a long dark thread between the icy lake and the grey sky.

"Four hours," said Joe, "and the wind's getting up."

He looked anxious, for it was blowing from the northwest. But I could see no sign of a storm coming, unless it were in the milky clouds floating on the horizon like a distant sea-mist. Pierre and I had taken our places on the sleds again. I found I could settle myself more comfortably, arranging a little space to stretch my legs when I got cramped; and by drawing the tarpaulin up over my legs I was well protected. The Indians had put their parkas on again—a warning sign. When an Indian or an Eskimo slips into his parka made of caribou-skin, one knows that it is going to be cold—for them. So for us it would be unbearable.

It was hardly noticeable at first, but as soon as we left the shelter of the islands the full force of the wind was felt; it was sweeping the snow across the frozen lake, which was very open and wide at this point—although we were crossing this inland sea at its narrowest point. But as I mentioned earlier, Great Slave Lake is as large as Belgium. The elements rage over this icy plain, across these frozen waters which would not thaw for another six weeks. Crossing the immense lake with a sled has always been a feat of stamina.

Joe Mitchell had taken the lead, Augustin Enzio was next, with his fine seven-dog team, and I was trotting along at his side. Now and again I exchanged a word or two with Pierre, who sat stoically on his sled, the bag containing his camera open in front of him, ready to go into action.

He gave me a rueful look. "I'm frozen. But what a wonderful sight!"

It was indeed wonderful to be gliding not just over the ice but over the windswept snow which was being blown at a furious rate.

The sleds in the distance seemed to be bounding through foam. Henri Catholique was a long way behind; he had only five dogs, and despite their great efforts he was finding it difficult to keep up with the rest of us.

Two hours went by, and we were still heading in the same direction but without seeming to get any nearer to the other side. The wind had increased in strength, and Pierre and I became little more than shrivelled mummies, buried among the things on our sleds with only our heads showing. I admired Napoleon who stood facing the wind like a captain at the helm, guiding the sled and encouraging his dogs. *"Cha-cha-cha! He-tet, he-tet!"*

His lead-dog was a carroty-red and white bitch with a pointed head like a fox. She answered to the name of Nancy, turning her head to glance at her master with intelligent eyes, then running on after giving a sharp little yelp. I gradually learned the names of the other dogs in the team—Silver, Goldie, Copper, Blackie—all names closely corresponding to the colour of their coats.

Napoleon leaned towards me now and again. "Cold?"

"Okay."

After three hours the distant shore began to get larger; and old memories of setting foot on a new continent returned, memories of reaching an unknown land after a long journey. The trees crowning the cliffs ahead had suddenly grown bigger, we no longer had a view of the whole width of the great lake, and the shore we were approaching was now seen to be jagged with creeks and inlets. A number of beaten tracks met at this point. A sled was coming towards us, loaded with skins and dried meat and with a woman lying on it. The man was walking at the side, for he had few dogs and there was a long way ahead of him. The thought came to me that he had in front of him the whole distance that we had just covered from Snowdrift. But what of it? The fur of his anorak was frosted over by the wind and there were little icicles on his beard, yet he smiled at us and accepted some tobacco with pleasure. He had been hunting and was on his way to the trading post at Snowdrift to exchange his skins for provisions for his family; they lived in a tent in some secret valley where he had his trap line.

We reached the shore at last, at a point where many other sleds had made a wide, deep track in the snow. This roadway pleased our guides. But there was a long steep slope to climb, and they respectfully asked us: "Can you walk?"

"Walk! We're only too glad to walk, after seven hours on a sled."

They smiled as we stretched ourselves, getting the circulation back into our legs and arms, numbed by the cold. It was pleasant in this sheltered and peaceful cove which we had reached by crossing the waves of ice thrown up by recent storms. The wind had dropped, though we could still faintly hear it howling in the distance. The forest was quite thick here, and some of the spruce trees were as high as an average pine in the Alps, about fifty feet. Our Indians were giving their dogs a breather after the great effort they had made.

"Go and walk," said Henri.

We followed the trail which went deep into the woods, becoming ever steeper, and as we walked we could read some of their secrets. Here a couple of moose had bounded across the trail; farther on were many signs of small fur-bearing animals, marten, ermine and mink; then we came upon large tracks, near some rocks, which might have been made by a small bear.

"Do you know what they are?" Pierre asked me.

"No, not really."

We learned later that they were tracks made by a wolverine, the devil himself, the hated enemy of all the denizens of the forest.

We reached the top of the ridge and before us was another lake, not so wide but which stretched east and west as far as the eye could see. Did this mean that we had not yet crossed the whole of the great lake?

"Have you got the maps?" said Pierre.

"Well, I'd better own up. All those maps we so carefully chose at

Ottawa were left behind on the table in the bar at Yellowknife, that evening when we had a long talk with Dr Tenner."

Pierre teased me, but took it well.

We heard the sleds coming up behind us—the yapping dogs, tinkling bells and shouting men. We all gathered at the top of the ridge, looking at the steep descent between two reddish cliffs, down a gully with firs growing in a quincuncial arrangement. The Indians started off on reconnaissance.

"Wait, wait a moment," cried Pierre. "I'll take some shots."

He dashed forward holding his camera, left the track, and disappeared into the snow up to his neck. He struggled out with some difficulty, then had to wipe the camera and examine it, and warm his fingers which had got numbed by contact with the loose snow. We thus learned that in the bush one cannot take a step without putting on snowshoes; the snow will not bear any weight.

While helping Pierre to struggle out, I fell into the drift as he had done.

The Indians burst out laughing. Remembering Father Marec's advice, we laughed even louder; and this all helped to keep the party in good humour.

One after the other, the sleds went dashing down the steep slope. The dogs raced away, urged on by their masters, but the heavy sled soon overtook and banged into them, which set up a howl of furious protests. Joe, Augustin and Napoleon skilfully negotiated the descent, but Henri hit a tree going round a curve and his load was scattered all over the snow. We gathered everything up and lashed it on again.

Eventually we all gathered at the bottom, in the calm of a small creek sheltered from the west wind by a cliff about three hundred feet high. It was a magnificent spot; the snow lying on the rocks made them seem coated with ivory. The distant shore looked to be covered with rocks and trees.

"Where are we, Henri?"

"On Great Slave Lake."

"But how's that?"

He laughed at my surprise, then traced a rough map on the snow. What we had done so far was to cross the great lake only to the sixty-mile-long peninsula which separates Christie Bay from Macleod Bay on the north, and then to get over the narrow part of the peninsula at the one accessible point.

"What do you do in summer, to cross the entire lake?"

"We have to go all the way round the peninsula," Joe replied.

This short halt allowed the dogs to get their wind, while the loads which had been shaken loose in the descent were packed more firmly on the sleds.

Then we were off again, running due west this time, and so straight into the wind, once away from the shelter of the high, rocky cliffs. The trudge through the woods had warmed us, and for a time the wind did not seem too bad; but after an hour it became almost unbearable, and I had only admiration for our drivers who stood stoically facing the blizzard. The dogs were trotting more slowly; now and again they seemed to be swimming through snow as it was blown thickly across the ice. Ahead, the lake was getting narrower, we were entering a bay about a mile wide; the southern shore was entirely rocky, while to the north there were hills rising by degrees to a high plateau. The forest was quite thick and came right down to the shore. The sun was beginning to set, dropping behind fleeting clouds and sending haloes of light and brief ir- radiations across the sky.

I had the hood of my parka drawn well over my head, and no sound came to trouble my thoughts. But I could tell the force of the wind by the way it was whipping at my face; and there were little icicles fringing my eyelids, mouth and chin. Even the dogs had their heads down; their fur was bristled and their muzzles were glistening with ice. Now and again one of them lapped quickly at the snow without stopping. It was like being in a dream world, so silent was everything. Our journey had no end; we should go on like this for days and days, without a change in the landscape. This impression of infinite travel seemed to loosen our last links with the quite recent past.

The poor Indian settlement of Snowdrift now appeared a haven of comfort and warmth. We had become wanderers on the face of the earth. Perhaps that was the reason Napoleon, who was pressing against my back to get a little protection from the blizzard, suddenly broke into song. He stopped singing only to shout smartly at his team. "Nancy! Ho, Nancy! *He-tet, he-tet! Cha-cha-cha!*" Eight heads turned to glance back at him, though without slackening pace; eight sharp heads with ears cocked, intelligent eyes, and tongues hanging from panting mouths.

But Napoleon was singing because he had sighted our destination for the night.

"Do you see the house?"

I searched the banks of the inlet and at last saw a cabin on the north side, half-hidden by trees.

"Aren't we going to sleep in the tents tonight then?"

Nap stammered some vague explanation. He could understand English quite well but spoke it badly. I had to be patient—Henri would tell me later.

Joe Mitchell had already shaken up his team and was dashing on ahead, and this caused the other dogs to quicken their pace. The wind blew strongly along this narrow inlet, as if whistling through a tunnel; it had formed the drifted snow into hard hummocks, and our sleds were bounding from one crest to another. Suddenly I was pitched off as the sled overturned. Nap jumped for the rope trailing behind and stopped the dogs by swinging the sled round.

I remembered instructions. "Okay, Nap," I said with a laugh.

Augustin's sled with Pierre on it passed us while we were righting ourselves. "No harm done?" he called.

"No, it's just a baptism. There'll be more yet. How are you?"

"Frozen stiff! Especially my legs. And the camera's got jammed— I wonder what I can do about it?"

He was worried, realising the many technical difficulties ahead.

Our sleds passed close to the bank and we could see stakes marking holes made in the ice for fish-nets. There must be a camp somewhere near. This was probably the reason for our turning west after crossing the lake, instead of heading north again.

The cabin was showing signs of life—our approach had been noticed. Some children came running out to meet us, in spite of the howling blizzard, and a woman appeared at the door. Our sleds ran up the bank, and the arrival of our teams caused all the dogs in the camp to set up a wild barking.

No sooner had we all come to a stop than Henri Catholique signalled to Pierre and me to follow him; without waiting for the sleds to be unloaded he made straight for the cabin and ushered us inside. What a delicious feeling of comfort! The one large room was like an oven, heated by a wood-burning stove that was glowing redly. A whole family of Indians watched us step into their home without betraying the least sign of our being unusual.

"We'll be sleeping here tonight," Henri told the woman.

Then he must have explained about Pierre and me. The family unbent a little, though still looking very reserved. Then the head of the family appeared; he was about forty and was Henri's elder brother. He spoke English very well and was obviously a cultivated and intelligent man. The ice was broken. His wife took our top-clothes and hung them up to dry. Pierre was chilled to the bone, especially his legs. He had refused to put on a second pair of trousers as I had done, a light pair that had proved an excellent protection. He had thought his buckskin breeches would be sufficient; but he changed his ideas now: "I'll get out my quilted trousers tomorrow."

This first evening of our trip was indeed a festive occasion for our four Indians. They would not have to pitch the tents nor cook a meal. The wife was heating up some caribou stew. I asked Henri to fetch some of our tinned food and fresh bread, also cigarettes—which the wife accepted with delight.

The children gathered round, looking at us with curiosity; but they were shyer and more reserved than the children at Snowdrift.

While drinking the welcome hot tea, I put a few discreet questions to our host.

"Have you been living here all through the winter?"

"Yes. I built this cabin myself. We could have had one of the cabins at the Tourist Lodge, but it's too cold there."

He and his wife went about their work. She was putting muskrat pelts into a wooden presser and then hanging them from the ceiling, where there were a good many other furs—martens, and a fine lynx—as evidence of her husband's trapping skill.

Sitting there freed of my heavy top-clothes, I listened to the blizzard raging outside, increasing in strength and howling through the forest. Our Indians were bringing in the sleeping-bags and supplies. Pierre and I helped to fetch the photographic material. The important thing was for the rolls of film not to be subjected to a high temperature immediately after being in the icy cold, for that might cause the gelatin to peel off. The package of exposed film was given every care throughout the journey; by always taking great precautions we were able to bring back our large collection of pictures safely. The stock of unused film was kept in a canvas kitbag with a padded interior. We found that during the day the temperature in this isothermic bag had not dropped lower than fifteen degrees Centigrade; this was fine, if it could be maintained. But the day had been a bad one for the cine-camera. Four hours after leaving Snowdrift, the speed-indicator had started to go wrong; when set for twenty-four shots a second, the camera was actually taking sixteen or eighteen, and so the film would have been over-exposed. Everything now depended on the electric camera, and we hoped that the batteries would last.

The precautions we were obliged to take with the photographic material caused us frequently to check the air temperature. I had bought a very good thermometer from the Bay at Snowdrift. It showed thirty-two below this evening, but the wind had to be taken into consideration. A temperature of twenty or even thirty degrees below is bearable, but as soon as a wind gets up, just a light one, it becomes unendurable. A temperature of twenty below, with a wind blowing at thirty miles an hour, can feel like fifty below.

Night comes very late in these latitudes. There was still a lovely violet light in the clearing, made iridescent by the low rays of the setting sun filtering through the trees. And the snow being swirled across it looked like spangled comets tumbling to the ground.

Our guides were now seeing to their dogs. Indians are sometimes careless and untidy, but they take great care of their dogs' harness. It was all gathered into loops and hung up behind the cabin, away from the wind. The sleds were turned upside-down so that the bottoms would not freeze. Then the dogs were tethered separately to stakes driven into the snow, all at some distance from the camp dogs to prevent any fighting during the night.

Henri obtained some frozen fish from his brother and fed our dogs. There was an abundance of fish in these parts; and no lack of other food either.

When the outside jobs were finished, everyone came into the cabin and the evening began.

What queer thoughts came over me! In the warmth of this rustic comfort I listened to the howling of the wind and the dogs, and through the frosted little windows I could just glimpse the landscape as stretches of black and white over which the night was beginning to fall. The secrets of the forest were quietly revealing themselves under cover of the encroaching twilight. While in the cabin each of us was smoking and meditating, our hostess was busy setting the table. A tall, upright young woman, she still looked handsome despite the hard life she led.

The men all ate in silence, then sat drinking or smoking. The children had got used to our presence, and the little girl was happily letting her uncle make a fuss over her, but she suddenly took fright and ran to the big bed, the only bed, at the other end of the room and disappeared under the pile of blankets and skins.

The moment had come to talk about our future movements.

I learned later that Henri had made the detour to the Narrows not just to see his brother Joseph but especially to obtain detailed information about the whereabouts of caribou.

"A few days ago a large herd passed a few miles from here," Joseph confirmed. "They were moving east."

The Indians discussed the matter at length between themselves. Even without understanding a single word of Chipewyan it was possible to grasp the sense of their conversation from their many gestures and the lines their fingers drew on the table. They knew all the lakes, portages and rivers in the district north of Great Slave Lake.

Joseph got up and fetched a large-scale map which was lying carefully folded on a shelf. He spread it out on the table and referred to it with surprising ease. His English was very good. He spoke with authority, and his younger brother seemed completely subdued by him. He was probably the head of the clan.

"The caribou passed at this point," he said to me, pointing to a place on the map. "But they're much too far away now for you to catch up with them. However, the herds from farther afield pass more to the north. If I were you, I'd make for there." He put his finger on the map, on Lake McKinlay, thirty miles north of where we were. "Then I'd continue north for a few days, and you're bound to come upon fresh tracks."

The others all agreed.

"It will be another long and tiring day tomorrow," Henri said to us. "You're not too tired, are you? Afterwards, the trips will be much shorter, and we'll go hunting."

"Tired? Of course not!" Pierre's reply made them all laugh.

I had an idea, and got out the four-bank harmonica that Father Marec had given me. The cabin on the shore of Great Slave Lake became filled with mountain airs and old tunes of Savoy. The children sat up in bed, the wife stopped in her work, the men sat and listened.

Then Napoleon held out his hand. "Give."

I passed the mouth-organ to him, and he started to play tunes he had almost certainly learned at the Mission, for they were solemn hymn-tunes. But he played them very well; and between us, playing in turn, we gave quite a concert. The door opened and more faces appeared; apparently there was another Indian family living in a tent close to the cabin. They had not spent the winter here, but had recently arrived in order to trap muskrat.

We were all relaxed now, and Joseph Catholique became more communicative. He told me about his life.

He was very proud of his cabin and showed me how he had filled the gaps with moss, paper and clay. It was very well constructed, with the planks overlapping, and he must have had a job finding the timber for it. In this region it takes at least a century for a spruce-tree to grow to a thickness of eight inches. Very few trees are more than six inches thick. The log cabin had two small winddows, one facing east and the other southwest, allowing Joseph to look out over the lake and the bush.

"What's this tourist lodge that you mentioned earlier?" I asked him.

He explained that there was a permanent camp for American tourists on a creek about a mile away. He did not just say tourists; in these parts it was generally thought that every tourist was American. He showed me the illustrated prospectus of an American tourist agency, and I read that "fishing safaris" were organised in July and August at various places round Great Slave Lake. They were package holidays; clients were flown to Yellowknife, then taken by a small flying-boat to Narrow Point, where Joseph acted as their guide and generally looked after them. He and other Indians did well for themselves by hiring out their motor-boats (the days of paddled canoes, alas, are no more) to the millionaires who stayed for a week or two to fish for trout.

And what trout! In Great Slave Lake, a decent trout weighs anything from thirty to fifty pounds. I was shown a photograph of the record catch the previous summer—a fifty-five pound trout. Every evening, Joseph carefully measured and weighed the best catches made by the holiday fishermen; photographs were taken of each fish, then it was prepared—not for eating but for sending home as a trophy. It was given an injection of preservative and put in cold storage until sent by plane to the United States, where it would be given a place of honour over the proud owner's mantelpiece, in a glass-case with a little plaque giving its size and weight and the date caught.

The Indians made a good thing out of all this, and Joseph Catholique led an enviable life. Instead of spending the winter at Snowdrift, he preferred to remain here alone with his family in the arctic night. He found that two months of continuous contact with white men was quite enough; and besides, he had not failed to notice that fish were most abundant in this part of the lake. When the tourist season was over, he cast his nets and got in a supply of dried fish to feed his dogs.

When the ice formed again, he went fishing, making a hole in the ice and lowering a harpoon on a long stick so that it floated on the water; attached to the harpoon was a long nylon cord, and by jerking at this he could work the harpoon along under the ice. The fisherman followed its progress by putting his ear to the ice and listening for the scraping sound it made. Obviously, the currents had to be taken into account, but an Indian knows his part of the lake like the palm of his hand. When the gear had travelled a sufficient length—150 to 200 yards—he would cut another hole in the ice and retrieve the harpoon and cord. Then he attached a weighted net to the cord—which stretched from one hole to the other—and drew the net along, fastening it to a stake at the edge of the hole. After that, all he had to do was to haul up his net every two or three days and gather the catch.

The Indians are expert at this method of fishing which calls for much skill, particularly in working the harpoon along under the ice; but characteristically they keep these secrets to themselves. Their reasoning has point and irony: the white men are apparently superior to us in everything, so they must know everything, and we had better let them get on with it in their own way.

I remember Father Pochat telling me with wry humour of his early days in the bush, of how he had to learn everything by himself from observing the Indians. He thus learned how to build a fire for the night, how to use snowshoes, find his way about in the forest, read the signs, trap game—and to fish with the harpoon and cord. But he had an unfortunate experience. He bought a fine new net, which cost him sixty dollars, and succeeded in working his harpoon from one hole to the other, which was no mean feat. The Indians watched him with great interest, but without offering any help or advice. He drew his net along and attached it at either end; but when he went to haul it up he found that it was stuck to the ice and impossible to move.

"Why didn't you tell me that I was stretching it too tightly?" he said to his Indians.

They burst out laughing: "Because you never asked us."

Father Pochat made the best of it and laughed with them.

I was once present at a wonderful catch, when Joe Mitchell hauled up one of his nets. Every yard or so yielded a great fish of ten to twenty pounds—salmon-trout or whitefish. The latter is highly favoured by the lakeside Indians; unlike the trout fished there, it is easily digestible and great quantities can be eaten at a sitting. The Indians are supposed to feed their dogs only with fish, according to regulations; the resources of the lakes are inexhaustible, and the caribou can thus be spared. But it is obvious that the passion for hunting predominates. In the course of our expedition with the Indians I saw them only once feed their dogs with fish, and that was on this first evening spent at Joseph Catholique's cabin by the Narrows.

Night had fallen at last. We fetched our kerosene lamps, and they shed an intimate glow over the wooden walls of the room and the shelves holding the crockery, and upon the lean faces of the Indians.

The children were all in the one bed, huddled under the covers. Pierre and I were feeling healthily tired after the long day in the bitter cold, and we should have been glad to get our heads down. But Indians sleep very little. The five of them had started to play cards, some kind of rummy, with great enthusiasm. Napoleon was shuffling and dealing the cards like an expert. By midnight, he had won a good part of Henri's wages, and Joseph brought the game to an end.

Pierre and I laid out our sleeping-bags on the floor. The wife turned her children out of the bed and they joined us on the floor, and our four guides stretched out wherever they could find a space. Joseph and his wife got into the bed, and everyone went to sleep. I lay listening to the purring of the blazing stove, then fell asleep too.

I woke up, shivering and chilled to the bone. It was daylight, and I could hear the howling of the wind and the dogs. The stove had gone out, and it must have been well below freezing point in the cabin. Then a female figure slipped silently from the bed, broke up some sticks and relit the stove. A feeling of well-being soon returned.

We left the cabin with some regret, for we should be sleeping in tents from now on.

I wished to pay for the hospitality we had received, but was not sure how much to give. Besides, they were used to being paid in American dollars. Perhaps they would have been surprised to know that the sum I gave them was the same as I had paid for a comfortable room for the night at the hotel at Yellowknife. Even so, I was indebted to them. They had not asked me to pay anything; none of the children had held out a hand. They do not know what begging is, and stand on their dignity as lords of the bush country. I offered the money to Joseph but he called his wife, and she took it with a simple smile of thanks. The Indian wife is no slave; in fact she seems to have an important position in the family. It is better that she should look after the money, too—if only to prevent its being gambled at cards.

In the icy morning air (the thermometer showed thirty below) Pierre was photographing the preparations for departure. A blizzard was blowing from the east. During the night it had covered the sleds, harness and dogs with a blanket of snow. The dogs were like large snowballs; they were asleep with muzzles tucked into bushy tails, but if anyone approached they would warily open an eye and snarl, disclosing formidable teeth. A frenzied barking broke out when they were being hitched to the sleds, an excited yapping from our dogs and a despairing lament from the dogs of the camp, a concerted effort which drowned the noise of the wind. Some of our dogs broke away and the Indians had to go and look for them.

The sleds were loaded in a more sensible manner than before, as our guides had been quick to notice the things we were always needing and those we used only at the end of the day. Pierre would now have all his material ready to hand. For the moment he was struggling with his cine-camera. He was surprised to find that the film had become as brittle as glass; and his fingers were numbed with cold, a painful handicap but one to which he would have to become accustomed.

The cabin and tents stood in a small clearing between the forest and the lake shore. The trees came down close to the cabin, and the forest was quite dense. Wolves were numerous, for many fresh tracks could be seen on the snow. The children played outside without any fear, but I had noticed the previous evening that when their mother accompanied the youngest to the outdoor toilet a hundred yards away, she armed herself with a cudgel.

The only wolves that Pierre and I had seen were from the plane when flying over the Wood Buffalo National Park. We should have liked to see some on the ground, but the wolf is the most elusive of animals, the invisible inhabitant of the forest. It avoids man, and only very rarely is one seen at close quarters. Yet the very day following our departure, Joseph Catholique found himself face to face with a huge grey wolf when less than five hundred yards from his cabin. He has quick reflexes and his rifle is always ready for use; he brought it down with one shot. On our return to Snowdrift we were shown the magnificent skin of this wolf. Stretched out, it was more than six feet long.

If I had properly understood Joseph's advice to his brother, we were going to travel due north for about one hundred miles, almost to the edge of the Barren Lands. Henri had warned us—it would be hard going, for there would be no trail to follow.

Joe Mitchell took the lead when we set out. I had already noticed that although Henri was the accredited leader, no decision was made without the agreement of Joe Mitchell, the eldest of the four and one of the best hunters of the Snowdrift community.

He followed the lake eastward for a dozen miles, and during this time the wind was in our faces; but Pierre and I had learned from experience and were muffled up to the eyebrows. After an hour and a half of easy going we reached a small creek and the wind suddenly dropped. There was an old trail leading into the forest, and this took us to a rocky ridge where we looked back for a last view of Great Slave Lake. The dogs were toiling at their task, especially the lead-dog, which was thrashing through the powdery snow as though swimming in deep water. Although the wind had dropped, the cold had increased; and Pierre and I were glad to be able to walk, keeping to the snow packed down by the dogs and sleds.

Our little party was travelling through an area without any distinguishing features, where there was a great number of frozen lakes in little rocky valleys, and where the trees got smaller and smaller. Now and again we reached the top of a rise which gave a fairly wide view, and our guides stopped to take their bearings; then we dropped down into a gully, slid across another lake to a bank where the place to cross was marked by Indian signs—broken branches, small spruce trees stuck in the snow—which only a practised eye would have noticed.

Tracks made by small animals were seen much more often, but with the exception of a few single tracks there were no signs of the passage of caribou.

"They're farther north," said Joe.

We stopped just before midday to light a fire. Pierre and I knew what to expect now; we watched the Indians chop down trees by the dozen, make a soft carpet of branches and get a great blaze going. We all stood round it, enjoying the warmth.

When we set off again the going soon became rough and difficult, and much skill and strength were needed to guide the sleds. The dogs kept getting caught up in the traces, and Napoleon had to stop the sled, plunge through the snow up to his waist and free the unfortunate dog, which had been mercilessly trodden on by his teammates behind. Then Nap encouraged his lead-dog, Nancy, who gave a few yaps and led the way forward again.

Suddenly the whole file of sleds came to a stop. I made my way with difficulty to the head of the line. Henri and Joe had halted because there were signs of an old camp—the remains of a fire, a battered stove and some cooking utensils on a flattened space where the tent had been pitched. Tied to a tree was a famished dog, howling. Henri untied it.

I heard the explanation much later. Henri had camped in this spot a fortnight previously, when on a hunting trip. It was he who had left the stove behind, with his usual carelessness; but as we had two tents with us, he decided to retrieve it. And he was the person, too, who had abandoned the dog, leaving the animal tied to the tree without the slightest scruple.

He now hitched it behind his sled, for it refused to work in the traces. Later in the day, the dog slipped away; it had had enough of bad treatment and preferred to go hunting on its own. But the poor animal would come to a sad end.

Late in the afternoon we reached the southern shore of a very large lake; it must have been Lake McKinlay, but our Indians called it Whitefish Lake. The names that the Indians give to the places they know differ from tribe to tribe, even from family to family, and in any case never correspond to the names on maps. Little did it matter. Our sleds drew to a halt in the centre of the lake, and the Indians took their axes and walked towards a heap of snow. It covered the remains of a caribou; much had been eaten by wolves, but there was still enough to feed our dogs. The Indians cut it up deftly, then put the pieces of frozen meat into a sack.

They carefully examined some tracks on the lake and discussed them at length, but said nothing of what they thought to Pierre and me. However, I recognised them as caribou tracks; a herd had crossed the lake here.

Henri informed us about the incident. "I killed six the last time I was here, but I left that one behind because the sled was fully loaded and the snow was deep."

"Will we find some?"

He shrugged his shoulders. "We'll see tomorrow."

Henri never said what he had in mind, at least not when asked. Perhaps it was better that way.

We set off again due north, and late in the evening came to the end of the lake. Here we were to make camp for the night, in the middle of a wood of small spruce which had just a branch or two on them, so that they stood like pikes, and in the dusk looked like a charge of ghostly lancers.

The long task of making camp began. Actually, the Indians were surprisingly swift and clever at it. Pierre and I would have liked to help, but on this first occasion we could have done very little. Besides, it was impossible to walk about on the deep snow without snowshoes; and the two pairs we had brought for our own use had been appropriated by Nap and Henri. They had deemed two pairs to be sufficient for six people—or else they had none of their own. Perhaps they had left their own behind somewhere, or had exchanged them for something else. In any case, Pierre and I were condemned to inactivity, sitting on the sleds until the snow was stamped down and a path made from one tent to the other. This made matters difficult for Pierre, who was trying to film the Indians as they went about their tasks; he could not get the best angles, despite plunging about in the snow.

Nap and Henri stamped out two rectangular places for the tents in the middle of a thicket. Meanwhile, Augustin and Joe had felled a dozen trees and lopped off the branches, spreading these over the snow to make a floor.

The tents had no relation to the modern isothermic ones of holiday-campers. Two poles were stuck in the ground a fair distance apart, another pole was attached to them horizontally, the canvas was flung over—and there was the tent. No guide-ropes or stakes. The canvas was torn in places and had burn-holes, but what matter. No one took any notice or tried to mend it. An opening had been made in one side, near the top. This was for the stove-pipe!

The stove defied the most elementary rules of fire-safety. It was no more than an old, eight-gallon petrol-can. One side had been flattened to make a base, and two holes had been cut, one for heating a saucepan and the other to take the pipe. The former plug-hole served as the draught. Four logs were placed on the carpet of branches, the stove was put on the logs, and the length of pipe was poked through the hole in the tent. And there it was, all ready.

It was filled with wood, a light was applied, and in a few minutes the petrol-can became red-hot, throwing out a terrific heat. The snow under the branches gradually melted and left a deep hole; this was to be useful as a rubbish dump. Now and again the heat set fire to the logs on which the stove stood, but a handful of snow quickly doused the flames.

However, there were several things to be done before lighting the stoves. When the tents were pitched, the bedding was carried into them. The Indians, like the trappers and gold-miners of the northwest, spread caribou-skins on the floor of the tent, then put down their heavy sleeping-bags, and placed blankets on top. It took up a lot of space, but was comfortable. They smiled at our quilted sleeping-bags.

The four shared the work between them, tackling it with a kind of frenzied urgency that was in marked contrast to their usual unconcern. Having pitched the tents, piled the baggage inside them and fixed up the stoves, our Indians turned their attention to the dogs, which had remained quietly curled up in the snow, just where they had been brought to a halt, while the work of making camp was progressing. They were exhausted, and growled menacingly when anyone went near them. Each was unharnessed and tethered to a stake, at a safe distance from the others. Then the harness had to be gathered up and looped over branches, the sleds turned over and their bottoms cleaned. Next, Joe and Augustin fed the dogs, while Henri set about getting a meal.

Joe and Augustin fetched the remains of the caribou recovered from the cache on the lake and chopped the meat with their axes. The dogs at once set up a great howling and whining, a yapping and mad barking. Augustin and Joe, wearing snowshoes, went round, tossing a huge lump of meat to each dog. They fell silent then; all that could be heard was the grinding of teeth on flesh that was harder than granite.

"Come in," Henri said to me. He was crouching by the stove, and looked up with his wide smile like that of a happy child.

Seeing this powerfully built man sitting there and looking so genial, who would have thought that he could be cruel and bloodthirsty when the passion of the chase was upon him? It was as though he had a Jekyll and Hyde personality. Yet this is common with all Indians, who are so very different when met in the peaceful atmosphere of their cabins or the indolence of their overheated tents from what they seem when hunting on the icy plains of the Canadian lakes.

Entering a tent when the stove is burning means stepping suddenly from a temperature of thirty-five below to one of twenty-five above. The immediate thing to do is to take off a lot of clothes, and this presents a certain difficulty; although an Indian tent in the backwoods is quite roomy and high enough for one to stand erect in, if care is taken, it also has to contain everything which might be affected by the freezing night—and this amounts to a considerable pile of bundles and sacks.

There were three of us—Pierre and I and Henri—under this thin canvas through which the twilight was shining. Henri was quite at home, which was only natural—he spent most of his life in this way. He had everything he needed close at hand; the supply of wood for the stove was stacked just outside, in the lee of the tent. Pierre and I were a little anxious at feeling the icy wind blowing in under the tent, and we set about making ourselves more comfortable. We had brought two tarpaulins into the tent, and we folded them to give an extra thickness on the ground and keep out the draughts. We were not wholly successful on this first night, but practice enabled us almost to seal the tent on later occasions. But that, too, had its inconveniences; the red-hot stove literally baked us, yet if the tent-flaps were opened only for a few seconds the cold rushed in and turned the tent into an ice-box. There were no two ways about it—we had to roast or freeze.

So we roasted while having a meal, and tried not to freeze during the night.

I let Henri do the cooking in the way he wished, and just kept an eye on the food supplies. He showed himself to be a perfect guide, though he was very free with the cooking fat. Fortunately we had plenty; but Henri used it liberally for everything, soup, meat and vegetables, and the pan swam with the stuff, which spilled over on to the stove. However, weeks later, when sitting cramped in an Eskimo igloo, without any fire and waiting patiently for thin soup from a tin to heat on a small flame from an oil-stove, I thought of Henri's meals with longing.

Here in the bush we had a fire! When man has the means of making a fire he possesses a great advantage. He can endure the cold.

I stepped outside when night had fallen—if the continuous twi-light can be called night. Through the trees I could see the lake shining like a mirror. Our camp was now in the middle of a clearing, for the trees had been felled over an area of a hundred feet all round the tents. Augustin was doing something to his sled and Joe was cooking a meal in the other tent; his silhouette could be seen on the canvas, squatting by the stove, and he was humming a lament. The dogs had eaten their fill and were sleeping. Fine dogs they were. My heart went out to them, and I stepped over to stroke one. As I put out my hand it leapt up and seized my arm in its teeth, growling furiously. All the other dogs reared up too, growling and howling. Augustin came running across and struck the dog down with a blow from his stick.

"Be careful," he said. "They are tired."

He gave me the stick and showed me what to do: raise the stick to the dog, and if it growls give it a swipe, then it can be stroked. But always be on your guard, and never show fear. A move to pick up a stone or a lump of ice usually makes the dog veer off. What a pity! I should have liked so much to make friends with one of our dogs. This time I escaped with nothing worse than a torn sleeve, the padding having saved me from the dog's teeth.

We had finished our evening meal, and Henri was putting away the utensils. Our mukluks were drying by the stove—part of the preparations for the night. (Pierre and I were amazed that during the day's long trek, and despite stumbling about in the icy, powdery snow, our feet had never been cold.) My three pairs of woollen socks, as well as the mukluks, had to be quite dry for putting on again in the morning, so this was another little job to do. Then I got out the mouth-organ and played a few tunes. The three in the other tent came and joined us, which made our quarters somewhat cramped. I made a present of the mouth-organ to Napoleon, and he proudly began trying to make up some tunes. I taught him the basic scales, and he was delighted.

We then talked about plans for the morrow. Joe Mitchell made the decisions, but Henri told me in English as though they were his own.

"Tomorrow morning the two youngest, Nap and Augustin, will go and make a reconnaissance. There are some tracks of caribou. We shall probably stay here for one more day. Whitefish Lake has always been known as a place for caribou."

Pierre and I were doubtful. We should believe it about the caribou when we saw them.

The other three went back to their tent at a late hour, and then we could stretch out in our sleeping-bags. The stove was still red-hot, and we had to be careful not to ignite our bedding. Sparks flew out now and again; the sizzling and popping of the burning wood made sweet music in the silence which had come at last. The bush and the tundra stretched for hundreds, thousands of miles around us; and we were a handful of men in search of meat, hidden away in this vast solitude. I thought of the nights I had spent in the desert, rolled up in my *burnous* and sleeping under the stars in the tropical heat; then I had heard the grunting of the hobbled camels, and strange night sounds had reached my ears, just as now, but how very different! Here, quite close, I could hear growling and the snapping of jaws and a crunching of bones—probably one of the dogs tearing at the last of the meat.

I slept like a log; then woke up with a start, cold and shivering. The stove had gone out and the cold had crept in. The temperature in the tent was the same as outside—thirty-five below. Yet Henri was still snoring happily and Pierre was sleeping peacefully with his face uncovered and close to the tent-flap. I was cold, and found it impossible to get warm again. I slipped on a sweater and wrapped a quilted jacket round me and slid deep into my sleeping-bag; but then my feet got frozen. There was no doubt about it—my sleeping-bag was no good. This was my own fault. I had thought it would do, for it had "done" the Sahara with me; but I had no idea how intense the cold was in these regions. Pierre had his "Himalayan" sleeping-bag, which had a lining making it proof against the wet and the wind. He could sleep out in the snow in it. I should have to see about the matter tomorrow. Meanwhile, I could only be patient.

Daylight was beginning to creep into the tent, although night had never really come, and the pale streaks were sidling up to me. Should I relight the fire, rouse my companions? No, Henri must be allowed to remain master in his own tent, especially at this early stage. He was sleeping peacefully, buried in a heap of blankets. But suddenly he threw them back and got up, saying "Good morning" to me with a wide smile. He chopped up some wood and lit the stove, then put more wood in until it was roaring away and seemed likely to burst at any moment. In a matter of minutes we went from cold to hot. Life flowed again, and we started to talk. Voices were heard coming from the other tent. I dressed quickly and went out; Augustin and Nap were about to start and were checking their rifles.

They set off across the lake, two slim, black silhouettes moving with the awkward, slouching gait of men on snowshoes—so different from the action of skiers. I watched them for some time, and understood the reason for Indians' choosing to wear black to go hunting, when they are otherwise fond of bright colours. In these tight-fitting black clothes, which made their lean figures seem even slimmer, the two had the appearance of a couple of fir trees when they stopped for a moment in the open; and as soon as they reached the wooded bank they merged into the background. They could have had no better camouflage.

However, Pierre and I felt anxious at the two going off in this manner. We had come here to photograph hunting scenes. If the Indians took the idea into their heads to go off by themselves and just bring back their trophies of the chase, that would be of no use to us. Pierre was fretting. Henri was enigmatic; he just smiled and started to repair a dog's harness. Joe went and joined him.

Joe had his look of good hunting in prospect, though I did not realise this at the time. But on later occasions, whenever I saw his lean, usually sad face suddenly light up, I knew I could not be mistaken: the excitement of the chase was in store for us that day.

However, I had to make things clear just now. "Why didn't Nap and Augustin take us with them? Or at least Pierre with his camera?"

"They have to find fresh tracks. It will take them a long time, they will have to cover long distances, and there are only two pairs of snowshoes."

I almost retorted *yes, and they belong to us*, but there was no point in embittering the atmosphere. Our guides had unbent considerably since leaving Snowdrift, and the night we had all spent together had established friendly relations. The thing to do was to try to understand them, not to push them and make some psychological blunder.

"You see, Henri, the important thing for us is not just to see a herd of caribou but to take part in hunting them as well. Pierre must be able to film the scenes before you start killing any."

Henri and Joe nodded and looked thoughtful.

"We're only at the beginning," said Henri. "Right now, we're going after meat; later on we'll go filming."

"We could do both at the same time," Pierre said.

They did not think so.

Pierre and I wandered about the camp, feeling a little peevish. Without snowshoes our range of action was very limited.

Joe came back from searching the undergrowth, holding up a splendid marten, caught in a trap and frozen stiff a long time ago.

"That's a fine catch," I said to Pierre. "Something for you to photograph."

"Later on," he grunted.

The marten was thrown on a sled and forgotten.

The two Indians, trying to please, showed us some traps which had been set more than two months previously. Nearly all were empty; a wolverine had eaten everything. The deep, distinctive tracks it had made—the animal is plantigrade on its front paws and digitigrade on its hind paws—led from one bush to the next. A wolverine gobbles up every kind of bait and the usual traps are of no use. To catch a wolverine a large wooden trap has to be built. Henri and Joe set about doing this, which gave them an excuse for felling three or four more trees, all tall and slender but more than one hundred years old. One has to keep reminding oneself—when thinking how rapidly forests in France would be depleted—that the Canadian forest and bush extend for many thousands of miles and are inhabited by only a few thousand people. The law of nature is maintained, and the clearings marking a camp are just a few widely scattered tiny spots in the vast area. No, there will not soon be a shortage of timber or of water in the Canadian woods.

The wolverine trap took two hours to build. It was a kind of little log cabin open on one side, with a tree-trunk held by a peg; this the animal had to push with its nose to get at the bait, whereupon the tree-trunk would fall and crush it. The fur had no great value, and in any case there was no certainty of finding the trapped animal, for another wolverine might come along and devour it.

We went back to the tents and let the hours slip past. It was very cold, but the wind had dropped. Suddenly, Joe cocked an ear, and so did Henri. Neither Pierre nor I had heard anything. But the two Indians were smiling and nodding at each other.

"Caribou!" announced Henri.

"Where?"

He pointed to some woods on the other side of the lake. "Didn't you hear the shots?"

I listened hard, and then distinctly heard two more shots. The Indians exchanged a few words. Joe got up, harnessed his dogs, then beckoned to Pierre. "Come on. We have plenty of meat to carry."

I passed the bags of photographic material to Pierre, and he took out the cameras to check them, making sure they were loaded.

Joe was impatient. "Quick!" he called.

Pierre jumped on the sled and the dogs bounded forward, yapping joyfully. I watched them crossing the lake until they disappeared from view.

"Do you think they've killed any?" I asked Henri.

He nodded. "Three."

He had heard three shots, so to him that meant three dead caribou. His confidence was truly impressive.

It was late in the evening when the hunters returned to camp. Despite the intense cold they had endured crossing the lake at such a late hour, they were highly pleased with themselves. Henri had been right—they returned with three caribou. Or rather, what had once been three splendid animals bounding through the woods but were now no more than bloody hunks of meat piled on the sleds and already frozen hard.

Pierre told me what had happened.

Joe had driven his sled straight to the spot where Nap and Augustin were waiting, close to the lake shore. The two had surprised four caribou searching for lichen under the snow among the trees. They had shot and mortally wounded two; the other two had also been hit but had been able to make off. Nap and Augustin had despatched the first two (with their axes), cut up the carcasses and loaded their sleds. As the chase after the two wounded animals might be a long one, Nap and Augustin had decided to explore another area.

They were completely exhausted when they returned to camp, having covered about twenty miles on snowshoes over deep snow.

Joe and Pierre had gone after the wounded caribou. The excited dogs followed the scent and led them towards a shape lying on the snow in a creek. When they were within two or three hundred yards, the caribou had struggled to its feet; one leg was broken, and the animal seemed exhausted. Joe jumped from the sled with his rifle and took aim to finish off the beast. But the eager dogs ran on with the sled—on which Pierre was still sitting—and gained on the wounded caribou as it hobbled away. Joe could not risk a shot, and so Pierre had been in on the kill, a horrible kill. The caribou turned at bay and held off the dogs with its hooves and sharp antlers. But there was no hope for the poor beast. Pierre had been caught up in the wild scramble, with the sled overturned, the seven dogs entangled in their traces, the caribou furiously defending itself. Then it suddenly stopped, became still and resigned itself to its fate.

Pierre had filmed the final scene. "But I don't guarantee the result," he said.

He is never optimistic. He always wants his work to be perfect and makes no concessions. I have complete confidence in him. "I'm sure it's good, Pierre," I said.

"You're cheerful, anyway," he replied, shaking his head.

He went on to describe the end of the animal—the dogs biting it furiously and lapping at the blood flowing from its wounds; the impassiveness of Joe Mitchell, arriving on the scene with his axe and killing the caribou with a single swing at its neck, and his smile as he cut it up.

Pierre was still affected by the scene. "The cruelty is unbelievable."

He was right, but such is the life of these Indians; they hunt in order to live, to eat. There had been four caribou, and they had killed three and wounded the other; if there had been fifteen they would have killed them all, even though they could not have carried away all the meat. But they hunt in order to survive. Can the same be said of the fox-hunting and stag-hunting in Europe, with all the pomp and ceremony that surround them; and are they any less cruel?

We feasted on caribou late that evening. I was expecting us to eat the loins, but the Indians preferred to cook the offal, tongue, heart and liver, which were fried on the stove. The choicer cuts were kept to be dried and smoked, and the legs were given to the dogs.

While Henri was doing the cooking, using plenty of fat and onions, the others fed the dogs; they gorged themselves, then curled up in the snow and slept soundly.

The second night in the tent was more comfortable, but I almost set fire to my sleeping-bag through moving too close to the stove. I folded a tarpaulin round my sleeping-bag and covered myself entirely, and in this manner slept very well and did not feel the cold.

In the morning, however, I found there was a thick layer of frost between the tarpaulin and sleeping-bag, formed by my breath and perspiration; but it soon melted when the stove was relit.

We were about to strike camp and a hard trek to the north was ahead of us. It was a bright, cold morning, but milky clouds trailing across the sky warned of a blizzard by evening. Setting off was always done in a great hurry. Having made up their minds to leave for other hunting-grounds, the Indians became very active. In next to no time the tents were struck, the sledges loaded, the hot stove thrown on the snow to cool, the stove-pipes were taken apart and slipped one inside the other.

The dogs, having eaten their fill, gaily waggled their tails. One of them set up an overture, howling with muzzle pointing to the sky, and at once all the others joined in. I was to become used to these weird sounds which the dogs made for reasons known only to themselves. In some mysterious way, they realised that they would be pulling through deep snow for the whole of the day, but also that at the end of it they would be rewarded with large chunks of meat. And so they voiced their joys and sufferings in anticipation. But overnight a whining, plaintive melody with varying undertones had been introduced into the raucous orchestration. Spring had arrived. An agitated bitch was appealing to the dogs, and they were rolling about in the snow, still tethered to the stakes, uttering fond, demanding, furious yelps.

The Indians hurried to and fro, roughly seizing the dogs and slipping on their harness, cuffing their heads and kicking them in the ribs, then dragging the sleds on to the trail already made. I took a last look around. Surprisingly, there was nothing which had been forgotten in all the litter and jumble left behind. The axes, which were always carelessly thrown down anywhere, were now safely back in their places, hanging from brackets below the steering-handles of the sleds; the rifles were also to hand, and the snowshoes were tied crosswise at the prow of my snow-vessel.

Instead of taking the agreed direction, we set off due west, passing a rocky islet and running into a quiet bay; the snow had been swept clean away by the blizzard in many places, and the ice was showing clearly. The sleds halted. Our Indians examined some tracks and held a discussion—then we continued for a few miles to stop again by a steep slope covered with dwarf alders and small spruce, and bordered by large granite blocks worn smooth by glaciers long ago.

Nap and Augustin put on the snowshoes and took their rifles. Henri turned to Pierre. "Caribou."

Pierre realised what was afoot, seized his camera and started to follow the other two, wading in the deep snow.

"Not far," Henri called encouragingly.

The three went up the slope, and Henri explained to me: "It's the fourth caribou from yesterday, the one they wounded. It must be hiding up on the hill, it can't have got far."

He was right, it had not got far. About fifty yards up the hillside Nap, who was in the lead, turned and signalled to the other two. The wounded animal was lying in the snow, half hidden among the bushes. Pierre raised his camera, the caribou struggled up, a shot rang out, and it was all over. Augustin returned to fetch his dogs; they were hitched to the caribou in their usual order and then dragged it over the snow to the sleds. The animal still had to be cut up, but that was soon done with the axes, and the half-dozen chunks were loaded on to the back of a sled.

"Why aren't you taking the skin?" I asked.

The previous evening they had skinned two animals, and the thick fur had made a very comfortable sleeping mat.

"It's no good. The heavy winter hair soon falls out, and it won't be of any use in a few months."

We soon knew only too well that the winter coat is shed. The thick mat of the caribou's winter fur is surprisingly light; the hairs fly off at the slightest breath of air and, fine and invisible, flutter into all the cooking utensils, stick to camera-lenses and are a real nuisance. But this fur is so comfortable to lie on!

We turned round and followed our own trail for a time. The day was already advanced and the sky had completely clouded over. The Indians were looking ill-tempered; there were signs of snow in the sky, and if there was a fall the dogs would have a hard time hauling the sleds.

We came to the northernmost point of Whitefish Lake. One of the Indians stopped to cut a few branches, then he arranged them on the ice to mark the place of passage to and from the lake.

"There's no trail marked, north from here," said Henri. "Tonight we shall sleep on the edge of the tree line, at the edge of the bush. Beyond are the Barren Lands. Bad, very bad," he concluded. "No wood, no fire." Fire—without which the Indians could not live.

We began to follow a winding river course which linked a number of lakes of various size; the going was easy crossing the lakes, but the passage from one to the other was a great strain on the dogs. There was no trail to follow here. Between snow-covered blocks of moraine were troughs of snow, traps into which the lead-dog suddenly sank with a howl.

Joe Mitchell had taken the initiative. Wearing snowshoes, he went on ahead to find the best route. We sometimes had to wait a long time for his return. The way he chose did not seem very sensible to me at first; I could not understand why he did not take the fine smooth path of the river-bed. But it was because the ice was thin; he had put his ear to it and heard the water gurgling beneath. So we had to cut our way through the woods, chopping branches as we went. The leading team broke the trail and the others benefited from the ruts made.

"Come on, Nancy! *Cha-cha*, come on, come on!" Nap coaxed his lead-dog. He was fond of his dogs and seldom beat them; even when he punished them it was done mildly, using his short whip. I never saw him beat them with the handle of his axe, as Henri and Joe did, usually drawing blood.

Nap signalled to me to wait; the way was too confused for more than one sled at a time. His dogs rested, crouched in the snow and lapping avidly at it to quench their thirst. It was a wonderful spot, a narrow, rocky gorge where the cliffs on the sheltered side were blanketed with snow all the way down, while the windswept side showed the famous arctic red stone, rich in minerals. The Indians looked closely at the veins (for they are prospectors at heart too), then chipped off a few fragments with their axe-heads and passed them round.

"Gold!" laughed Henri.

"Copper," retorted Joe, who was the best educated.

Never mind, if this was not the day when they would strike it rich, they were happy enough out here with their dogs and the great wind of freedom blowing over them from the forest.

But it could hardly be called forest, nor even woods, now; the landscape had abruptly changed. Round the shores of Whitefish Lake there had been clumps of firs and some quite tall trees, but here the northern slopes were almost bare, with just a few dwarf birch and arctic willows growing in the dips and crevices between the smooth rocks, with a tangled spread of bilberry bushes. We had almost reached the tundra, although the southern slopes were still covered with spruce.

It was our turn to go forward. Nancy, grand little animal that she was, scrambled over rocks with the aid of her sharp claws, staggered into troughs and regained her balance, frequently glancing back as though seeking her master's opinion. Her intelligent eyes seemed to be saying "Are you satisfied?" The sleds behind us were rocking and swaying over the rough, uneven ground. Nap was exerting all his great strength on the steering-handles to help his dogs, and I often had to give a hand, lifting the back of the sled clear of obstacles or prying loose the front when it got wedged between two rocks. Sometimes we had to use the sled as a bridge to cross a gap in the rocks.

I no longer felt the cold. All this activity was fine; Pierre and I had forgotten our state of hapless civilised men and were sharing the joys and labours of our rugged friends. And as they saw this, the last traces of aloofness vanished from their faces. We had succeeded, we were all one team now, not white men and Indians. We were all men on the move, struggling to reach new hunting-grounds by nightfall.

We regrouped at the end of each gully, and Pierre and I rode on the sleds again when crossing a lake. Pierre had been filming continuously and was looking very pleased.

While Nap and I were waiting at the beginning of another portage (in summer, the Indians have to carry their boats round these rapids to get from one lake to another), Nap pointed out to me a splendid ptarmigan perched on the branch of a young birch tree; it looked almost tame. Ptarmigan, a species of arctic grouse, have a plumage of pure white in winter; you could almost tread on one before seeing it. This bird was watching the men and dogs quite unconcernedly. Pierre was some way behind, and before he could arrive to photograph the bird it flew off and landed on the snow about twenty yards away, and at once disappeared as though by magic, so perfect was its protective colouring.

We came upon a group of them a little later. Pierre had his camera and crawled towards them; the ptarmigan were strutting about on the hard snow and could be made out only by their moving shadows. Pierre could not see a sign of them when he put the camera to his eye. He took some shots of them blindly. "White on white—with a pure white sky," he growled.

We worked our way along this succession of gorges and came to a high windswept plateau which was almost entirely lake. Joe Mitchell brought us to a halt. There were distinct and recent tracks of caribou on the ice, of a herd of at least fifty, about the maximum in winter.

But Joe was not very pleased. "Wolf!" he exclaimed.

On one side of the caribou tracks, then on the other, and sometimes merging with them, were the marks of a large wolf. It was either following after or running behind the herd, waiting for an animal to drop out or fall behind; then it would attack.

Cutting down spruce for the fire

The Indians' camp

A caribou herd on Lake Ptarmigan

Nap and Augustin going to look for caribou

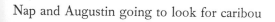

A caribou

Nose to nose

Joe Mitchell

Henri Catholique

Napoleon Mitchell

The author and Henri in their tent

Two hours later we came upon the remains of a caribou. Master Wolf had had its meal and then continued the chase. I wondered whether we should catch up with the herd; the Indians were doing their best.

The going became easier, for the river now formed a narrow lake about eight miles long. I asked what its name was, and opinions were divided. Henri thought it was Lake Ptarmigan, but Joe maintained that it was not. They were not really interested in place-names. In the minds of these nomads, places were remembered as being connected with some hunting or fishing exploit, an unexpected meeting or an accident.

We had not noticed the change in the weather during the struggle and effort along the gorges, and now the wind had risen and a storm was threatening. Wisps of snow skated across the ice, there was a sudden drop in temperature—which had not been so bitter, because of the clouds (probably about twenty below)—and then the blizzard was upon us, right in our faces. The drivers put on their parkas—a bad sign. Instead of being carried along like Roman charioteers, they trotted behind their sleds; Pierre and I did the same, whenever we could. Pierre was in his thirties and a good strong walker, he could keep up the pace for a long time; but five minutes of this loping run were enough for me, though I could walk for hours at the steady, slow pace of a highlander.

When we finally stopped, the sun was setting behind a line of spiky little evergreens, trees twisted and gnarled by the wind of the arctic winter, yet miraculously coming to life again in the spring. Slender and tapering like spears, they formed a sombre screen to the long white stretch of frozen lake. To the north were low, rolling hills, ice-topped and with a greyish fringe of dwarf alder or birch.

Joe had chosen our camping site very carefully.

The average height of the spruce was no more than ten feet, and I had a distinct feeling of having reached the limit of nature's growth. A few miles to the north were the Barren Lands, where the

Indians venture only in the summer, but where the Eskimos still live.

In this open and windswept country, the snow piles up against all natural obstacles. The trees here seemed to have stopped all the snow from the tundra. The drifts were so deep that the dogs had to give up after a few minutes of struggling forward. Joe and Henri put on the snowshoes—it was their job to make camp; the young men, Nap and Augustin, were the hunters. Pierre and I waited in the biting wind for the snow to be stamped down. In order to keep ourselves warm we ran about on the frozen lake, where the herd of caribou had left tracks, a pattern ten to twenty yards wide. Only the tips of their sharp hooves had marked the hard snow. Following along at the side were other tracks, those of wolves, but so large that when I saw the first of them I wondered what great beast had passed this way; there were also the small, light tracks of a white arctic fox which had been following the wolves that were following the caribou. Everyone is invited to the hunt-feast. Freshest of all the tracks were those of our dogs, pads outspread on the snow, tight and pointed on the ice.

Henri and Joe were going to have a difficult task to obtain the six poles needed for putting up the tents, and also the leafy branches for spreading over the snow. The spruce were little more than a thin, tapering trunk with a few branches less than a foot in length.

The cold was becoming intense, but the Indians were going about their tasks without any sign of fatigue. According to the thermometer it was thirty below; with the wind that was blowing, the actual temperature must have been considerably lower. I was glad of the light, supple mocassins which were such good insulators that my feet never felt cold. Pierre and I whiled away the time by running on the ice and flapping our arms, while in the twilight the few trees protecting us from the bitter wind were being chopped down one by one. In an hour, the tents would be pitched on their carpet of leaves, though in this case the leaves were more like fine thorns; still, their lace-like covering would protect us from the snow.

Henri and Joe showed us a great mark of friendship by concentrating on one tent first, instead of putting up the two at the same time. Their first thought was to provide shelter for us, to fit up the stove and light it.

"Come in," they said with a smile. "Come in. It's too cold tonight."

We were only too glad to get under the canvas with our sleeping-bags and equipment.

In the gathering dusk the camp site looked a weird place. The Indians had destroyed the trees over a large circle, chopping them off at waist height (a regrettable habit of theirs, to save themselves the trouble of stooping), so that we were surrounded by jagged stakes and might have been in a wood that had been heavily shelled.

While we were relaxing, melting snow and making the tea, Henri and Joe put up the other tent, fed the dogs and gathered up the harness. Nap and Augustin had put on the snowshoes and gone off on reconnaissance to the west. It was very late when they returned, having followed the caribou tracks and discovered the whereabouts of the herd. It had run westwards before the wolves, then turned south towards a large lake. The Indians could not put a name to the lake, but they were sure that we should find the herd on or near it next day.

Nap and Augustin hung their rifles on a branch, shook the snow from their mukluks, then came and drank some tea and ate dried meat.

In spite of their fatigue, they all gathered with us in Henri's tent after the evening meal. We handed round cigarettes, played the harmonica, and discussed the morrow's hunting programme. The Indians seemed quite happy. However, a slight altercation broke out between Napoleon and Henri. During the day, Henri had proudly pointed out to me that he now had six dogs. Until then, his had been the smallest team. But he was an unstable character and a spendthrift who would gamble his shirt; and there he was with an extra dog. He told me that he had given his wrist-watch for it. And my big chief's team had suffered in prestige, for it had only seven dogs instead of eight. But in the gorges and scrub we had been travelling through it was almost impossible to control a large team; six dogs were quite sufficient if the sled was not loaded too heavily.

So all would have been well if Napoleon had not noticed that the watch he had received in exchange was not working properly. He asked me the time, and found that his watch was twenty minutes slow. The others made fun of him, and he was furious.

"Give me my dog back!" he shouted at Henri. "Here's your watch." He made as though to dash it against a log.

"Here, wait a minute," I said. "Let me see it."

It had an automatic action, and normally should never be wound. However, to give a turn or two every evening would do no harm. I put it right. Nap held it to his ear like a little boy, but did not seem entirely satisfied. "Do you think it'll go all right now?"

I could not swear to it, but I refrained from telling him so.

Henri was grinning away happily, so I damped him down a bit. "Henri, if the watch doesn't go tomorrow, you'll have to give back the dog."

Nap went one better. "It's a lead-dog and a jolly good animal, worth at least twenty-five dollars."

"How much is the watch worth?" I asked Henri.

"Thirty-five dollars."

He had bought it the day we left but was already tired of it; more particularly, he felt ashamed at having the smallest team. Actually, he was not telling the truth; the watch was a cheap fifteen-dollar one from the Bay. I checked this later.

Henri consoled himself for having parted with his watch by naming his new dog Timex. I think he had made a good bargain, for when Timex was put in the lead to give Blackie a rest, he did his work very well. The watch kept good time, too, and could be expected to adorn Nap's wrist until he lost it at cards. But that would not be for some time, as he was a very clever player.

After a very cold and windy night we woke up to find an inch of snow on the tents and a sky that was milky white, streaked with grey.

Pierre and I were given back our snowshoes.

"Follow the trail that Nap and Augustin made," we were told. "It's a long, hard climb. Then wait for us on the mountain."

Pierre took the pack containing the cameras and I carried the other photographic equipment, and we went on ahead while the Indians struck camp.

Our progress on snowshoes was made much easier by our having a trail to follow; but the moment we stepped aside we sank deep into the snow, and I realised why skis are not used. Everyone has seen pictures of Canadian snowshoes, so I need not describe them here. But there are several different kinds: short ones are used for crossing hard snow, and very long, wide ones for crossing deep, soft snow. The snowshoes are kept on by a single leather or canvas strap, which leaves your foot fairly loose and gives it plenty of play; and as you walk, the toes of your mukluks sink into the snow through an opening in the netting. It takes some time to get used to snowshoes, but being skiers we did not find any difficulty. The chief thing is for your leg-muscles to become accustomed to walking with the feet wide apart—though less wide than it appears—and especially to taking long sweeping strides. The Indians never use sticks, they keep their hands free for their axe or gun. You sometimes find yourself sinking up to your neck in some trough or pit, for everywhere there are fallen branches and rotted tree-trunks covering some hollow but hidden by the snow. It would be impossible to disentangle skis from these traps, but snowshoes can be lifted out fairly easily. Moreover, the snow slips through the netting, so that your feet do not get weighed down by an accumulation of it. Snowshoes are perfectly suited to the hunter's or trapper's need to leave the trail and go where one could not help sinking with ordinary footwear.

In little more than an hour we reached the top of the "mountain". It was an altitude of about twelve hundred feet; but Great Slave

Lake is five hundred feet above sea level, so that the prominence on which we were standing was not a great deal higher than the surrounding plateau. This was enough for it to provide a commanding view. On three sides there stretched an undulating landscape of rocky ground and frozen lakes and thin lines of spruce; to the south was a large lake, and beyond were high hills worn smooth by wind and weather. These were the rugged barriers to the northern shores of Great Slave Lake. The plateau looked as if it had suffered a colossal air-raid, for it was covered with hundreds of large craters which were now frozen ponds or lakes, glinting where the blizzard had whisked away the snow.

To the north and east, the line of forest—if it could still be called such—dipped into gorges, bordered the lakes and girdled the rounded hills. It made me think of a very fine, black-and-white lithograph. To the south, and nearer to us, the slopes were much more wooded; the dark mantle covered everything, except where white blankets indicated the dormant, frozen waters.

Right on the top of the hill was balanced a huge, erratic block of granite, scored by glaciers. It fitted in with the landscape like a monument on a specially selected site.

We were sixty feet above the tree limit, standing on this barren, windswept summit. The bald top dominated a vast emptiness, and here indeed it was possible to grasp the idea of infinity. All around was the hunting-ground of Indians and wolves. In a few months the big brown bears would be coming out of hibernation, as well as the grizzlies of the Barren Lands, which are more dangerous than wolves and can kill reindeer. But at this time of year they were still in their winter hibernation, hidden away asleep.

We should see neither bears nor beavers in this region; but the caribou herds had already set out on their long trek to the northeast. Once the thaw begins, they can no longer find the food they need in the bush, and so migrate to the Barren Lands where grass and lichens grow during the short summer. Caribou gather in countless herds and, guided by instinct, make their way north and east, crossing rivers as wide as any in Europe, and, whenever possible, keep to heights where the wind drives away the mosquitoes that pester them.

In summer, caribou herds numbering several thousands have been counted in the Thelon River reserves by zoologists of the Northwest Territories administration.

The caribou population was once estimated at two million, but now it is about one-sixth of that number. Nevertheless, their migration still follows the same ancient and sometimes disconcerting pattern. One year, the herds from the region of Great Bear Lake cross the Barren Lands to the District of Keewatin near Hudson Bay; but another year, for some reason unknown to man, they follow a different route. Most mysterious of all is the manner in which the scattered herds gather for their winter migration to the bush; their instinct leads them to districts where climatic conditions have produced the vegetation which they need.

The secret of these migratory routes is, however, known to the Indians. They observe the herds during the winter, and when the arctic night comes to an end they follow the tracks of the caribou and estimate the route being taken. In this particular year the herds which had wintered south of Great Slave Lake had crossed that vast stretch of ice and were heading north; while herds from the forests along the Mackenzie River were heading east.

The does leave the herd to have their young on the high barren plateau; then does and fawns join the bucks to form a huge wandering herd, until the approach of autumn.

The Canadian authorities are making attempts to replenish caribou stock, and expansive reserves have been created. The habitat of the caribou is so vast that it is difficult for Europeans to imagine. It covers a triangular area from Lake Athabasca to the mouth of the Mackenzie River, and from the lake to Hudson Bay, encompassing thousands of miles.

Two different species are found. The wood caribou (which we were hunting) migrates between the southerly forest and the tundra; the barren-ground caribou has its home in the North, on Melville Peninsula, Victoria Island and Baffin Island, and rarely moves south.

The four teams were coming up the slope towards us, straining at the traces. It had been a hard climb and the dogs needed to get their wind. The way down was going to be a rough scramble for a hundred yards, to reach the big frozen lake stretching to the south. This time our Indians were in agreement—it was Ptarmigan Lake, though not named as such on the maps.

The teams rushed down the slope one after the other, each driver clinging to the steering-handles and guiding his sled as best he could to avoid the little trees and the rocks. Pierre and I made our way down on foot, and once on the lake we were able to take our places on the sleds again.

The episode which made this day so memorable began when we were out in the middle of the lake. One of the dogs gave a peculiar whine, and at once all four teams streaked forward.

"Caribou! Caribou!" yelled Nap behind me.

I looked hard but all I could see was a sort of thin grey line which blended into the rocky, far shore of the lake. But for the Indians there was no mistake—it was a large herd of caribou. And the herd stood still, watching our approach with curiosity.

We were far from quiet or cautious. The dogs were barking madly, the Indians were yelling to excite them even more. Nap fired his rifle into the air to speed on the dogs, who strained harder when they caught a whiff of gunpowder. The four teams spread out fanwise to cut round the herd, which still was not moving. I heard Pierre shouting: "Don't shoot yet!"

Pierre had his telescopic camera ready, and from a distance he looked like a hunter himself, as if armed with a heavy rifle. That was the last I saw of him until evening.

Nap was driving his team towards the rear of the herd, and when we were about five hundred yards away I saw the caribou start to trot off in small groups, going in different directions. But whichever way they went, from their position in the middle of this large lake dotted with wooded islets, they found themselves facing a speeding sled and a team of excited dogs barking furiously. The herd broke up and the dismayed animals galloped in circles, trying to reach the safety of the woods.

Suddenly, Nap stopped the sled by turning it on its side, and I was thrown on to the ice. Two, three shots rang out. Nap had hit three caribou; one fell and remained there, the other two limped off. Nap righted his sled and whipped up his dogs in pursuit of the caribou, leaving me behind. And there I was alone, out in the middle of this great lake, seeing the four teams disappearing in different directions, chasing caribou.

Rifle-shots kept echoing across the ice. Half the herd had made off to the south, pursued by Augustin, Joe and Pierre. To the north, Henri was chasing a dozen or so bounding animals which disappeared from my view behind a headland. Nap had driven the remainder of the herd, about sixty, back towards the middle of the lake and was in pursuit, keeping between them and the shore. More shots rang out, then came a pause. The sleds were no more than specks on the great expanse of ice. I heard a few shots in the distance, saw some terrified caribou go bounding past and plunge into the woods, then complete silence reigned.

Alone in the middle of the plain of ice, a feeling of sadness came over me. In spite of the north wind that was blowing, I was not cold; the activity, the pursuit, had warmed me. But all this carnage had transported me into some age of barbarism, and I had to stifle any tender feelings. There were three animals lying on the ice. I went towards the nearest, a splendid doe that was in fawn; she had been hit in the chest and was slowly dying. Seeing me approach, she summoned the strength to stagger to her forelegs, then dropped down again, finished. I had no weapon on me, not even a knife. All I had picked up after the sled overturned were Nap's parka and rifle-cover.

This wounded animal ought to be put out of her misery. But I doubted whether I should have the courage to do it.

I went and looked at the other two. One was a doe, also in fawn, about seven or eight years old to judge by her magnificent antlers; the other was a young buck. The doe had both hind legs shattered by a bullet, and had dragged herself for fifty yards over the ice, leaving a bloody trail. The other had a broken shoulder. The ice round these wounded animals was gradually turning red. I shall never forget their astonished gaze as they lay there dying, covered with sweat, and the memory is a constant reproach.

I don't know how long I remained there, waiting patiently for someone to come.

The hunt must have long been over, for it was some time since I had heard any rifle-shots. At last I saw a sled moving about in a bay on the far side of the lake; one of the four was probably cutting up carcasses and loading the meat. Then an excited team came streaking across the ice towards me. It was Nap, drunk with success. He had killed another caribou. I pointed to the dying animals: "Finish them off, for God's sake!"

But he was impervious to such an appeal.

"They can't go far," he said.

Their sufferings did not matter, so long as they could not get away.

He decapitated one caribou with a single blow of his axe, and I was expecting him to do the same to the other two. The doe with shattered hind legs was dragging herself over the ice, terrified by the dogs. But Napoleon, joyful Nap, began methodically to skin and cut up the dead caribou. He threw a few chunks of meat to his dogs, and when he had finished he went towards the other two animals. He killed them, skinned them and cut them up, all in the same precise manner.

Henri came across the lake to join us, urging on his dogs. He had the caribou meat piled on his sled. That made five already.

The two Indians baited snares with the entrails and left them on the ice, for tracks of more than one white arctic fox could be seen about the lake.

"Where are the others?" I asked.

"We'll see them this evening. Over there." Henri pointed towards the southern end of the lake, where there was a high, dome-like mass of rock capped with ice.

He and Nap loaded their sleds with the caribou meat, threw a skin over one lot, and I sat on the bloody heap which was already staining the canvas sides of the sled. We set off across the lake moving at a slower pace, for dogs and drivers were tired after the long chase. The day was drawing to a close when we reached the shore and could see a long band of blue smoke curling above a clump of slender trees. We found the others at the end of a narrow creek, where there was probably a sheltered beach in summer. The high bank on the south side was sparsely covered with dwarf birch, but the north side ended in a high rocky mass blanketed with hard snow and ice. The sun was just sinking below the hilltops, and its last rays were colouring the snow and blinding us with their reflection.

Joe and Augustin had lit a fire and made some tea. They greeted us with wide smiles; they, too, had had a very successful hunt, each having killed two caribou. They had wounded others, which had escaped into the woods.

That was the tragedy of it. Nine had been killed, but how many had been wounded and would die a miserable death in the bush, succumbing to their wounds or to the wolves?

The Indians were excellent shots. They needed to be to bring down a galloping caribou at a distance. But in fact they adopted more simple tactics, firing at a herd where it was most closely grouped, knowing quite well that they would do no more than wound a few. Then they chased after the wounded animals to finish them off—as had happened this day. Nine from a single day's hunt. No wonder our Indians were looking pleased.

I saw Pierre for the first time since morning, and opened my arms wide in joyful greeting. "You got the caribou this time, then. I bet you're satisfied now."

He looked cross. "I've got nothing at all. How d'you expect to take pictures in those conditions? When you're shaken about over the hummock ice, it's like being in an outboard motorboat going at full speed through a rough sea. The only thing I got in the box was a solitary caribou. We saw it lying on the ice and thought it was dead, but when the dogs drew near it sprang to its feet, held off the dogs, then fled. After that, there was a mad scramble, like the other day."

"But the herd. You got some shots of the bunch? You were closer than I was, this time."

"I told you—it was impossible to use a camera."

"You should have tried, all the same."

I left it at that. I knew Pierre aimed at perfection. Still, what a chance for our film—that herd, sixty strong, fleeing across the lake. It was worth trying. But I kept my thoughts to myself. I had sworn to leave Pierre to do what he considered best.

"There'll be other opportunities," I said to console him.

He shrugged his shoulders. "What good will that be, if it's the same thing over again? What's needed is for me to have the camera set up on its tripod when a herd comes past. And that means not chasing after them as soon as they're sighted—just rounding them up and waiting for a bit. But try getting the Indians to do that!"

"Yes, I know."

However, Pierre had in fact filmed the mad stampede of the caribou, though he did not tell me so at the time. He showed me the results three months later. There were shots of bounding, terrified caribou, of dogs and sleds, all racing in front of a jolting camera; an action film that had all the atmosphere of the hunt.

The tents had been pitched and the Indians were busy preparing the caribou meat for drying over a big fire. They were singing and laughing. Nap, who had got four caribou with four shots, was the hero of the day. But all the meat was put in a common pool.

A blizzard began to blow and the cold became intense. It was a sign of snowstorms tomorrow, I was warned. Never mind. We were quite at home under the patched tents now; each of us had his own place, was not in the way of the other two, and had everything he needed close at hand. Any stranger looking into our tent would probably have thought what a disorderly jumble everything was— but how wrong he would have been. Henri had the things that mattered, his axe and the sacks of food, within easy reach; Pierre had the cameras in their pack as his pillow, and I had the kitbag containing the spare film. It was not very soft, but I used it as a bolster and it was most useful to keep my head out of draughts.

The Indians were in high good humour, so I seized the opportunity to put our plan to them. What Pierre and I wanted, I explained, was for them to find another caribou herd and drive it past a place where we should be waiting to film it—and we'd wait a whole day, if need be. But the essential thing was for them not to start shooting at the herd until the filming was completed. It was a lot to ask, I knew, but was worth trying.

The evening was spent feasting on caribou meat and playing the mouth-organ. I brought out a bottle of pure alcohol from the bottom of my pack. I had kept it hidden as people had warned me against giving the Indians strong drink. "They never know when to stop," I was told, "and then they start fighting, and you'll get no more work out of them." Yes, but if I kept a tight hold on the bottle . . .

I poured a good ration of spirits into each man's tea-mug. The liquor was over-proof and ought to be drunk diluted with three parts water. In this case, we diluted it with tea. But Joe was artful; he drank the tea first, then held out his empty mug. He added some tea to the spirits, but very little:

"It's too sweet."

I put the bottle back in my pack for a later occasion. I ought to add that the Indians never tried to get hold of it, to have a swig in secret. They must have found it difficult to understand why we did not empty the bottle that evening, for the custom among outpost Canadians often is to go on drinking a bottle, once opened, until it is empty. Our sense of moderation was beyond them, but they made no comment.

Late in the evening, Henri went and joined the other three in their tent to discuss the possibility of doing as I had asked.

During the night the dogs suddenly broke into a frenzy of whining and barking that drowned the howling of the wind. It was the pack's love chorus, and Nap had to make sure that one of his bitches did not get over to Blackie, the big lead-dog, who was pulling desperately at its chain. The dogs fell silent again after a few minutes, and we were able to get some more sleep, lulled by the deep calm all around us.

In the morning, Joe told me that Nap and Augustin were going to look for tracks of a herd of caribou, while he and Henri dried the meat over a fire. This suited Pierre and me, for it would give us an opportunity to take some background pictures.

Nap and Augustin returned without anything definite to report. The tracks they had found indicated that the caribou had continued moving eastward and that there was no chance of overtaking them. However, Joe thought that other caribou might be following the same route, and that we should go next day to a lake on the other side of the hill. The string of lakes formed a natural path for the caribou, who found the lichens they needed along the shores.

It was a day of relaxation for all of us. The cold was bearable, and in fact by midday the snow began to melt—another sign that spring was not far off.

A special structure was needed for drying the caribou meat, and this gave the Indians an excuse to chop down some more trees, and then still more to serve as fuel. The best of the meat was cut into very thin strips, then placed on a roughly made trellis and held over the smoky fire. The meat thus treated became lighter to carry and took up much less space on the sleds.

Pierre and I went to look at the snares with entrail bait which had been left out on the lake, but no fox had been caught in them. Pierre took some interesting shots of the landscape and of the strange patterns made by the wind on the hard drifted snow; then we returned to the camp and he photographed the Indians at work and in their tents. The bitches were almost mad with desire, rolling in the snow and whimpering. The Indians soon put a stop to it all by distributing blows right and left.

At mealtime, Henri wanted Pierre and me to have some of his "Indian turkey"; this was the unborn fawn found in the doe, and was considered by the Indians to make the tastiest dish of all. The practice of firing into the midst of a herd from a distance means that the Indians never know whether they are killing bucks or does. I should add that the dead does I saw had antlers that were quite as large as those of the bucks. A doe gives birth to only one fawn a year, and she is carrying it when the herd migrates north to the tundra, which is the period when the Indians hunt the caribou.

I refused Henri's "Indian turkey", but Pierre, who will eat almost anything and always has a keen appetite, tried some of it and said it was very tasty.

Pierre even ate muskrat on a later occasion, and when the Indians asked him what he thought of it he said: "Very good; tastes like rabbit." They exclaimed in horror at this—comparing muskrat, fattened and sweetened by all the aquatic herbs it feeds on, with the despised rabbit! I wish, now, that I had tried these dishes and so added to my gastronomic experiences.

The following morning, the Indians took us over a rise and across another lake, south of our camp. The lake had its issue in a narrow gorge, one side of which formed a headland dominating the lake by about one hundred feet and giving a wide view. The Indians found some fresh tracks which indicated that a herd of caribou had passed this way less than twenty-four hours before. There was a good chance of another herd following the same trail.

The Indians had fully understood what Pierre and I were hoping for; the spot was ideal for posting ourselves with the camera on its tripod. The snow had been trampled down by caribou searching for moss and lichens around the dwarf birches. When we looked more closely we found many wolf tracks; one of them was worthy of respect—it was nearly four inches in diameter. However, that was unlikely to be the size of the animal's paw. When a wolf is running over deep snow it spreads its toes, and the furry paw leaves prints that are much larger than the actual size.

The stream flowing from this lake in summer joins the Indian Mountain River, which runs into Great Slave Lake.

Henri had his trap line in this area (we visited it later, before returning to Snowdrift) and he tried to find one of his traps for us, saying that it was close at hand. But the snow was so deep that he had to give up the search. The total snowfall that winter had been much greater than was usual for the region. The depth of snow rarely exceeds two feet.

The Indians lit a big fire for themselves and spent the rest of the day smoking, eating and sleeping, while Pierre and I remained on the height, cameras at the ready, keeping a lookout in the hope that a magnificent herd of grey-and-white caribou would appear. We stayed at our observation post from nine in the morning to six in the evening. The sky gradually clouded over, the temperature dropped and a strong wind began to blow. A storm was threatening; it was time to return to camp. It had been a long day and our patience had not been rewarded, but we resolved to make a similar attempt if another favourable spot were found.

I congratulated Henri and Joe on having organised this ambush for us. It had brought no results, but they had understood our aim and done their best, and had sent the two young Indians to explore the terrain over a wide area. They were pleased at receiving our thanks and were happy to have done what we wanted. There was no longer any awkwardness between the Indians and us; we were all out on the same hunting expedition.

It was the Indians, in fact, who came to ask us to give up and leave our observation post. "It's too late to hope to see a herd now.

The caribou will have taken shelter in the woodlands, since this wind got up. It's going to be very cold. Are your feet wet?"

There was danger of getting wet feet from the melting snow. Mukluks kept one's feet warm only when the snow was hard and the weather was very cold. The Indians were wearing rubber boots, and I decided to follow their example if the thaw continued.

Dusk was beginning to fall as we all set off to return to camp. The dogs had had a good long rest and pulled strongly up the ridge, so that we did not have to get off the sleds. Then they went full gallop down the other side, which resulted in a number of spills; but all this gave us much to laugh about when we gathered together in the evening.

Nap was most distressed. His watch was losing a minute or two each day, and he seemed to attach great importance to this—which was very surprising in view of the fact that one hour or one day more or less made little difference to these Indians. I suspected him of wanting to cancel his deal with Henri, so I settled the matter to everyone's satisfaction.

"Take back one of your dog's legs. Then the watch and the dog will both hobble along."

They all laughed, and the matter was forgotten. Though Joe kept teasing Nap about having got the worst of the deal.

The wind blew hard during the night, covering the dogs and the sleds with snow. When daylight came, there was a low, grey, leaden sky, and the wind was moaning out on the lake.

I wanted to push a little farther north, to see what the Barren Lands were like, but the Indians were opposed to it.

"There's no wood, no fire."

Instead, they proposed going east, to the upper reaches of Indian Mountain River. We might come across caribou in that area.

I left it to them. They had given proof of their willingness and desire to help us. The decision had to be left to them. Actually, not even they knew exactly where we were, and their longest hunting trips had never taken them into the country ahead of us now. I looked at the one map I had, but the scale was so small that it was like trying to find the paths through the forest of Fontainebleau on a map of the whole of France.

The Indians took their direction from the sun. It was not shining, but they could tell its position from the light in the clouds. They also took notice of the vegetation, which was distinctly different on the north from that on the south slopes of the slightest hillock. And there were the long parallel hummocks on the lakes, which indicated the direction of the prevailing winds.

The temperature had risen during the night and was only ten or twelve below. The snow was turning slushy, and the dogs were going to have a hard time. We crossed the lake to its eastern end and found ourselves on a large bare patch of ice as slippery as glass. Dogs and sleds began sliding all over the place, but the Indians stopped and played like children, seeing who could slide the farthest. It was a difficult game, for the ice was not as smooth as glass; it had been rucked up by the winds and currents. Taking photographs became something of a balancing trick; the gusts of wind sent one drifting about like a loose buoy.

Once we reached the bank we were again among small trees, gorges and frozen streams. The going became very arduous, but the dogs had been well fed and worked with a will; it became necessary, however, to change the lead-dogs fairly often. The landscape was almost arctic, with sparse clumps of small spruce and high, bare, rocky hills.

Suddenly we came upon the springtime. Joe's lead-dog broke through a bridge of snow and fell into a raging torrent. We retrieved the unfortunate animal with some difficulty. It was the first flowing water that we had seen. The river seemed to be quite large, gurgling and roaring along under the ice, and we had to turn aside and find a way round, scrambling over heaps of granite covered with snow and ice. Ptarmigans fluttered up from all sides, and then some large black crows flew over us, their hoarse croaking suddenly filling the silence of the gorges.

The clouds were sweeping low, just clearing the hilltops, and we seemed to be making our way through an icy tunnel. The wind was blowing in our faces; the dogs' breath froze on their jaws, and little icicles formed round our hoods. There were many tracks of game in these forbidding surroundings—chiefly of wolves, foxes, wolverines, martens and ermines. But none of caribou, except for one or two single tracks under clumps of dwarf birch, and occasionally signs of where a herd had nosed among the snow some time previously.

We struggled on. Joe was leading the way on snowshoes; he recognised some landmarks, having come prospecting in the area the previous spring. Nap had shown great confidence in me by allowing me to drive the sled, and I was soon aware of the physical effort required. It was like ploughing a field deep in snow. The dogs knew me by now, but they were not used to my voice; and besides, I expect I gave a faulty intonation of the key-words.

Nancy stopped, flopped down in the snow and turned her fox-like muzzle in my direction as if to say, *Now just what is it that you want?* I kept shouting, "*He-tet, he-tet!*" but she did not budge.

Nap, some distance ahead, called to her softly, "Come on, Nancy, come on." The intelligent animal got up and stretched her back, then yelped at the other dogs to get them moving. I lifted the sled by the steering-handles, and off we went again. Sometimes the dogs ran on too quickly, and I slipped from the little platform into the soft snow. Fortunately, a rope was always trailing from the back of the sled; I grasped it, got pulled to my feet, and regained my place as driver.

This long stage across lakes and along gorges brought us at nightfall to a small wood of firs which was thicker than any we had seen for the last couple of days. I reckoned that we had made a wide curve to the east and south during the day.

Now we had to make camp. There were some deep snowdrifts close to where we had stopped, and we soon found ourselves up to the waist in them. However, less than an hour after arriving, there was a clearing dotted with tree-trunks the height of a man where previously a thick copse had stood, and in the middle were our two tents with smoke coming from the stove-pipes. It was snowing. Our clothes were wet, and we spent part of the evening drying them.

While I was enjoying the peace and rest after the day's long effort, an unexpected sound came to my ears. I listened hard, and there could be no doubt—it was the sound of an engine.

"The mine," was Joe's casual reply to my question.

A mine near here? This was surprising news. It marred the feeling of solitude and complete freedom that had been with me since leaving Snowdrift. A mine meant white prospectors, drillings, buildings.

Then the wind changed, and I heard only the familiar sounds of the bush.

In the morning, Joe said to me, "Would you like to go to the mine?"

I felt little inclination, I must say. It would mean an encounter with civilisation, the shattering of part of my dream.

"Is it on our way?"

"No, just a short detour."

I had a good idea of what a short detour meant to an Indian.

But Joe was insistent. He went and spoke to Henri. It was obvious that the Indians were disgruntled. Finally, Henri came to tell me, "Joe will go with his sled to buy some food supplies at the mine."

"Food supplies? But we've still enough left."

Henri hung his head. We had hardly anything left, other than caribou meat. And he had a sudden longing for all the things he knew to be obtainable from white men—dried milk, canned goods.

I gave in. Joe would go to get supplies, while the rest of us continued on our way. Joe knew this district very well, having worked at the mine last summer, so he said. And I had thought that Indians never took jobs of that kind.

When we struck camp there was a lowering sky and snow-showers were coming up from the east, blotting out the landscape.

It was comparatively mild, and the mushy snow presented a new hazard for the dogs. Great care was needed, not on the lakes where the ice would remain thick and solid for another month, until May, but along the gorges where we were passing over river-beds much of the time.

An hour on the trail brought us to the end of a high rocky ridge, and just then the sun began to shine through the thinning mist. Henri pointed ahead, at the southern shore of a small lake, and I could just make out two long buildings and a few tents. "The mine," he said.

It was not a mine, but simply a prospectors' camp. We were nearer to it than I had thought. As we were crossing the lake I saw a man riding a skidoo, or motorised sled, which was dragging a wooden triangle to flatten out the hummocks of snow on the ice. Some other men had seen our teams and sleds and were waving to us. It would have been most impolite not to have paid a visit to these lonely people.

The man on the skidoo came towards us, stopped and introduced himself. He was a fair-haired young man with a smiling face and frank expression. Finding two white men with the Indians, riding on their sleds, surprised and amused him.

"You'll come and have a cup of coffee, won't you?"

His name was Bob Earhart; he and the other men had arrived here by plane a few days earlier. The buildings had been put up the year before, and he was in charge of the preparations for another season of prospecting for mineral deposits. There were four or five colleagues with him, and they had half-a-dozen Indians to do the cooking, build and repair cabins and, later, to act as guides to the prospectors. Joe Mitchell had been one of them the year before—this was what he meant by "working at the mine". It was a way for him to continue his rambling life in the bush and also get a guaranteed wage.

The main, prefabricated building was divided by a partition; on one side were the kitchen and dining-living-room, on the other were the men's cubicles. It was real camp life, with little comfort but plenty of food. A plane was expected in a day or two, bringing the mail, more food supplies and materials for repairing damage done by a bear.

Bears were still hibernating; this damage had been done in the autumn, after the prospectors had returned south. The bear had broken into the main building, pulled down partitions and raided the kitchen.

"You're sure it was a bear?"

It seemed to me that to leave a sturdy building well stocked with food throughout the long arctic night was a temptation to the passing traveller.

But Bob was in no doubt; the bear had left its tracks and mess all over the place.

Chatting with him, I realised once again what a small world this is. Bob had spent some of his long vacations skiing in Europe and knew Chamonix and its ski-runs very well; he was delighted to talk about them again. He promised to come and see me the next time, and we would go skiing together.

My Indians had made themselves quite at home, and I knew why they had wanted so much to come here: the cook was Henri's brother. There were a good half-dozen of his brothers scattered about the bush.

Henri and the other three were given plenty to eat and devoured the lot.

I asked Bob if he could sell me some canned food. "They've eaten a fortnight's supply in a week," I told him.

He laughed; he was used to that sort of thing.

He knew Joe, and told him to fix up what he needed with the cook. Poor Bob! If he only knew what I found on our sleds that evening . . .

It was late morning when we took to the trail again, and we made slow progress through the woods. The dogs were tiring, and we halted and lit a fire on a rocky headland by a long, narrow lake hemmed in by steep slopes. We were still following the course of the Indian Mountain River, but our direction was now due south.

Nap and Augustin went off on reconnaissance while the rest of us were having a meal. They put on snowshoes, took their rifles, and disappeared into the woods. Pierre took advantage of this un-expected, long halt to set up his camera and take some pictures. He left the camera on its stand, for there was no risk of its freezing in the comparatively mild air. Then suddenly we heard a couple of rifle-shots in quick succession, a mile or two away.

"Caribou!" cried Joe, leaping to his feet.

The dogs began jumping about and barking, and he silenced them with a stick.

"Come on, Pierre!" he said, pretending to be pointing a camera.

"The caribou will turn towards the lake," said Henri.

Nap and Augustin must have surprised a herd and got round behind it. Henri knew from experience and from the terrain and direction of the wind that the caribou would come our way.

We hardly had time to run to the positioned camera before the first of the caribou appeared. They came slowly down from the woods and on to the lake, at least thirty of them, keeping close to-gether and sniffing at the wind; but they had not sighted us.

Visibility was poor, with a whitish-grey sky; there was no sun, no light and shade. Joe loaded his rifle and posted himself next to Pierre, while Henri knelt on the snow with his gun ready. Then the dogs started howling frantically. Joe gave me a stick and motioned to me to go and quieten them. For a few minutes I tried to be like an Indian and hit at the dogs until they cowered down, growling softly. The caribou had now become aware of our presence. Joe called to me to take off my red quilted jacket. He was quite right. The bright colour showed up against the grey surroundings, whereas the dark clothing of the Indians blended with the trees.

The herd was slowly moving across the lake towards us. Their behaviour was strange—they had been hunted from the woods and had fled to the lake, but had forgotten their alarm almost at once, had herded together again and were advancing in close formation. Pierre's telemeter showed them to be about half a mile away. Joe badly wanted to fire at them, but contained himself. This time, we had them in the lens. An opportunity like this would never occur again.

The caribou were still advancing towards us in serried ranks— eight hundred yards, seven hundred——But suddenly they became startled and trotted in circles. Our dogs were bounding about, straining at their chains. Pierre was filming for all he was worth, and I was taking photographs too.

"Can we shoot now?" said Joe. It was almost an entreaty. If this crazy waiting continued much longer, all that good meat would disappear into the distance.

"Just another minute, Joe."

I had a distinct feeling that the minute lasted only a few seconds. A shot rang out, then two, three, four. Joe and Henri emptied their magazines into the herd; and the terrified animals broke away, ran around and gathered again. The two Indians fired at the compact mass; it broke into two groups, and one made straight for the opposite bank, scrambling up the steep slope; a wounded caribou hobbled in the rear. The other group came running back, then turned and bounded into the woods.

The lake was empty of caribou, except for two stretched out on the ice. One was dead, the other only wounded.

I turned to Pierre. "Are you satisfied this time?"

He would not admit it. "Even with the telephoto-lens, they were a long way off! Of course I took them, but you can see what the light is like. Have to have another try."

Pierre could not conceal his satisfaction, though. He turned to Joe and Henri and shook them by the hand. "Thanks, Joe. Thank you, Henri. It was nice of you to do all that for us."

What they had done was to select a good position in which we could lie in wait while the other two drove the herd in our direction;

and Joe and Henri had contained themselves for at least five minutes before firing at the caribou—the best proof of friendship that they could give us. The waiting must have been torture for them. I could still see the beseeching look in Joe's eyes as he asked like a little boy, "Can we shoot now?"

The rest of the day was spent in skinning and cutting up the carcasses. There were four altogether, as Nap and Augustin had killed two in the woods.

This made a total bag of thirteen.

"I said we'd have good hunting," Henri exulted. "But I brought this with me."

He produced from a pocket, carefully wrapped in a handkerchief, a sort of brownish nut shaped like a large date and polished to look like amber. It was his lucky charm. He explained to me that if a hunter is lucky enough to find one in a caribou's stomach—which happened rarely—he could be sure of killing many other caribou. The object was a concretion resulting from the caribou's gnawing at the bark of trees.

Henri and Joe were both fervent Catholics, but I had the impression that when it came to hunting Henri had much more faith in his talisman than in prayer.

The Indians appeared to have finished with hunting for the day, so I said, "I saw a wounded caribou making for the woods. Aren't you going after it?"

They shrugged their shoulders. There was enough meat for the dogs. They were right about that. Chunks were being tossed to each dog, as much meat as a European family eats in a couple of months. But Indians do not often think of stocking up, of looking ahead. The dogs were well fed, we had plenty of food—why go after one wounded beast?

The abundance we had was largely due to the raid on the kitchen that morning, as I saw when Henri started to prepare the evening meal. He produced a huge crate of pork sausages and fried mounds of them for us. Enough to put one off pork sausages for good.

"You cook too much food, Henri. You should think of the days ahead."

This only made him laugh.

The sleds were full of food. He unloaded tins of coffee and packets of tea, bread, sugar, canned meat, and two more crates of sausages. He must have liked them.

You mustn't hold it against me, Bob, I thought. *Neither Pierre nor I knew anything about this sack of your kitchen. It happened between Indians. After all, when you've a brother who is a cook for the white men . . .*

We headed back towards Snowdrift. The sleds were laden with fresh and dried meat, and the dogs had a hard time hauling through the slushy snow. Pierre and I had finished our work as cameramen, though if we came across another herd, and if the light was good . . . But then the firing and the killing would begin again. We shouldn't be able to restrain the Indians another time. They probably thought, and rightly so, that they had kept to their part of the bargain. We mustn't ask too much of them. Henri had promised to take us to his trap-line, which was beyond the "mountains". He meant the bare hills which were the highest in the region, but were at an altitude of no more than twelve hundred feet.

This high, broken landscape was just ahead of us, and the Indians decided to wait a few hours for the snow to harden. The temperature was falling, the cold weather was returning. At this time of year there often were temporary thaws.

I decided to use my free morning exploring—or tracking down the wounded caribou I had seen limping away yesterday, perhaps.

I put on snowshoes and soon found where the caribou had beaten down the snow and bushes in their headlong flight. The snow was very deep so progress was slow and exhausting even on snowshoes. If I were a born hunter and knew the habits of caribou, I should probably have been able to spare myself much effort by making directly for the place where the herd had gathered to take

refuge. But that was something only the Indians knew. So I followed
the beaten trail, which was marked by bloodstains every so often. It
was possible to see where the caribou had turned back, had gathered
together and then scattered again; and the track of the wounded
animal could easily be distinguished, though the loss of blood
seemed to be diminishing all the time. At one point the animal had
lain down to rest, leaving a red patch, then had hobbled on. But the
deep tracks it had left were marked by blood only at the edges. So
the wound was not mortal.

My pursuit brought me to a rocky bluff from which I had a
view of more hills and frozen lakes. The feeling of solitude was overwhelming, but I savoured it to the full. I could imagine what the
life of a trapper must be like. What a sense of infinity and of absolute
freedom! If I were an Indian I should certainly not stay in a settlement.

I had been following the trail of the caribou for three hours, and
it was time to turn back. I understood better why the Indians had
not pursued the wounded animal. They would have been taken
much too far. Now a wolf would probably pick up the scent and,
more persevering than I, overtake the wounded caribou.

I recognised some landmarks on the way back and then cut
across, taking my direction from the sun which was just visible
behind the clouds, and rejoined my companions.

Our teams were on the move again, picking their way along gorges
and through thick undergrowth. Then we followed a long ridge
for more than an hour, finally descending a steep slope to an ice-
covered, small lake set among rocks and cliffs. Henri took his axe
and beckoned to Pierre and me to follow him. This was the beginning of his trap-line and his own hunting-ground. Two families
rarely set traps and hunt in the same area, and there is no poaching
on another's territory.

Henri had set his traps in clefts between the rocks at the foot of the
cliffs, but had underestimated the fall of snow; the traps were deeply

buried and caught in the ice. Henri searched for a long time. He had an amazing memory, but there were no signs to show where the traps were hidden. Sometimes he was guided in his search by a tree, a branch or the outline of a cliff. One by one he uncovered five or six traps, but they were all empty. Wolverines had passed this way and devoured the lot. Henri shrugged his shoulders philosophically. One might have pointed out that he had let four months go by before coming to inspect his traps.

But what were four months, or a week or a year? Time exists for the northern Indians only as two seasons, winter and summer, night and day. Henri would set other traps, then forget about them; and would only happen to remember them if some such opportunity occurred as had this day.

"Look, there's a tent!" exclaimed Pierre.

It was standing in a small clearing. There were also a home-made stove and some lengths of stove-pipe lying about, together with cooking utensils and a few traps. The tent in this abandoned camp was almost new, decidedly better than the one I had been sleeping under.

"It's mine," said Henri proudly.

I was expecting him to take it down carefully and carry it away. But instead, Henri was suddenly possessed by a kind of destructive frenzy. He slashed at the canvas with his axe, broke the poles, smashed the cooking utensils and the stove. The only things he spared were two lengths of stove-pipe; he probably needed these, as our pipes were almost burnt through.

"Why on earth did you do that, Henri?" asked Pierre. "That tent was new, and the one we're using is nearly worn out."

Henri shrugged his shoulders. "My mother will make me another."

Pierre probably thought as I did: that would mean buying more canvas, quite a lot, which cost money. Henri's stupid act was beyond us. Was Henri angry at having caught nothing in his traps? Did he think the place was haunted? Or was it just to show off in front of us, to demonstrate that material things mattered little? Probably the last was nearest the truth. The Indian puts little store in material things, not even in money.

We continued along the course of the Indian Mountain River, descending towards Great Slave Lake in a series of great steps. Along this deep gorge the river-bed sometimes widened to become a lake, sometimes narrowed to a defile, but all was frozen solid. The bottom of the gorge could get very little sun, except in summer. Occasionally we came upon running water, but that was because the current was so strong and the flow so fast that the water could not freeze over. Woe to any man or dog who fell into it! The Indian Mountain River is one of the shortest of the thousands of rivers in the Canadian sub-Arctic, but its outflow is considerable in summer.

It was the way followed by all living things in winter. Our dogs were passing over tracks made by caribou herds, wolves, foxes and wolverines. Now and again some ptarmigan seemed to blossom forth like magical flowers from the carpet of snow on which they were so well camouflaged, flying up to perch on a branch and then swooping down to the snow and becoming invisible again.

Nap pointed out to me an eagle's nest halfway up the cliff-face. It was empty, for its occupant had migrated to Florida for the winter. The eagle would soon be returning, together with the thousands of migratory birds which descended like snowflakes on the lakes and brought life to them during the short season of running water.

Henri's team, which was in the lead, suddenly came to a stop and he investigated the way ahead. There was a steep drop, frozen solid. The drifted snow had piled up against it, but the Indians apparently thought it was negotiable. To take dogs and sleds down there seemed exceedingly rash to me.

"*He-tet, he-tet!*" Without the slightest hesitation the dogs plunged down the steep slope, the driver clinging to the steering-handles of the sled, which banged into the dogs. The driver acted as a brake by letting himself be dragged along in the snow. The ice began to show after two sleds had gone down, and the others went even faster, the last tipping over. Then we assembled on the lower reach, among rocky and wooded surroundings that were most impressive. The dogs, which had howled and whined during the descent, now licked their wounds and had a rest while we straightened the loads and tightened the ropes again.

Pierre joined us, smiling all over his face. He gave the thumbs-up sign. "Fabulous!" he said.

I thought that we had seen the last of our difficulties. The gorge widened out into a fine, thickly wooded slope which extended into the distance, and beyond were vast white flats stretching away to the far horizon.

"Great Slave Lake," said Nap.

It was like being back on familiar ground again. But we were not there yet.

Ahead of us, the course of the Indian Mountain River disappeared into a very thick forest, a real forest. The trees were protected from the north winds by the heights we had just crossed and were as tall as those farther south. The silvery trunks of willows and birches rose well above the spruce. There was dense undergrowth—broken branches intertwined, fallen trunks, bushes and tall dry grasses. The watercourse here divided into several runnels to work its way through this jungle, which must be a large swamp in summer but was now deeply snowed under. Henri went ahead on snowshoes to break the trail, following the largest of the runnels. Nap took over his sled, and I took Nap's place at the steering-handles. Pierre went on filming, up to his waist in snow and branches. Progress was slow and difficult. Henri could be heard at work with his axe some way ahead, chopping trees and breaking branches. Then a sled set off, the dogs hauling strenuously. They howled in despair and came to a stop. We all helped to get each sled over fallen trees and large rocks. It was more like a steeplechase than a sled ride, with dozens of natural obstacles to get over.

After two hours of this slogging it was thought preferable to blaze a trail through the forest, where there were fewer obstructions than along the runnel; and we soon came out into a clearing which gave us another view of the boundless vistas of Great Slave Lake. Here we collected together and gave the dogs a rest. Their coats were soaked in sweat, and very soon they were covered in hoar-frost.

I should have liked to continue driving the sled, but Nap was firmly opposed to it. "No, it's too difficult now. Ride on the sled, but be careful. Don't put your arms outside the canvas."

The other teams had already streaked off, dashing down a long, steep, wooded slope with many dips full of snow. Now it was our turn. "*He-tet, he-tet!*" The dogs bounded forward, the sled gathered momentum and overtook the dogs, knocking them off their feet. We brushed past trees and the sled skidded over on one side. Instead of speeding over snow we were sliding over bluish ice which covered the undergrowth, for there had been floods here in the autumn. The snow which had fallen later had remained powdery and was lying loosely on the ice. We could neither steer nor stop the sled. Nap was amazingly skilful in avoiding a good many obstacles, but the sled sometimes scraped past a tree and I instinctively drew in my arms to avoid getting one broken. Nap saved us from a serious accident by steering the sled into a thicket, and it came to a stop with a snapping of branches. We disentangled the harness and set off again.

The river here widened before tumbling into Great Slave Lake, 150 feet below. From this vantage-point we had a splendid view of the vast lake, its great white stillness stretching to the far horizon, with its wooded islands and peninsulas.

Snowdrift was on the distant southern shore, invisible to us. It would take us another two days to get there.

We all assembled on this plateau of bare ice, which had colours ranging from emerald green to ultramarine, all amazingly clear. Below us was the waterfall, an impressive sight with the great mass silent and stilled in its flow.

"How are we going to get down there?" I asked anxiously.

"Straight on." Henri laughed. "When you can't stand, you sit down and let yourself go."

It was going to be an uncontrollable descent all right, for there was no chance of digging in one's heels wearing mukluks.

Pierre got out his cine-camera.

"You be careful, Pierre. You might have a bad fall."

He laughed as loudly as the Indians. He is a real acrobat on skis.

I decided to try to slide down by the left bank, where some hummocks of snow could soften my fall. But I wondered how the dogs would get down.

Each driver turned his sled on its side, to have more chance of checking its progress. The dogs sped down, slipped, staggered and fell; the sled dragged them along as it swung from side to side like a dead tree drifting down a fast-flowing river. The drivers hung on desperately. The team—if one could call this mad scramble of dogs a team—slid down the slope like an avalanche.

Pierre had filmed the start, and came sliding down skilfully to join me. Two sleds were mixed up in some bushes, and while they were being extricated he told me that he had just managed to get to the bank to avoid having a bad fall.

We had not yet reached the bottom; there was still a steep slope of about sixty feet to negotiate. I slid down on my back and managed to arrive feet first. Fortunately, a snow-bank brought me to a stop. I was glad to have finished with these acrobatics, but the sleds and dogs were still up above, and I hurried to get out of their way. I took shelter behind a stout birch, and from that position saw a cascade of dogs, sleds and men, with much shouting and laughing, yelping, howling and barking. Three sleds got mixed up, and the drivers were trying to sort them out when Henri's came rushing down. Trying to avoid them, he turned several somersaults and scattered his load all over the ice. The kitchen utensils and caribou-skins rolled down, and Henri lost his cap and sun-glasses.

Then Pierre came sliding down with legs apart like a skier, holding his camera at arm's length for safety. He just missed the sleds, overbalanced, fell and went sliding on for another hundred yards. He had thought only of saving his camera and had fallen very heavily. He picked himself up and walked back to me, bent with pain. He felt the effects for a month.

"What a crazy thing to do, coming down like that!"

"You don't think I did it on purpose, do you? I was taking some shots when I began to slip, and the only thing to do was to carry on. Let's hope the cameras are all right."

The bag containing the other cameras and accessories had skated more than fifty yards over the glassy surface. By a miracle, nothing was broken.

When order had been restored, we set off again. Out on Great Slave Lake our only enemy would be the cold; the temperature dropped rapidly after sunset. The ice was thin and dangerous for more than a mile where the Indian Mountain River fed into the lake, and we had to make a wide detour. Then we were able to get up speed over solid ice which had a covering of hard snow. The teams streaked along, and for several miles it was a race between the four. Nap fired his rifle to spur on his dogs, and our sled gained a few lengths. The others entered into the spirit of it, shouting and singing. Pierre and I cowered in our sleds, trying to shelter from the cold. The Indians had warned us, "We shall keep going until ten o'clock tonight."

We made a halt on a long, low island covered with spruce. The Indians lit a fire, and we melted snow for tea and grilled some caribou-cutlets. We also dried our clothes and mocassins, which had got wet during our several falls. Then off we went again.

Henri led the way, driving eastward towards the end of the long peninsula which divides the lake into two large bays each the size of the Lake of Geneva. We were going into the wind, and the hoods of our anoraks became fringed with the ice formed by our breath. The dogs pulled marvellously; it was extraordinary what reserves of strength they had.

It was dusk when we reached the narrow part of the peninsula, and I thought this was to be the night's halt. Beyond, I could see a long bay several miles wide with high cliffs on the far side, which I had taken for the southern shore of Great Slave Lake. But it was still part of the winding shore of the never-ending peninsula, which could be crossed only at the one point, and that was where we were headed. Riding on a sled for hours on end, one loses all sense of time. Gliding across the lake, I was in a state of somnolence most of the time, only kept awake by the cold.

As we drew near the shore I could just make out the dark mass of the spruce, the snow-clad hilltops and grey rock-face, before the evening shadows fell.

It was about ten o'clock when we reached land, and I thought thankfully of our night's bivouac. But there was no question of that for the moment. We had reached the one place where the long peninsula could be crossed, thus saving a journey of one hundred and twenty-five miles to get round it. We headed towards a small, sheltered cove.

"No wood," said Nap.

Yet there was enough wood for Lapps to camp there for a fortnight. What our Indians wanted was plenty of spruce. They saw a wooded bank at last, and drove their teams up the slope. In the twilight of the arctic night, the Indians took only half an hour to pitch the tents in this gloomy spot. Trees fell as though a tornado had struck them, the axes flashed and the fire soon blazed up. As we crept into our tents we suddenly felt the searing cold, for the temperature had dropped to thirty-five below.

It was to be our last night under canvas before arriving back at Snowdrift. We were a cheerful company, and in spite of our fatigue we kept it up very late, drinking a lot of tea and gorging on caribou meat.

The last day's journey was indeed a long one.

We set out very early in the cold and wind which had continued throughout the night. We had to make our way along an inlet which was more like a Norwegian fjord, with cliffs that were over six hundred feet high in places.

When we were out on the open lake, Nap pointed to the faint outline of a reef with a distinctive shape, far to the west. That was where we should make a fire.

It took another three hours, without a single halt for the dogs, to cross the open breadth of frozen lake. The distance covered was about twenty-eight miles.

As we drew nearer the shore we could see thick forest coming right down to the lake. The reef, which was shaped like one of the Emperor Napoleon's famous hats, stood out a few hundred yards from the shore. The fire was lit on a large rock. Steaks were hacked for us from the meat on Henri's sled, and the dogs were fed. We were all in high spirits. The Indians sang and shot off their rifles.

The snow around us had been trodden down by moose, which was proof enough that we had left the bush of the north for the forests to the south. A long afternoon's drive across the lake brought us within sight of Snowdrift. When we were still a long way off I recognised the deforested peninsula on which the settlement is built; then the houses became clearer and the small belfry stood out against the sky. It was like returning home after a long journey. No sooner had the sleds drawn up in front of our cabin than Mrs Jackson came hurrying across. "Come and have coffee with us," she said to me.

Father Helcoat left his work to welcome us back. The Indian children, who had been the first to sight our sleds when they were no bigger than ants out on the lake, came running round us, clambered over the sleds, cracked the whips and helped to unload our equipment. It was a real home-coming.

I took leave of the Indians, and, as it was late, said to them: "Thanks a lot. You've been wonderful. Now go and rest, and I'll settle up with you at dinner tonight."

Henri had been beaming broadly, but now suddenly looked cross. The rest looked at each other, not daring to say anything, Finally it was Henri who blurted it out. "The Bay shuts at five."

So that was it! They had only just arrived back, and already wanted to start spending their money, to buy things before the store closed.

"Okay, boys. We'll go along together."

I gave each of them his due, plus a good bonus, and at once they were all smiles again. The notes I had given them began to pass into other hands, into the till at the Bay. Henri, who was a bachelor, roamed round the store wondering what he could buy. Nap had vanished. Augustin and Joe were looking rather embarrassed, and I wondered what was the matter now. Then I turned round, and smiled—their wives had come into the store. They were determined to have some of their husbands' pay before it all vanished. However, the men's rueful looks soon disappeared. Within an hour of our return, each had returned to his cabin with his sled laden with provisions.

Mr Jackson was rubbing his hands. "You've been the great provider for the Indians."

"And for you, too," I laughed back. "Everything the Indians earn finds its way into your till."

"Well, that's chiefly why we're here," he said with a frank smile.

It was good, after all, to be back in our little log cabin. The stove was crackling, we had fetched water, taken off our outdoor clothes, and were having a very necessary clean-up. Each of us had grown a beard, and this was the moment of decision.

"You ought to keep yours," said Pierre. "You look like a patriarch."

I looked in the glass. My face was red and roughened by the wind and cold, I had a stiff, prickly beard; I hardly recognised myself. *I must shave all that off*, I thought. Pierre compromised and kept his moustache.

We spent the evening with Father Helcoat. There were a dozen children in the one room of the Mission, listening to the record-player, singing, shouting and playing games, while he sat there in his armchair looking on benevolently. Indians kept dropping in, some to seek his advice.

Father Helcoat was glad to talk about world affairs with Pierre and me, for he rarely had an opportunity. He had a weekly paper sent to him from Brittany which had one article written in Breton and gave him news of his home locality. It was a welcome relief for him to be able to talk in his native tongue, for he had few opportunities to speak French.

We slept erratically that night; the camp-beds were too soft and the room seemed overheated. But, weighed down by the accumulated fatigue of the weeks in the bush, I was at last able to relax and drop into a long, deep sleep.

It was Palm Sunday, and the Indian families were assembled for Mass in the room of the Mission. The tables had been pushed to one side; an opened cupboard disclosed the altar. Father Helcoat, having robed himself, took the service. My guides were present with their families, and I was surprised by their reverence and piety. An old Indian led the responses in Chipewyan. Some of the congregation followed the service in tattered prayer-books printed in that little-known language. It was a simple, dignified and homely service.

As soon as it was over, the cupboard was closed again, the card-tables were pulled out into the room and the record-player began blaring out modern tunes.

As events turned out, we had to wait at Snowdrift a whole week for Ptarmigan Bill to come and fetch us in his plane. Unfortunately, weather conditions were against him, for while we had been away the warmer weather had transformed the settlement. When we had left, snow and ice held everything in their grip; but now little streams were flowing down the slopes and the snow was turning to slush. There was a fresh snowfall daily.

We called on the schoolmaster, Douglas Macdonald. He came

from Halifax, Nova Scotia, where many Scottish families have been as long established as the French in Quebec. He could have taken a less rigorous job in the south, but he chose to remain in this lonely outpost. Indeed, he never went away; he was going to spend his next holiday painting and making improvements to the school-room. He served as law officer, for the nearest post of the Mounted Police was at Hay River. Like Father Helcoat and Mr Jackson, he had a radio transmitter, his only link with the outside world.

A tall man, who looked younger than his forty years, Macdonald taught young Indians the rudiments of the English language, the three Rs and drawing. We filmed his class during lessons. In a French primary school this would have caused much commotion and excitement, but not so here. We set up the camera and Pierre filmed without respite for an hour, but not one of the children even looked at us. Their whole attention was focused on their teacher, and all their efforts were directed towards mastering numbers. Previously, these children had found the number ten (ten fingers) quite sufficient for expressing all the amounts and measurements in their world; and even now they could count only in English, for in their Chipewyan tongue there was no word or sign for anything higher than ten.

Mr Macdonald was helped by an Indian, a lovely, distinguished-looking girl who corrected exercises and gave individual help to pupils who had not properly understood the lessons.

The classroom was big, airy and warm. It even had a coffee urn for the children. The walls were covered with their paintings and drawings: sleds, dogs, caribou, moose, wolves and hunting scenes, inspired by tales told at home in the evenings. They also drew the small aircraft that landed on the lake from time to time, bringing the mail and taking sick people to hospital.

A Stinson had just landed, the sound of the engine startling me as I was finishing my letters. I ran down to the lake with them, but arrived too late. I saw the plane taking off, and learned that it was transporting two sick girls to the hospital at Yellowknife. Nap was on board too, as I heard later; he had gone to spend his money at Yellowknife.

Pierre and I decided to go and film the Indians trapping muskrats, and I arranged the matter through Henri. The rate of pay would be the same as before. But on the morning when we should have set off, nobody turned up.

Later, Henri rather shamefacedly told me that they could not set out as the snow was too deep for the dogs. This was a poor excuse, for the trapping area was only about fifteen miles away. The truth was that the Indians had spent the night in a drinking bout. They had somehow concocted a horrible beer (for there are no intoxicating drinks on sale at Snowdrift), and that morning they were sleeping it off. So we put off the expedition for another day. The weather was still bad, and Bill would not be coming to collect us.

We hired two teams, those of Henri and Augustin. On the way we joined up with Joe Mitchell and his family, who were going out on the lake to haul in his nets. I saw a miraculous catch: three hundred pounds of fish in one net. That was enough for Joe, and he left us to return to Snowdrift.

We drove on westward, passing a headland on which a large cross had been erected. It was here that the first Mission chapel had been built, before Snowdrift existed. Father Marec used to come from Yellowknife by sled in winter, by canoe in summer, to visit the Indians who then lived scattered along the shores of Great Slave Lake or in the wooded valleys. A few families still lived in these isolated spots, and we were going to visit one of them, on the bank of a small lake amidst rocky hills.

There was no need to make a trail, for other sleds had made one, which climbed steeply to a wooded pass, then dropped down into a wide valley of lakes and ponds surrounded by rolling, rocky hills. The trees were very tall: it was like travelling through a forest of conifers and birches.

We were heralded by the barking of dogs, then children came running to meet us. The camp, like all those we had seen, was at a safe distance from the lake and at the foot of a hill. Wisps of smoke were curling up from two tents pitched on a slight rise. A woman who must still have been young, as she was suckling a baby, but who looked well over fifty, was scraping the fat from a moose hide. She spread it out for us to admire. The couple in the other tent had several children. The husband had just returned from his trap-line, and was taking half-a-dozen muskrats from his sled. We had arrived too late for filming; the traps had been emptied.

Before continuing, we made some tea and invited the Indian families to join us. Henri and Augustin told about our expedition. After we had left the camp, Henri said to me, "That was my brother."

Another of them. I had lost count.

Five or six miles farther on we came upon a solitary tent in-habited by an Indian about fifty years old and his wife. There were no children. The man caught fish in the lake and dried them over a fire, and also trapped muskrats. He was an open, friendly man and invited us to a meal in his tent. His wife was roasting muskrat; it is apparently very good to eat. Fish and game were being dried over a fire just outside the tent. He had still to go trapping muskrats, and willingly agreed to our accompanying him to visit his trap-line.

The muskrat, like the beaver, builds a sort of hut with mud and grass on the frozen lake and enters it through an underwater tunnel. The Indians trap muskrats in the spring before the ice melts and these fur-bearers take to living in burrows in the banks of rivers and lakes. The trapper looks for the little conical huts and goes to each one, opens the top, puts his trap inside, firmly tied to a stick, then carefully closes the opening he has made. When the muskrat enters its hut from below, it gets caught in the trap and starts squeaking. The trapper goes from one hut to another, bending down to listen at each snow-covered top. If he hears squeaks he knows he has made a capture, and he has only to re-open the top and kill the rodent.

Our Indian made a good haul. He was out of tobacco and was going to Snowdrift next day to replenish his supply.

Our dogs put up a fine performance on the run back to Snowdrift—fourteen miles in one and a quarter hours.

The days went by and there was still no sign of an improvement in the weather. I went regularly to the Bay to make radio contact with Ptarmigan Bill. His replies were always full of common sense. The weather had to be clear at Yellowknife to take off, and at Snowdrift to land; similarly at Baker Lake and Igloolik. And as the weather was variable over the fifteen hundred miles, we just had to be patient. There was no point in leaving Snowdrift and then having to wait a week at Baker Lake. Besides, it was a tricky flight; navigation would be difficult as the radio stations extended from south to north, and we should be flying east. In short, we had to wait.

Pierre and I were better known and accepted in the settlement. Children played outside our cabin, old Indians stopped us to say a few words in English. Augustin proudly showed us his litter of pups. Joe Mitchell's wife embroidered mocassins for us, and his father, old Dry Geese, asked us for photos of our families.

We spent the afternoons at the Bay, which was always very busy. It was the season when furs were being brought in by Indians from all over the district. Muskrat preponderated, and each was expertly examined by young Mr Jackson. The price paid was one and a half or two dollars a pelt, three dollars for an exceptionally fine one. While we had been away, Jackson had received a splendid lynx and some fox skins, some sables and a wolf skin. All these would be packed and sent to Yellowknife by plane. Business was conducted in the manager's office in silence. A ruled board was used to measure the skins. The price offered was usually accepted without argument; it had of course been fixed by the Hudson's Bay Company in consideration of world fur prices and the current supply and demand. When supply was high, prices were naturally lower. But the Indians had no means of selling their furs other than to the Bay, and so were obliged to take what was offered. However, they found it difficult to understand why they got only one dollar for a pelt when the previous year a similar skin had fetched two dollars.

Trapping muskrats is the mainstay of these Indian families. They are prolific and easy to trap. Other fur-bearing animals, such as marten, skunk, ermine and fox, are much more chancy. The depredations caused by wolverines had become familiar to me—they usually visited trap-lines well before the trappers.

The caribou used to provide most of the food of the Indians who live around Great Slave Lake, but now merely supplements it. Few indeed are the families who go on hunting expeditions to the Barren Lands in the summer in order to be sure of having enough to eat during the winter. In recent years, working at summer camps for holiday fishermen or for prospecting parties, and trapping at other times, have enabled the Indians to earn fairly good incomes. They buy much of their food and clothing at the Bay. So the old way, the hunter's life, is gradually disappearing.

However, in spite of their acquiring any modern gadget that pleases them, the Indians have not yet really settled down to a regimented, white man's way of life. They may well send their children to school at Snowdrift, but that is partly in order to be sure of receiving the Federal Government's family allowances. Despite this useful addition to income, they are often unable to resist the call of the forest and set off with their families to pitch their tents by a river populated by beavers, or in some isolated valley in the bush. Both teacher and missionary have tried to hold them back, but are helpless before this overwhelming urge periodically to be on the trail, to journey through the vast extent of forest and bush, to cross the lakes and live in freedom in this huge hunting territory.

How can one blame them? They have all the pleasures of freedom and run very few risks. Indeed, as my expedition with the Indians proved to me, their hunting life is a splendid one. You come back with the feeling that at last you have been free to go wherever you wished and to do whatever you felt like doing, to throw off, if but temporarily, modern civilisation.

The Indian holds his happiness in his own hands without being obsessed with it. He leads a human life. He does not just survive in this part of the Northwest Territories; he lives fully.

PART TWO

The Eskimos of the Arctic

3

A Flight over the Barren Lands

BRIEF SNOW-SHOWERS had been whipping across Snowdrift throughout the morning; low clouds kept drifting over the lake, with just a short bright period now and again.

Pierre shook his head. "We won't be off today."

"Well, don't go too far away. You never know."

The evening before, Ptarmigan Bill had told us over the radio that weather conditions were improving from the east, but at Yellowknife it was still too bad for him to take off. For a free-lance pilot not to be able to take off, the weather must have been bad indeed. "Still, be ready to leave," he had added.

We had been ready to leave for the past week. Our luggage was all ready, the rolls of film carefully packed. We had said our fare-wells three times already—it was getting a bit wearisome. We seemed condemned to stay at Snowdrift for weeks, waiting for a break in the weather. At one point we had thought of making a wide detour to the south, flying 4,300 miles instead of 1,500 in order to get to Igloolik. But the mere thought of finding ourselves back at Montreal had been enough to put us off the idea. We were acclimatised to the North by now, to the cold and our new way of living. There was only one thing to do—wait patiently.

I went across to the Bay as usual, to pass the time and have a chat with Jackson. I knew all the Indians of the settlement by now, and they showed me the furs they had brought to sell. I had thus learned to judge the thickness and quality of the pelts. I found Jackson in the back room, sitting at his transmitter. He spent much of his time keeping in contact with the outside world. He signalled to me to wait.

"The plane is coming," he said.

"Yes, but when?"

"It will be here in half an hour. Bill took off from Yellowknife in spite of the bad weather, and he radioed his message while in flight."

I hurried back to the cabin. Pierre, bored with waiting, had unpacked his equipment and was cleaning his cameras.

"Pierre! We're off! Bill will be here in half an hour."

"Tell that to the marines. You've been saying that all week."

"But I tell you it's true."

"What, in this foul weather?"

"Listen. Here he comes."

The drone of a plane could be heard faintly but distinctly. We went outside. The sound was louder, but no plane could be seen. Then there was silence again.

"It was probably the electric generator at the school," said Pierre.

Suddenly there was a roar overhead. This time there could be no doubt. The plane appeared from low cloud over the lake, flew round the bay, landed smoothly on the ice and slid across to the loading platform.

We ran towards it, and saw Bill climbing out.

"Are you ready?" he cried. "We must leave at once. Be quick."

Of course we were ready. Well, almost. Pierre had to repack his photographic equipment; then we had to get dressed for the flight, and say our farewells again.

We started to carry the big packages to the plane, and Jackson came out to give us a hand. Indian children gathered round, bombarding us with questions. "You're going to where the Eskimos live? Is it very far? How many days by sled?" How could we explain that we were going to fly to a quite different world from theirs? To a land where no tree grows, where the sea is always frozen over.

On the trail in the backwoods with the Indians

Baker Lake. Warming up the engine. Under the wing can be seen a boat caught in the ice

The fishing-port of Igloolik

Igloolik, one of the major Eskimo settlements in the Canadian Arctic. The top
half and middle right is all frozen sea

After five days in a
blizzard, with the
temperature forty
below zero

Tatigat, Giuseppi and the author on their sled

The author

OVERLEAF: By Eskimo sled
along the northern coast of
Melville Peninsula

These children knew about Eskimos from tales told by old men, far more than from their schoolbooks. Indians and Eskimos did not always get along well together, but they knew their differences and for the most part stayed out of each other's way. Eskimos were splendid hunters, but were not interested in warfare. An Eskimo proudly called himself *Inuk*—man.

Our luggage and equipment had been securely stowed in the back of the small Cessna-180, a single-engined aircraft, sparkling new.

We found it hard to leave our new-found friends. Father Helcoat had come to see us off, and Jackson was there too, puffing slowly at his pipe. Mrs Jackson came running up with a parcel—she had made a big cake for us to eat on the way. We had still to say goodbye to the schoolmaster, but he was with his class. Bill was growing impatient, so all we could do was to leave a message thanking Douglas Macdonald for his quietly efficient help in the making of our film.

We suddenly realised how attached we had become to this small Indian settlement. On our return from the long expedition in the bush we had been received back in this community so simply and naturally that we felt quite at home.

But now it was farewell to Snowdrift. We were leaving for new adventures.

Bill opened the throttle and the engine throbbed. He knew its every change of tone. Our long flight depended on this one engine. We were well aware that if Bill had to make a forced landing, weeks might pass before we were found and rescued. But Bill had no anxieties; the point of his waiting so long was to be sure that flying conditions would be reasonably good.

"We'll have poor weather until we reach the Barren Lands," he told us, "but then it will improve and we shall have fine weather the rest of the way. I don't think we shall get farther than Baker Lake by this evening. That's five hours' flying time from here."

We were soon airborne, despite all the weight on board. Bill flew

Tatigat looking for seals at the floe-edge near Igloolik

over the settlement, then headed due east. After an hour's flight we were over the eastern end of Great Slave Lake, having admired from a great height the splendours of lakes and forests where Pierre and I had travelled in recent weeks.

The plane dropped down towards the lake, flying over an archipelago of wooded islands. Bill was preparing to land. The nose of the aircraft pointing towards two buildings, from one of which the Canadian flag was flying. This was Fort Reliance, though a more apt name would be Fort Solitude. Three Mounted Policemen and a white trapper lived here. There was no sign of any settlement or even a camp. Our pilot flew low past the outpost and came down on an arm of the lake, all rugged with hummock ice, then ran the plane on its skis towards a small beach where drums of gasoline were stored.

"We fill her up here," said Bill.

Eastward from here, to the shores of Hudson Bay, was a great white desert. It reminded me of the Sahara.

Pierre and I helped Bill as best we could. The plane had to be moored facing the wind. Then Bill rolled some gasoline drums across, climbed on to the wing, and we lifted the drums up to him. He filled the tanks, checked the gauges and smiled. "We're okay for a five-hour flight now."

We got aboard again and Bill taxied the plane out on to the lake, past the police post where three men were waving to us. I threw the mail-bags out on the snow. Bill swung the plane round for take-off. It was longer before he got it airborne this time, for the weight was greater and the many ridges of hard snow shook us up; but soon we were above the trees and gaining height. The immense expanse of spruce and snow was on all sides, obscured by a thin mist.

We were on a course east-northeast. The hillsides became barer and the spruce ever smaller. Before long the only signs of vegetation were a few stunted trees growing in river-beds. Then there was nothing at all, just a vast whiteness everywhere. We were beyond the tree line now.

Bill was flying at more than three thousand feet, the map spread out on his knees. He was out of range of the Yellowknife radio transmitter and would be flying for two hundred miles before being able to pick up signals from Baker Lake. He kept on a compass course but relied on his knowledge of the region, having flown over it many times on scientific missions. The Thelon River and Game Sanctuary stretched below us, a desolate landscape of tundra indented by gorges and hollowed out by ponds and lakes.

Suddenly, Bill put the nose down. "Musk-oxen!" he cried.

He flattened out at three hundred feet, which was as low as he dared go without danger of crashing, for the snow and mist made heights confusing.

"There they are."

There at last were the musk-oxen we had so much wanted to see—about a dozen grouped in a defensive circle. Pierre got out his camera, while I held the window open with some difficulty. Bill flew low in concentric circles over the small herd, which was stamping about in the deep, powdery snow. But the animals suddenly took fright, galloping off through the snow, pursued by this huge bird roaring just above them. Pierre was filming away, but it was all too fast. He wanted to land and get near the herd. But Bill was adamant: "It's impossible in this visibility and with so much snow."

We had to accept his decision. He flew over the musk-oxen three or four times, then turned back on his easterly course. We sighted three other herds in different places, and I wondered how they managed to live in this land which never thaws to any depth, which is either covered with heavy falls of snow or swept by winds that lay bare the age-old rock.

We were now flying over the arctic wastes, and would see no more plant life of any kind until we returned south. It was as though the earth were dead.

Bill was trying to make radio contact with Baker Lake. Occasionally he picked up faint signals from the DEW Line, far to the north, but they were of little aid to him for the moment. He changed course slightly, repeatedly calling "Hello Baker Lake. Hello Baker Lake."

"Baker Lake; we read you," came a friendly voice at last.

Bill was given his exact position. The musk-oxen had caused us to make a dip to the south, but now we were guided towards our destination, drawn by the invisible thread of radio communication. In an hour we should be at Baker Lake.

When Bill at last reduced speed and went down to land, we caught sight of Baker Lake and its large asphalt runway.

To look at Snowdrift and Baker Lake on a map, one would expect each to have a similar landscape of wooded hillsides and lakes. Yet Baker Lake, on a latitude only slightly more northerly than that of Snowdrift, belongs to another world—the tundra, where no tree grows. Whereas Snowdrift and Great Slave Lake are south of the tree line.

Baker Lake is one of the most important transport bases in the Arctic. Its airfield is equipped to handle any type of aircraft. Eskimos had helped with the construction of it, and there are now about five hundred of them living at Baker Lake, in a village of log-cabins. They are mainland Eskimos, who previously existed solely from hunting in the Barren Lands. They have gradually become fishermen, going out on Baker Lake or Chesterfield Inlet, where the waters from the lake flow into Hudson Bay.

Our small plane came to a halt and Pierre and I got down, passing at once from the relative warmth of the cabin to the intense cold sweeping in from the lake. Bill motioned to us to go inside. The huge hangar, more than a hundred yards long, was almost buried in snow. Entering it was like going through a tunnel of ice, an elongated igloo. We went along corridors where the electric lights were on, because all the windows were blocked by snow, and came to the canteen.

A few men were drinking coffee. "Help yourselves," they said.

"Where have you come from? Where are you going?" the others asked us, though without real curiosity. They were used to aircraft of all kinds, civilian and military, arriving and departing every day. We were people in transit, part of the routine.

A sergeant recorded our names and addresses and asked the name of "the organisation which would pay for our stay."

"We'll pay for it ourselves."

He looked surprised. It was not often that he saw people who paid for themselves. Most of the accounts went to various government departments, industrial organisations or other bases. "Freelance?" he said.

"That's it." Like Bill, we worked for ourselves. All was in order, and we were each given a room.

"Just for the night," I added.

"Or for a week," said someone ironically.

"Yes, of course, it depends on the weather."

Bill hurriedly drank his coffee and went out again, into the bitter cold of the evening. He filled his fuel tanks for the next day's flight would be even longer, perhaps seven hours. He covered up the engine and made sure that the small plane was securely anchored on the open space which was constantly swept by the wind. Out on the runways there were bulldozers at work, keeping them clear of snow.

The Eskimos' cabins could be seen along the lake shore for more than a mile. Beyond them were the Mission and the Bay's trading-store. Eskimo children were tobogganing down the hillside, shouting and laughing. They did not feel the cold. The white men worked in the offices, ran the radio and weather stations. Ropes had been stretched from some buildings to others, for guiding people when a blizzard was blowing; and several tunnels led into the headquarters building.

We left Baker Lake the next morning. Bill spent a good hour at the weather station and in drawing up his flight plan. We were in luck—there was fine weather to the north. Ground crew had been warming up the Cessna's engine with a heating apparatus. Then we took off with full tanks, to fly direct to Igloolik in one hop.

Baker Lake is about two hundred miles west of Hudson Bay, at the head of Chesterfield Inlet. So Bill had to fly across the empty wastes of the Keewatin District to the southern end of Committee Bay, then fly north across Melville Peninsula to its east coast and Igloolik. It was a long flight and one that took us right across the Canadian tundra, the forbidding Barren Lands.

Bill had been in radio contact with Baker Lake, but now began to pick up signals from stations along the DEW Line, from Pelly Bay, Hall Beach and elsewhere. He gave the thumbs-up sign. "Okay now."

It was as though all these unknown voices were uniting to help us; every minute or so, Bill was given his position. He increased altitude, then suddenly we saw the sun shining on a flat stretch of open water. We were approaching Committee Bay. Jagged pack-ice showed where the land met the sea. The flowing water was a sort of canal, with a few ships in it. But there was little of it: this was a floe-edge, one of the curiosities of the Arctic. Such stretches of water are sometimes found even in mid-winter.

We caught sight of a small building and a runway on the east shore of Committee Bay, one of the many stations forming the DEW Line. The radio messages that Bill had been receiving had come from that forlorn little building. He sent a message of thanks, then called up Hall Beach; that large airport on Foxe Basin took charge of us for the rest of the flight.

We were flying up the west coast of Melville Peninsula, then our course took us across the flat, monotonous landscape. Bill was searching for a sign of the eastern coastline that would indicate we were nearing Igloolik. Used as he is to the Arctic, he was nevertheless at a loss. He called up Hall Beach, and received a slightly ironic reply.

"Igloolik? Right ahead of you, about fifteen miles away. Can't you see it?"

"What, that?" muttered Bill.

A few marks on the snow grew larger as we approached, and Bill went down to land at Igloolik, one of the largest colonies of

Eskimos in the Canadian Arctic. We could see a church and some prefabricated huts half-buried in snow.

Our plane touched down, and we wheeled to the end of the runway—which was in fact no more than a wide path marked out on the frozen sea. Some Eskimos came racing out to us on skidoos, each carrying his wife and the wife carrying a baby in the hood of her parka.

A youngish man greeted us with a smile as we got out of the plane. "Welcome, gentlemen! My name is Jim Hennings, Northern Affairs officer."

We shook hands. He had been expecting us for a week, but without impatience, for he had been stationed in the Far North for twenty years. However, he was a little surprised to see that we had come from Snowdrift in such a small plane, and congratulated Bill.

"I've given you the Transit Cabin," he said to Pierre and me. "I think you'll be comfortable there. I'm expecting you to dinner this evening. You'll want to meet Father Fournier too. We'll be happy to help you in any way we can."

The Transit Cabin was a new building; half of it was an office, the rest living quarters consisting of two rooms with bunks, a bathroom and a fully equipped kitchen, the whole being centrally heated. Waiting for us was Mr Bartels, an ex-German prisoner of war, who had settled in Canada and married a charming Peruvian, whom he had met through their being pen-pals. He was the general factotum of the place, looking after the electrical installations, the heating and the vehicles. "If there's anything wrong, come and see Bartels," he said as he left us.

But everything was fine. We went to say goodbye to Bill, for he wanted to start on his return journey. There was no fuel supply for him at Igloolik, so he intended to make a detour to Hall Beach, forty-five miles to the south, and from there to reach Pelly Bay before nightfall. In the morning he would fly on to Cambridge, then straight back to Yellowknife, a total flight of sixteen hundred miles. However, Bill thought that the most difficult part of the trip was over: "Along latitude 69 I'm in radio contact all the time, as there's a station every sixty miles."

I settled up with him—a small fortune, for the return journey had to be included, of course. The trust and honesty of these men of the North is truly wonderful. Bill had never asked me for anything on account. Not a cent. We had agreed on a price, and he had given his word as I had given mine.

Bill took off. Having much less fuel weight on board, the plane was airborne after a hundred yards. It quickly gained height and headed due south.

Pierre and I walked slowly back to our cabin. Our second adventure was about to begin.

4

Igloolik

IGLOOLIK, THE "place of the igloos", just south of latitude 70, is not a new strategic base. As the name implies, it was one of the important winter centres of the Eskimos in the Canadian Arctic archipelago. It was often visited by polar expeditions during the search for the Northwest Passage, being on a bank of sand and gravel at the entrance to Fury and Hecla Strait, which leads into the Gulf of Boothia. These storm-swept waters are free of ice for only a month or two in summer. This hazardous route was abandoned when the Lancaster and Barrow Straits were discovered to the north of Baffin Island. The search for the Northwest Passage, begun by Frobisher in the late sixteenth century, did not end until the opening of the twentieth century, when Amundsen succeeded in his little ship of forty-six tons, the *Gjoa*. It was the first time a vessel had passed from sea to sea. During those three centuries, dozens of ships had been lost or were trapped in the ice; some crews spent as many as four years trying to get out; those who attempted to make their way south on foot died of starvation in the Barren Lands. The greatest disaster was the Franklin expedition in the mid-nineteenth century. More than one hundred men lost their lives in territory between King William Island and Cape Herschel. But they completed the discovery of the Northwest Passage.

Until quite recent times, the Eskimo had always led a nomadic existence. In summer he pitched his tent on the shore of an island frequented by caribou, polar bears and other game. He could also hunt the seal, whale and walrus; and sometimes there were wildfowl to supplement his diet. When the sea froze again, he struck camp and moved across the ice-fields to settle for the winter near a floe-edge—a stretch of water never freezing over entirely, and the home of seals, the Eskimo's basic food.

Some ten to fifteen miles east of Igloolik is one such floe-edge; its size varies with the winds and currents, but there are always enough breaks in the ice-floe for seals to surface. The Eskimo waits patiently at the side of one of the breathing-holes—sometimes for several days—and harpoons the seal when it comes up for air.

Igloolik is on an island between Melville Peninsula, which is the home of caribou, and Baffin Island, which has game in summer. It had therefore been a suitable area for Eskimo life for centuries. Before the time of Christ, it is thought that the Eskimos built huts of stone on this island.

The Canadian authorities have built a large school, which is attended by several hundred Eskimo children. There is a Catholic mission, an R.C.M.P. post and a trading-post of the Bay—the usual trilogy. There were altogether seventeen non-Eskimo Canadians resident at Igloolik when Pierre Tairraz and I were there.

We had arrived in time for the Easter festivities, the most important of the year. Some Eskimo families had come for the occasion from their camps on Melville Peninsula, Baffin Island, Jens Munk Island and elsewhere. These visitors could be distinguished from the Igloolik Eskimos by their more rugged appearance, by their faces deeply lined by the wind and cold. Their clothing was rough and ready, whereas the Eskimos living permanently at Igloolik were wearing their festive dress of embroidered, white woollen parka and light, elegant boots.

We were fortunate in being present at one of the largest gatherings of Eskimos, as Mr Hennings told us after dinner that first evening.

"You can film all you want to here. It's not often that we see the Eskimos who still live by hunting. Some of them come here only once a year."

I must have looked disappointed, for Hennings said in surprise: "You had something else in mind?"

"Our intention is to go and see Eskimos hunting in their own surroundings. We were told of a few families living at the other end of the Straits, on the Gulf of Boothia."

"That would be a tough journey at this time of year."

"I'll ask you about it later."

His large and comfortable living-room was full of guests who had come for the Easter festivities. Igloolik has the advantage of being an isolated settlement in the midst of ice-fields; yet it is connected with the outside world by the airport at Hall Beach, forty-five miles to the south, which can always be reached by caterpillar snow vehicles.

Still a little dazed by the long air journey, I now found myself at a worldly social gathering. Soft music was coming from a record-player and elegant women were serving drinks. There were journalists who had seen a good story in the Eskimo gathering, and officers from military bases who had brought their families to see the festivities.

Hennings was a perfect host, smiling and serene. He was a confirmed bachelor, a philosopher of the frozen North, who had not always known such comfortable living conditions. He had worked for the Bay in his early years, managing the most northerly trading post, at Arctic Bay, in the north of Baffin Island. Then he had joined the Northwest Territories administration, where his knowledge of the Eskimos and their language was most useful. He was happy in his work, had no intention of changing, and went to Ottawa only when summoned. Although his methods and point of view in dealing with the Eskimos were not always in accordance with those of his friend, Father Fournier, he was equally devoted to the task of finding the best way of life for the Eskimos in the years to come.

Pierre and I, reclining in deep armchairs after an excellent meal, found difficulty in making polite conversation with the other guests.

We found ourselves back in the atmosphere of cocktail parties at Montreal and Ottawa.

"It's not always like this," Hennings said to us with a smile. "Fortunately, there are many days when it's a lot quieter. We see no one at all during the six months of winter. This is the first party of the year."

Miss Harper, the young school-teacher, nodded agreement.

As I discovered in the next few days, she worked hard teaching the Eskimo children. She shared a comfortable prefab with her colleague, another young woman from Ottawa, and her evenings were spent in reading, listening to music on the record-player, and receiving visits from ex-pupils now married, who brought their babies to show her. To think that the Canadians stationed at Igloolik lead a gay social round would be completely erroneous. But they are excellent hosts and, like all Canadians, know how to make people feel at home; a party such as the one I found myself at that first evening was just a nice change for them, a relaxation from their long and monotonous life in the seclusion of the Arctic. How many of the guests and reporters laughing and drinking in Hennings' warm and comfortable lounge, I wondered, had any real idea of the other side of the coin? Of the long arctic night and terrible blizzards?

However, it was not the hell of Sartre ("Hell is other people"), which I had sometimes experienced in posts in the Sahara, where the climate almost drove people mad; where each European hated the sight of the others and only spoke to them when obliged to by official business. Here at Igloolik everyone kept to himself, but everyone helped his neighbour too.

The Canadian authorities provided excellent living-quarters for their personnel. All prefabs have central heating, hot and cold running-water (and obtaining fresh water in these parts is difficult), and are comfortably furnished. These conveniences must be of great help as one endures the long winter, the dark and cold, the isolation and solitude.

Hennings suggested that we should go and see Father Fournier, although it was then ten in the evening. Apparently time mattered little here.

"He speaks French," Hennings said, "and he knows the Eskimos as well as I do, if not better. He's in touch with what's happening at all the Eskimo camps. I'm sure he'll be very helpful to you and be able to give you good advice."

Despite the late hour, we met several Eskimo families out for a walk. Children were playing in the snow, young men were riding skidoos at full speed, charging over the hummock ice. This motorised sled is much admired by the Eskimos. They will spend all their money on one. It costs about six hundred pounds, or fifteen hundred dollars, a huge sum for an Eskimo; to save this amount he has to sell a good many white fox skins or a large number of stone carvings. Yet there seemed hardly a family at Igloolik that did not possess at least one skidoo. It was used for everything, with a small sled as trailer. But more especially, it was a plaything. The Eskimos rode their skidoos up and down the hillsides night and day, jumping obstacles on them, racing at full speed across the ice-fields. And what joy the skidoos gave during the Easter festivities! Their drivers showed off to the crowd, revving-up engines, and taking the whole family for a ride—wife and children too, with the youngest in the mother's parka.

"In five to ten years," a friend said to me, "the skidoo will have replaced the Eskimo's huskies."

That may well be the case. Some Eskimos have already ridden hundreds of miles across the ice-fields, and several have hunted bear on their skidoos.

On the way to the Mission we had to step over several dog-teams curled up in the snow. Their owners had always tethered them in a certain place, and the fact that it had become a public walk made no difference. The huskies were used to people walking past them, and did not even bark.

The church is the largest building at Igloolik, and has the shape of a ship with the keel uppermost, the belfry being at the bow. In a couple of hours' time, Midnight Mass would be celebrated here, and the Roman Catholics among the Eskimos had already gathered at the Mission. This long, solid building of various materials was standing for many years before the Canadian government established a post at Igloolik, and during that time the Roman Catholic Church was alone in exercising any influence over the Eskimos, an influence which has steadily increased. The priest at present in charge of the Mission, Father Fournier, has great responsibilities. The Eskimos look upon him as one of themselves; they know instinctively that he is there to help them, that he will not leave them, and this they find reassuring.

The door of his Mission is open day and night. But nobody living at Igloolik ever locks his door; that would be breaking with tradition. When the Northern Affairs officer, Mr Hennings, goes away for a few days or for several weeks, anyone can enter his home. I discovered this for myself when I knocked at his door one day. There was no answer, so I tried the door, opened it and went in. The place was empty. On enquiry, I found that Hennings had gone away for three days.

Pierre and I never locked the door of the Transit Cabin, although all our photographic equipment, film, money and other belongings were inside. Theft is unknown at Igloolik. What a wonderful feeling of security and trust this gives one!

Pierre and I went into the Mission, passing along a corridor with rooms in which there were Eskimos playing billiards, chess or checkers, and their wives and children were drinking lemonade and nibbling cakes bought at the Eskimos' Co-operative. There were some furs left in a heap on a counter. In the back room we came upon half-a-dozen Eskimos sitting round a table. A score or so of small sculpted objects were lined up on the table. I learned later that these were some of the carvings which bring the Igloolik Eskimos part of their income.

"Is Father Fournier about?" I asked.

A man with greying hair turned on his chair. He was huddled in a thick black sweater and his dark trousers were tucked into sealskin mukluks. He had a small pointed beard, and his tanned, weather-beaten face expressed those twin qualities of men of the Far North, willingness and good-heartedness.

"I'm Father Fournier," he said with a smile. "Why, you're French! What a godsend. I'll be able to talk my own language. I forget it all here. But what brings you to these parts? Ah, of course, the Easter celebrations. You must come to Midnight Mass. It'll be out of the ordinary. If you're looking for local colour you'll find plenty of it."

He spoke French with a strong southern accent, and I was not surprised to hear that he came from the Lozère. I told him of our aims, and the Eskimos around the table listened attentively as he translated our conversation for their benefit.

"So you would like to go to Agu Bay. That's a long journey, and the spring storms are bad just now. Have you travelled by sled before; are you properly equipped for it?"

He thought for a minute or two. "I don't see why you want to go all that way. If you want to photograph igloos, there'll be an igloo-building competition here tomorrow, and some sled races too, all very picturesque. And if you want to see an Eskimo camp, there's one only twenty miles from here. Why go any farther?"

"Because we've been told that the Eskimos at Agu Bay live apart, only coming here once or twice a year to get supplies, sell their furs and collect their family allowance cheques. Is that true?"

"Absolutely. We don't see them here very often. They just refuse to join our community. I won't go so far as to say that they don't like white men, but that's what it seems. Their chief is one of the best bear-hunters in the Arctic. He's an intelligent fellow, and holds sway over all the families at Agu Bay."

"Do they live in igloos?"

Father Fournier questioned the Eskimos sitting with him. "Yes, those at Agu Bay still live in igloos. They winter on Prince Frederik

Island in the Gulf of Boothia, south of Agu Bay, with their wives and children."

"That's where we should like to go," I told Father Fournier.

"Well, if you really want to. But it's a long way—150 miles on the map. With detours, you can reckon on nearly 200 miles each way. Pacôme! How many days by sled?"

Pacôme was the manager of the Co-op store and the head of the Eskimo community at Igloolik. A few years ago he had been the best hunter, and it was this title which had caused him to be regarded by the Eskimos as their chief. Unfortunately, he knew only a little English, and no French at all.

Father Fournier spoke to him in Eskimo, then translated his reply. "Three days—or a week. It depends."

"Indeed it depends," the missionary said to me. "For an Eskimo, three days means three times twenty-four hours. He's capable of travelling without a rest, not even to eat, all that time. But if he decides to take it easy, you'll find yourself taking ten days to make the journey instead of three. If you do go, remember this: time doesn't count for an Eskimo, neither does money or gain. He likes to be free to do what he wants."

"Would you be kind enough to organise this journey for me? Mr Hennings has to go away tomorrow afternoon."

"And I shall be going off on Wednesday. However, we'll see. The chief of Agu Bay is here just now. His name is Tabatiak. I'll get in touch with him. But you'll need two teams, and then you'll want to have men who get on together. All that requires time, much discussion. There's also the question of payment."

"Have no fear about that. I'll pay the men as we did at Snowdrift, at the official rate. I could deposit the money with anyone you wish —perhaps yourself, or the manager?"

"That's all very well, but I've Mass at midnight. It's amazing how people from the south are always in a hurry," he said with a laugh. "However, don't worry. There's plenty of amusement for you until Tuesday. Come and have lunch with me on Monday, and I'll tell you how far I've got with the plans. In any case, after Mass tonight, everyone will know that two strangers have arrived, that they want to go to Agu Bay and are looking for guides. There'll be lots of talk about it in the Eskimos' cabins. Until Monday, then."

Pierre and I walked across to the church. There were several teams of huskies resting in front of the porch, having brought Eskimo families from far afield. The large church was already packed. The timbered roof, stained glass, and the huge white bear-skin in front of the raised altar, all made it a house of prayer of which the Eskimos could well be proud. Everyone was wearing his best parka. The rounded, smiling features of the girls contrasted strongly with the weather-beaten faces of old hunters.

The service was followed with devoutness, yet there was a sort of fair-ground atmosphere to the proceedings, a continual coming-and-going of mothers attending to their children. Then there were the babies, in the hoods of their mothers' parkas. When one became too restless, the mother bent forward and extracted the babe from the hood, then held the infant on her lap. Children were running about everywhere, playing and shouting, weeping or singing. The moisture from people's breath was forming a halo round the candles. Loud, wracking coughing continued throughout the sermon, but Father Fournier did not seem put out by it; he went on in the same even tones. The service was going to be very long. But if Father Fournier ventured to cut down the length of his services he would be severely criticised by the Eskimos.

Easter Day is a time for presents. After church, Father Fournier distributed handfuls of sweets to young and old; then everyone went to the Mission to feast on frozen raw caribou. The meat had been supplied by the Co-op. Men, women and children alike sliced with their knives at the mounds of pink flesh. More than one young woman, who had seemed so polite and refined a short time before, was now seen chewing the raw meat with delight, her face smeared with blood.

Later in the morning we saw more of these strange, restless and smiling people. Whole families were arriving on sleds from all directions. Their huskies were put in an enclosure some distance from the settlement; by order, no dogs were allowed to stray about the place. Those belonging to the inhabitants were chained to stakes outside the cabins. We had been warned so often how ferocious they are, that we gave them a wide berth. But only stray dogs running about together were likely to be dangerous, and the act of picking up a stone or brandishing a stick was enough to make a husky cower away.

It did not take us long to walk round Igloolik. The main street, so to speak, was a sort of wide drive with great ruts of hummock ice. The large administrative buildings stood out above the snow, but the smaller dwellings of the Eskimos were almost buried. Each cabin was full of relatives and friends who had come from a distance for the Easter Day sports and dancing.

Jim Hennings had organised a real field-day, with races and competitions for men, women and children. It was all held out on the frozen sea, and the landing-strip was used for the sled race. More than fifty teams took part in this, and there was apparently no regulation about the number of huskies to a team, for they varied from six to twenty. The competitors drew lots for the teams they were going to drive; consequently each man had a team that was not his own, huskies who did not recognise his voice. All this added to the fun. The race had hardly begun when several teams started fighting, the traces got tangled up and sleds were overturned, which caused loud laughter among the onlookers. The teams that got away streaked across the ice towards the buoy about a mile distant, then turned around it to race back. But one driver deliberately turned back long before reaching the buoy—to the great delight of the Eskimos, for the team belonged to the 'Mounties', though it had a new driver.

Jim Hennings calmly continued judging the races and distributing prizes. He is one of the very few officials who can speak Eskimo fluently. So the missionaries are still the main pillar of every settlement, and probably the most stable influence on the Indians and Eskimos. Hennings is happy in his job. When I asked him where he came from, he slyly replied, "From the Arctic." Unlike many of his colleagues, he does not envisage returning south; he is not interested in promotion. Among the Inuk, he feels as free as they.

The highlight of the day was the igloo-building competition, which took place in the afternoon on a slope where the snow had been judged by experts to be of the right consistency. A space was marked out for each competitor, or rather couple, as each entrant had an assistant. The previous year's winner had built his igloo in fifteen minutes; he was the favourite in this contest, and most of the spectators gathered around his space. Eskimos love this kind of competition, and they have their champions at it.

The signal was given, and each couple began quickly making snow-blocks. The igloo rose as if by magic, one man disappeared inside to fit the keystone, while the other filled in the gaps between blocks. Then the entrance was properly cut out, the man inside came crawling forth and hurried to the judges to be timed. The winner's time was twelve minutes. He was not the favourite, last year's winner, who had felt so sure of himself that he had waited for a few minutes after the start, lighting a cigarette and engaging in animated conversation with friends. He apparently thought it unworthy of him to appear to be in a hurry. He accepted his defeat with a smile.

The winner received a handsome tent, and the other competitors were given primus-stoves or kitchen utensils. All were very satisfied.

The school-teachers had told us: "Whatever you do, don't miss the Eskimos' dance."

So we went to the dance-hall, the recreation-room, which was packed with about three hundred people and so overheated that it was impossible to see across the room because of the wreaths of moisture. Couples were dancing to the strains of an accordion played by a woman; the airs were easily recognisable as minuets and polkas. It was a most unusual spectacle to see an Eskimo woman with a baby in the hood of her parka dancing a minuet and curtseying to a perspiring partner whose shirt was gaping open, or who had taken off his shirt altogether. But there was nothing particularly Eskimo about it, except that it stemmed from contact with whaling crews and Hudson's Bay Company traders nearly a century ago.

On Sunday evening, Father Fournier and the Anglican minister (an Eskimo) held a joint service in the church. It was a great success; all the white population of Igloolik attended the service.

Easter over, Igloolik settled down to its usual calm existence, though first there were the departures of all the visitors. The Eskimos had been paid their family allowances, and the store was busy all day long.

Father Fournier had been looking out for our interests, as we learned when having lunch with him in his kitchen, together with Mr and Mrs Bartels.

Our host was worried by the thought of Pierre and me journeying across the ice and being entirely dependent on Eskimos.

"I know you've been on many expeditions," he said to me, "and that your young friend is an accomplished mountaineer, but travelling with Eskimos is a very different matter. You need to understand them; the slightest mistake can cause an irremediable misunderstanding."

"Yet I've been told, and I've noticed it myself, that they're always laughing."

"That's true, but their continual smile is a mask, and has no meaning except to themselves. An Eskimo would think he had lost face if he showed pain, dissatisfaction or anger. You must have noticed that yourself, during the competitions. The losers laughed more heartily than the winners. Eskimos have been called big children, but what a mistake that is! Their mental processes are so different from ours that we can't grasp them, any more than they can understand our way of thinking."

Father Fournier thought for a moment. "I can't let you go off with just Tabatiak, but the difficulty is to find another Eskimo who gets on with him but does not belong to his camp—someone to bring you back here. However, I've had an idea. I'll tell you later. I'm worried about your equipment, too."

Like Father Marec and many others we had met, Father Fournier had little confidence in our lightweight nylon clothing.

"I'll lend you my parka with a double lining and my trousers of caribou-skin," he said to me. "You'll be all right in those. If you weren't in such a hurry, I'd have some boots made for you by one of the Eskimo women. But she won't have time to chew the skins, to mould them into shape, before you leave. You'll have to make do by buying some felt-lined rubber boots that you can put on over your mocassins."

"What worries me," I said, "is the question of food."

"There's really only one solution when travelling by sled, and that is to eat like the Eskimos—frozen raw meat. However, your digestion will need a little time to get used to that. It took me several years. Yet from the day I ate some frozen raw seal, which was going bad, I never felt the cold any more. For you'll be cold, very cold, colder than you can ever imagine. You'll see. Even the Eskimos get cold when the terrible north wind is blowing."

This was not very encouraging for us. But Pierre and I were obstinate.

"So, how about a little trip by sled to the nearest camp?" Father Fournier said. "To Jens Munk Island, for instance. Won't that do you?"

"For our film, perhaps. But for us to get first-hand knowledge of what the life of Eskimo hunters is really like, no, I don't think so. We want to make a complete break with modern civilisation."

"All right. I'll make a list of the supplies and equipment that you ought to take. And don't count on what the Eskimos will have. They'll take just what they need for themselves—perhaps not even that."

Father Fournier's list was of the greatest use to us, and particularly because of the detailed thought given to it. For instance, we were instructed not only to buy a primus-stove but also a spare burner and a packet of needles to clean out the burner. We had to take plenty of tea, sugar, instant coffee, dried milk, flour, some canned meat and sardines.

"You're going away for ten days, but take enough for a fortnight," Father Fournier had said to us. "Take a big sack of flour, for your men to cook bannock for you. And some sweets to give to the children; cigarettes and tobacco for the wives."

Pierre and I spent the next two days preparing for our journey. We divided our purchases between the Eskimos' Co-op and the Bay. The manager of the latter, a Scot, had a young assistant who had arrived from Scotland only a few weeks previously and was making his first acquaintance with the Far North. He did his best, but still had much to learn. I bought the primus-stove from him, still in its cardboard box. Fortunately, I opened the box: it contained a whole lot of burners. The lad had taken the wrong box. His other mistake was not so serious. Included in Father Fournier's list was "a case of biscuits", to take the place of bread (there was none to be had at Igloolik). But the young assistant brought me two cartons of cocktail biscuits—enough for a party every evening for a week. I hardly thought that Father Fournier had meant me to have these tiny things, but I asked the manager to telephone to him. The conversation was in English, and the manager soon got impatient and called to his cashier, an Eskimo: "Here, you talk to him. I can't understand his blasted French accent." The cashier and Father Fournier spoke in Eskimo and the matter was soon sorted out.

We made our final arrangements at the Mission that evening. We were to leave the following morning at ten. Father Fournier was himself leaving for Hall Beach in a few hours, to attend a conference at Povungnituk, on the east coast of Hudson Bay. I deposited with the Co-op manager the amount to be paid to the Eskimos who were taking us. The rate of pay was the same as for the Indians, fifteen dollars a day per man. Then we checked the list of supplies.

"I haven't taken any meat for the Eskimos, Father."

"No, they'll have their own supply of seal or caribou meat, or frozen fish—don't worry about that. But for them you need tea, sugar, milk, flour, cigarettes."

"There's plenty of all that."

"This young man will be your interpreter. His name is Giuseppi Tatigat. He speaks very good English. He's an intelligent pupil but as lazy as a dormouse. The leader of the expedition will be his father, whom you'll meet tomorrow. He has the task of taking you to Tabatiak's igloo-camp and bringing you back to Igloolik. He's very dependable and a fine hunter, and he knows the straits and the Gulf of Boothia very well."

"What's your final advice to us, Father?"

"Always be cheerful, whatever happens. Adopt the Eskimo's smiling mask. Don't interfere with driving the sleds. The Eskimo's sled is nothing like the Indian's; it's heavier and can be dangerous on the ice-fields. Beware of the huskies! Leave them to the Eskimos, too."

Father Fournier left for Hall Beach later in the evening, speeding south in a snowmobile driven by Pacôme. Pierre and I were sad to see him go. Hennings was away too. There was still Bartels, fortunately, for we suddenly felt at the mercy of these small men with slanting eyes. I began to regret having decided on this crazy expedition. Why go so far in all this cold? We could get some Eskimos to build an igloo here and to perform before the camera. But I chased such ideas from my mind.

Pierre and I sat up late in our cabin, checking the cameras and the rolls of film, making sure that they were properly packed. We did not want to take more than was strictly necessary. Through the wide windows we could see the moon shining on the ice. A few sleds were leaving the settlement, disappearing into the distance. The following day, we should be doing the same.

Then the wind rose, and great gusts shook the cabin. The thermometer outside dropped to thirty-five below.

"Doesn't look too good," said Pierre.

5

To the Igloos on
Prince Frederik Island

WE HAD been waiting all morning. The blizzard which had raged
throughout the night had not abated, and merely to walk to the
Bay, barely a hundred yards, was enough to freeze one to the bone.
The driven snow blotted out the landscape, and only a few odd
shapes could be seen: a trawler caught in the ice, a bulldozer that
the strong east wind had clothed in snow.

"They told us they'd be here at ten o'clock," said Pierre.

"That doesn't mean a thing. All we know is that we'll be leaving
today—or perhaps tomorrow."

All our luggage had been stacked near the door. Igloolik was
deserted; everyone was staying indoors. Suddenly, a sled drawn by
a dozen huskies came dashing along the shore and up towards
our cabin. The driver, wearing a parka with the hood drawn
over his head, threw out the anchor and stopped his team in front
of us. He snaked his long whip over the huskies to make them
lie down, then came waddling towards us. Giuseppi was with
him.

"My father," said Giuseppi casually.

I had seen the man before. During the festivities he had gone
from one group to another, easily distinguishable by his sealskin
clothing and particularly his peaked cap, which was not very suitable. He smiled as he shook hands with us. He had a round, pleasant
face with a thin moustache, and the air of a sly old peasant. His son,

who was now wearing a parka, had lost some of his dandified appearance of the previous evening.

So here at last were two of our travelling companions.

"We set off at twelve," said Giuseppi.

Tatigat took our sacks of supplies and such of our equipment that we could entrust to him, and loaded them on his sled. He cracked his whip, and the sled seemed to fly over the snow.

We had been half expecting the delay. The remarkable thing was that it should have been only two hours. Giuseppi returned just before midday. "We go," he said, as casually as before.

Picking up the cameras and other equipment that we had preferred to keep with us, we followed the young man across the hummock ice and the smooth patches to the top end of the settlement, where two sleds were waiting. We had no time to make the acquaintance of the chief of Agu Bay, for Tatigat signalled to me to get on his sled, and off we went. There were three of us sitting on the load, which was covered with a splendid white bearskin.

"The Father give it for you," said Giuseppi.

Then I saw that it was the handsome skin that had been in front of the altar.

During the expedition it was used as a carpet each night, to protect us from the snow on the floor of the igloo. What a kind thought of Father Fournier before he left for Hall Beach!

The teams trotted quickly up the slope from Igloolik. I was at once struck by the strength and speed of these Eskimo huskies. They were pulling a load three times as heavy as the Indians' dogs had hauled; but each team was harnessed fan-shape instead of single-file, each animal on a separate trace about a dozen yards long. I counted Tatigat's team—eighteen huskies, and a fine lot.

We came to a flat-topped hill used as the settlement's cemetery. The corpses were covered with heaps of stones to protect them from being eaten by wild animals. Then we passed a small lake frozen to a depth of seven feet and more. The Igloolik Eskimos came here to cut lumps of ice and so obtain supplies of fresh water.

Giuseppi, concerned for my comfort, kept asking me, "No cold?"

No, I wasn't cold—not yet. His father said something, and Giuseppi felt my nylon clothing, then made a face. "No good." He had no faith in synthetics.

We glided along for over an hour without any slackening of pace, crossing the island westwards and coming down to a shore where the winds and tides had formed some pack-ice. Visibility was poor. When I looked back I could just see Tabatiak's sled with Pierre sitting on it, some distance away. We headed across the frozen sea, which held many rocky islands in its grip. The expanse of ice was touched with vivid colour here and there as the brilliant light broke through the clouds. We had the wind behind us, and were already covered with a fine layer of snow. However, I still had enough re-serves of warmth to keep out the cold. But after our first stop, the cold got into me and remained with me for the rest of the journey.

We halted at the mouth of a narrow inlet. The Eskimos began at once to build a low, semi-circular wall as a shelter for the primus-stove. Giuseppi got out some tins of sardines and packets of soup. I ought to have helped him, for he wasted half the food and ended by upsetting the saucepan with its contents. Remembering Father Fournier's advice, I burst out laughing; Tatigat laughed, Pierre laughed, and Tabatiak smiled slightly with a glint of disdain in his eyes.

The renowned chief of the Agu Bay Eskimos was certainly impressive, with his smooth, round, Asiatic face, an inscrutable mask, and his haughty attitude. I was surprised to see that he was wearing a blue cloth parka of modern design, and furlined nylon trousers. He must have found some advantages in white men's clothes.

We had our little snack standing in the cold wind, which was increasing in strength and whipping the snow about our legs. Occasionally the sun emerged dimly through the clouds. We were only two hours out from Igloolik, but I knew that if I had to return on foot I should never manage it in this weather. The cold had gripped us all, and we were stamping about to get warm. Giuseppi had started to shiver, and his father made him put on a caribou-skin parka, then gave me the parka and trousers lent by Father Fournier.

I tried to put the parka on over what I was wearing, but got my head caught in the hood. I was dancing about like a puppet, my arms waving in the air, when Pierre noticed the difficulty I was in. It took three of them to get me out. The parka turned out to be a double one. The outside was made from the thick winter fur of the caribou, and inside was a thinner parka which was usually worn next to the skin. But that would have meant undressing, and the present was certainly not the time. So I compromised, removed the inner parka and succeeded in getting into the warm but encumbering garment. I felt warm at once, though I could hardly move in it.

Just before we set off again, Pierre took the temperature. It was thirty-five below—without allowing for the strong wind that was blowing.

We continued westward, passing ice-capped islands. I was numb with cold and weariness. Giuseppi, too, was quite overcome by the cold. He curled up on the furs like a dog, pulled his hood over his face and went to sleep. Tatigat, gazing at the boundless horizon, urged his team with short cries. "*Oe! Oe!*" The huskies trotted along evenly. By now I could pick out the gallant, intelligent leader, who occasionally turned to bite or yelp to bring the team to order. The youngest huskies were on the shorter traces; but the fan-shape of the team kept closing up and opening out again, so much so that after an hour we had to stop to disentangle the traces. I took the opportunity to get off and trot alongside the sled, but not for long. The pace was too much for me, the snow was uneven, and the bitter cold took my breath away. I jumped on the sled again and began another long struggle against the piercing wind.

The Eskimo sledge is very different from the Indian to ride on. The passenger just finds a place among the heaped load and tries to keep his balance despite the bumping, the swaying and the speed. He usually sits sideways, but then dangling legs sometimes get bruised against blocks of ice, as I soon discovered. Having found a more or less comfortable position with one's back to the wind, one gradually becomes drowsy. Then a sudden jolt throws the passenger

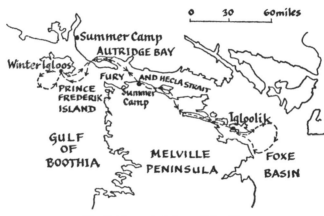

By Eskimo sled from Igloolik

off the sled. He rolls over in the snow, runs after the team and climbs on again, out of breath, lungs aching with the icy air.

The first few hours of the journey seemed very long. Yet we were travelling at a fast pace, as I realised when I tried to trot along by the sled and soon dropped behind.

Late in the day, some cliffs showed through the mist in the distance, and I thought we were approaching the west coast of Baffin Island. But Giuseppi soon put me right. "Mainland," he said.

In the evening I was able to consult the map, and saw that we had travelled almost due west and were in a long inlet on the northeast coast of Melville Peninsula.

"Two more days before we reach Fury Strait," our interpreter told me.

We stopped for the night at the foot of a high cliff. Tatigat and Tabatiak probed the snow for some distance, looking for a suitable place to build an igloo. Finally they decided on a spot near some hard drifted snow, which could quickly be cut into blocks. We were near the shore, marked by a mass of jagged and broken ice. I was about to walk across it when Tatigat signalled to me to get back on the sled. Pierre was some way ahead, with his cine-camera, and I suddenly saw him sink to his knees in water. He had broken through a layer of soft snow that our sleds had passed over without any trouble. But there was nothing to show that it was just a flimsy bridge and would give way under a man's weight.

The preparations for making our first Eskimo camp were quite new to us. First of all, the Eskimos unhitched the teams. They tethered only one husky, attached to an anchor and heavy chain. This was a bitch, and all the other huskies gathered round her, rolling and gambolling in the snow, as lively as could be after this first day's haul. Then Tatigat and Tabatiak got out their tools, knife and snow-saw, and tested the wide, supple blade. Tatigat was the builder, and a very skilful one. He began by cutting out a block about three feet long, two feet wide and eighteen inches deep. Then he continued the trench thus formed, passing the blocks to Tabatiak, who stacked them near him. The next operation was to build the first circle of blocks, all leaning slightly inwards, then the second layer, and so the dome began to take shape, a perfect curve. Tabatiak was shaping the blocks and Tatigat was fitting them into place; the latter had removed all his top clothes and was in his cotton shirt, but was sweating even so. Pierre and I, who had nothing to do but watch, were slowly freezing. Tatigat, inside the igloo, put the keystone in place. The gaps between the blocks were filled with snow, which was packed tight and then smoothed off with a knife.

Tabatiak went to see to the huskies and to turn the sled upside down. An hour and a half after our arrival, the igloo was ready for occupation. A far cry from the twelve minutes of the winner of the competition! But this igloo, which stood only a little higher than the hummock ice on which it rested, was our only shelter for the night. Our comfort depended on its being solid and airtight. Tabatiak carried in the caribou-skins, the white bear-skin and our equipment. When Pierre and I stepped inside, we at once appreciated its comfort; out of the wind, the cold was bearable. There was a sleeping-bench, with the bear-skin spread over it, on which we sat rather awkwardly. Giuseppi, who had given no help with the work, would not even reply to our questions. He pointed to his head. "Bad," he said, and then stretched out on the bench and lay still.

Tabatiak took the right-hand side of the igloo, which was the chief's place. He lit his primus and melted some snow. Pierre set up our primus on the left-hand side, the strangers' place. Tatigat and his son would sleep in the middle. Beneath this dome of translucent ice, muffled sounds reached us: the barking of the huskies, the moaning of the wind, the flurries of hard snow against the igloo.

We all prepared for the night, taking off our mukluks and putting them to dry at the bottom of our sleeping-bags. Pierre had made tea for the two of us and managed to heat some soup; with a tin of sardines, that would do. Tabatiak had only his tea, which rather surprised me. I questioned our interpreter, Giuseppi, but he was dead to the world. I wondered whether he was fooling us or whether he was really ill; he seemed to have no strength left. We managed to make him drink some tea and take some aspirins. He had probably caught a chill during the Easter festivities, when he had wandered about clad elegantly in just a linen jacket.

"And what are you going to eat?" I asked the other two.

Giuseppi replied for them, with an effort. "They'll eat what you're eating."

Father Fournier had assured me that the Eskimos would prefer their raw seal and fish, but I found that they had brought nothing with them. So I shared our soup, tea and sardines.

"No meat," I said. "Have you some seal?"

They did not understand, and Giuseppi made no further effort.

Luckily, Pierre was still cheerful. He showed an interest in everything; he turned cook, and seemed to get on very well with the two Eskimos. They found that they all had the same first name, which tickled them immensely.

Then began a serenade which I was to hear every night and morning. The three Eskimos were caught by a violent bout of coughing: they groaned, spat and spewed, and this went on for almost an hour. Tabatiak made me understand that he was tired. I learned later that they all suffered from chronic bronchitis. Pierre and I just had to get used to it.

Tatigat had sealed up the entrance to our igloo with a big block, and the heat from one primus was enough to send up the temperature; the snow wall began to melt, but froze again almost immediately. The thermometer showed fifteen below, which was twenty-five degrees warmer than outside—as I discovered in the morning. It was this difference which gave us some feeling of comfort. However, as soon as we put out the primus in order to economise on fuel, the cold crept in.

I had profited by my experience with the Indians and had bought a second, very big sleeping-bag into which my own easily fitted. This time, I was really warm. And what a wonderful feeling it was! The Eskimos had gone to sleep with their feet pointing to the wall and lying on their stomachs; in the morning they would only have to raise themselves a little to reach out and light the primus. This was the age-old position adopted in all the igloos of the Arctic. Pierre and I lay on our backs, which amused our friends very much. Moreover, as we are tall and the igloo was made for the smaller Eskimos, our feet stuck out beyond the end of the sleeping-bench. A box was put to support them, and then we all went to sleep.

That first night in an igloo was very comfortable. In the Indian tent, the wood-burning stove had given out a great heat, but as soon as it went out the temperature inside the tent had dropped to that outside. But here, there was no such violent change in temperature; in the morning it was just as cold as when we had gone to sleep, but no colder. The warmth from our five bodies had kept the temperature in the igloo at ten to fifteen below. I felt in fine form, and so did Pierre. We knew that we should be able to sleep at night. Some of our doubts about the trip had disappeared.

"We shall be able to stick it," said Pierre.

"I'm sure we shall."

Eskimos either sleep very little, or for many hours at a stretch, as if to catch up. They also still possess primitive man's amazing capacity to go without food for several days, then tuck away pounds of meat in one enormous meal.

Our three woke up very early, and at once began their coughing and spitting; it was very distressing to watch, but quite normal for them. When they had thoroughly cleared their tubes, one of them decided to make the tea and slipped a lump of snow into the saucepan. The igloo became filled with steam; luckily, we had put the cameras away safely. The morning light was filtering through the wall, only slightly dimmed by the sooty smoke from the kerosene flame. All that could be seen of Giuseppi was a motionless heap of furs. His father bent over him as solicitously as over a little child. He himself was well and smiling.

Tabatiak sat up in his sleeping-bag like a Buddha and solemnly read a passage from the Bible. Tabatiak was a Protestant and the other two were Roman Catholics. They did not want us to think that only Tabatiak was a Christian, so Tatigat recited the Pater Noster and his son joined in feebly; then they made a perfunctory sign of the cross and that was that.

Tatigat lit a cigarette, then we got breakfast. Pierre and I had white coffee, the Eskimos had tea, into which they dipped biscuits, and we all finished with big bowls of porridge. The Eskimos seemed to like this. And so we idled away a couple of hours. Then Tatigat suddenly took his snow-knife and cut a little opening, through which he inspected the outside world. He turned and smiled broadly at me, as much as to say, "It's all right now, the wind has dropped."

He cut a space in the leeward side of the igloo and crawled out. In a moment, the cold penetrated. Tabatiak quickly replaced the block, but the cold remained and we found it impossible to stay in the igloo.

Outside, I had my first good look at the arctic landscape. The evening before, with the driving snow and the north wind, I had been too frozen to take much notice of the surroundings. Now I saw that we were close to an inlet that seemed to continue a long way westward. Opposite were rounded hills made stark by the eternal winds; the bare earth and rocks showed everywhere. The huskies were prowling hungrily about the igloo. Tabatiak and Tatigat were busy glazing the runners of their sleds, made of rough lengths of wood to which the snow soon sticks. The Eskimos first smeared them with frozen mud, then applied a layer of ice. To obtain the right sort of ice, they made some water and then dropped small lumps of snow into it. These melted and then partly froze. They applied this glazing with a seal-skin glove and smoothed it with a pad of caribou fur. The temperature was forty below that morning, so the sled runners soon had a shining, smooth glaze as hard as iron.

This long, fastidious task sometimes has to be repeated once or twice in the day, according to the state of the snow and ice. Some Eskimos now shoe their runners, but they are very much in the minority. When I returned to Igloolik I mentioned the matter to Father Vandervelde, who has been at Pelly Bay for twenty-five years. I told him how surprised I was to see this method of glazing still in use, when it would have been so easy to tar the runners at the beginning of a journey, to last throughout. Drums of tar could be sent to these regions as easily as drums of gasoline. The Lapps tar their sled runners and find the method satisfactory.

"They just haven't thought of it," said Father Vandervelde. "Perhaps it is too simple. Besides, Eskimos are traditionalists by nature, doing as their forefathers did before them, and it doesn't occur to them to change. But the coming generation will go straight from the dog-sled to the motorised skidoo."

Although there was hardly any wind that morning, it was bitterly cold. The Eskimos took great care in getting ready for the day's journey, and their main concern was to have dry mukluks for their feet. The preparations for departure took several hours. There were the sleds to be loaded, the harness and traces to be thawed out, and the huskies caught and hitched. Some were most unwilling and only allowed themselves to be harnessed after a hard struggle with their masters, who distributed a good many blows and kicks. The Eskimos, however, seemed to me to be less cruel than the Indians.

Pierre's great concern during that first night in the igloo had been to keep his camera batteries from freezing. We had two cine-cameras, one of which ran on batteries; we were relying entirely on this one, for the other's mechanism had been affected by the cold. The batteries had been fully charged before leaving Igloolik, but everything depended on their surviving the next ten days.

The only way to prevent freezing was to carry them about under one's quilted jacket when not in use. Pierre kept the batteries in his sleeping-bag at night and inside his jacket during the day. It was not the height of comfort, but only through such care was he able to continue filming.

There was also the difficult business of loading the camera. This could not be done inside the igloo because condensation and moisture on the metal parts and the lens would have made them unusable. So the operation had to be carried out in the open. Gloves could not be worn, not even silk ones, as 16 mm. film is very brittle and breaks like glass. By the end of our expedition, Pierre's finger-tips were hardened from frostbite while reloading his camera.

These were small inconveniences hardly worth mentioning, but which got one down in the end. The cold affected every normal activity and the slightest gesture was painful—to say nothing of relieving ourselves. The Eskimos did their natural functions in front of us in the igloo, but we could not bring ourselves to do likewise. So we had to go out in the cold and wind, holding off the huskies which gathered in a menacing circle, baring their teeth. It was no laughing matter in a temperature of forty below.

We were ready at last. Tatigat disentangled the traces for the last time and came back to the sled; Giuseppi was already lying on it, obviously very ill. Tatigat gave a vigorous kick to free the runners. This was a signal to the huskies, who darted wildly forward so that I had to leap for the sled and cling as best I could. Eighteen huskies all bounding forward at the same time constitute considerable pulling power. I hardly had time to gain my balance before the sled was speeding over the ice, past the glazed cliffs.

That first night in the igloo had marked a complete break with ordinary comforts and everyday habits; I was now a part of the extraordinary world of arctic solitudes, and sense of time and bodily fatigue were forgotten. There was a primitive feeling of having become a sort of thinking animal, acting only on reflex.

There was no real sense of motion. The huskies went trotting on with maddening regularity for hours on end, so that finally my mind went blank and I seemed to be drifting.

Always there was the cruel, biting cold. Yet what a marvellous day it was! In the morning we made good progress up the inlet and then across the land. We were following a kind of tectonic furrow which was bordered to the north by a high range of hills separating us from the strait. To the south was a rolling landscape to high rocky plateaus swept bare by the winds. The bitter cold of the morning became less acute. The sun was shining but there was no warmth in it; the rays struck us like jets of cold light. We were each crouched as comfortably as possible on the sled, backs turned to the direction being taken, for even on such a windless day it was painful to remain for hours with one's face turned to the front, catching the current of air. Our speed was about ten miles an hour.

The drivers, however, had to watch their teams. Their faces had haloes of frost; there was a pretty row of icicles on Tatigat's moustache.

We went along this trough formed by a glacier, getting higher at each lake we came to, and passing two or three igloos on the way. Tabatiak had built them on his journey to Igloolik the previous week. He had left a cache of meat here and there; our huskies had had nothing to eat since we left, so we stopped at one crumbling igloo and the Eskimos took their hooks and pulled out a huge chunk of walrus, frozen as hard as granite.

Pierre and I had already got used to the tea-break. Tabatiak built a snow wall and we sheltered behind it. Crouching around the small flame of the primus, we could take off our gloves and use our fingers. But not for long. After a few minutes we had to rub them vigorously to restore the circulation. Still, it was a pleasant place to stop; the range of hills gave shelter from the north wind, and the sun was full on us.

When we continued our journey, I was able to sleep for a good part of the afternoon, lying among the furs and across Giuseppi's legs. Tatigat pulled the hood of his parka down over his eyes and dozed at the front of the sled, while the huskies trotted on. I had a good nap. It was really pleasant—only twenty below in the sun, and thirty-five below in the shade. It was the one comfortable day of the whole journey, and the warmest. But by evening there was a great change.

We were climbing a small, windswept pass where the snow lay only in the hollows. The slope seemed interminable; it was a strain for the huskies, but they pulled as willingly as ever. The sun was hanging just above the horizon, the perpetual mist of snow in the air was drifting as though the earth were on fire. The flurries were sometimes so thick that the huskies were blotted from view. For hours we had been huddled up in our furs, with only one thought in mind— to keep out the cold.

We reached the top of the pass and a new landscape was revealed. This sight of fresh horizons roused some strength in me, a desire to enter this new world. It was like the one we were leaving, yet quite different, for it slipped away ahead of us, the features changing shape, disappearing and coming into view again, as though the ice and the rocks were playing with us. We were going to the end of the world.

It was too cold to stop. As we went on down I caught sight of the sea stretching away to the west. It was covered with appalling pack-ice, with the massive grey bulk of icebergs. We were coming down to Fury Strait east of Amherst Island, whose outline was now merged with the coast of Melville Peninsula. To the north could just be seen the white blur of Baffin Island, pointing towards a snow-filled sky.

I thought we should stop as soon as we reached the ice-covered sea, but Tabatiak urged on his team and went ahead. Tabatiak never said a word to me, he just smiled; but he had an air of great authority and Tatigat readily accepted his leadership. I wondered how much longer he intended to continue and where he was leading us.

We worked our way through the pack-ice for another two hours. Tabatiak seemed to know it like the palm of his hand, leading the way without hesitation from one wall of ice to another, finding a passage where the going was easier, approaching the shore and then turning away from it, all for no apparent reason but always finding the best route.

The huskies trotted on, lapping at the snow in passing, sweat running down their flanks and with a glaze of ice on their fur. Tabatiak stopped his sled at last, in front of yet another wall of seracs, the pointed, jagged divisions of a glacier. He flicked his long whip over his team, not touching them but instantly making them drop down and sprawl in the snow. It was then seven o'clock. The sun had gone down behind the clouds drifting over the distant hilltops, and only a pale light remained. Tabatiak and Tatigat began to probe the snow to find a suitable place to build the igloo. The snow was crumbly and not very deep, so their search took some time. This long wait at the end of the day's travelling was always wearing.

At last they found the best spot, where the wind had piled up enough snow between two towering seracs, and began to build the igloo methodically and without hurry. Tatigat took off his parka and worked in his shirt as before. But Tabatiak seemed to me to be much less hardy; he kept all his clothes on and went at it gently. He cut the snow-blocks, and the other did the building. Young Giuseppi was lying on the sled looking very ill, spitting and coughing. He was just a passenger now, and I was beginning to feel very anxious about him. The school year at Igloolik had not fitted him for a return to the hard life of hunters. The poor youngster was poised between two civilisations. What would it do to him, I wondered?

Now that we were away from the shelter of the hills and out in the strait, the wind was blowing strongly and the cold increasing to the point of becoming unbearable. Pierre kept reading the thermometer. The figures rose but the temperature went down—thirty below at seven o'clock, thirty-five below at eight, forty below at ten, when we were at last able to go into the igloo, close the entrance, light the primus and make some tea. Tatigat had built this igloo much larger than the first, and there was more comfort for the five of us. This was why he had been so long building it.

That night, April fourteenth, was one of the coldest we had. A blizzard raged and roared. Inside the igloo the noises were muffled, but we were aware of the battering wind. We heard the huskies scratching outside. They must have sought shelter in the little snow-hut made next to the igloo for the harness and equipment which could not be taken into the igloo. I was very anxious for our invalid. Giuseppi was tossing and groaning. Pierre and I kept giving him aspirins with hot tea. The other two seemed tired and dispirited after their work in the cold night air. Tabatiak was shaken by a violent fit of coughing. The idea of going back came into our minds, but that would be a pitiful failure after two days on sleds.

The blizzard kept us in the igloo for twelve hours. Some time during the morning, Tatigat cut a little opening in the wall and saw that there was an improvement in the weather. He told Tabatiak, who cut away the block covering the entrance. Outside, the huskies were little snowy mounds; they barely raised their heads at our approach. The two Eskimos got out the harness. So we were going to make a start. Nothing could be seen of the ice-bound landscape except the seracs, towering like phantoms. Snow was falling and the wind made the cold as intense as ever; though the thermometer showed a mere twenty-eight below.

Tatigat got his son ready for the journey as though he were a complete invalid, putting a second pair of mukluks on his feet and making sure that his gloves were in good condition. Giuseppi lay motionless, and made no answer when I spoke to him. Tabatiak was busy outside, spreading out the traces and loading the sleds. Pierre and I helped him as well as we could; we now knew the main things to be done and tried to be useful. Pierre managed to get the harness on some of the huskies, who growled ominously all the while. But living at close quarters with the Eskimos had given us some of their smell, so we were no longer strangers to the dogs.

We did not travel very far that day.

Tatigat led the way through the snow and gloom. We circled some difficult pack-ice, then crossed the rocky Amherst Island and came to a bay at the narrowest point of the strait separating Baffin Island and Melville Peninsula. Visibility was never more than fifty yards. We reached a flat stretch where old tracks could still be seen. The huskies were tiring. Now and again one of them refused to go on, but the driver clipped it with his whip, and order was restored.

We were now well into the third day, and when I looked at the map I saw that we had barely covered a third of the distance. Father Fournier was right. In the Arctic, when you set off on a journey you never know how long it is going to take.

I had the impression that we were picking our way across a tortuous glacier. The powdery snow added to the difficulty, masking crevasses and hiding sharp ridges of ice. The two Eskimos were making superhuman efforts to avoid serious accidents, sometimes straining to stop the heavy sled at the very edge of a crevasse.

Tatigat had to stop in the middle of the pack-ice. The huskies had had enough, and had got their traces into a tangle. Pierre got busy with his camera, while I helped Tatigat disentangle the traces. When the huskies were pulling the sled, they kept crossing each other's path, so that after a time the eighteen traces became twisted into one thick rope.

We finished, and I was about to get back on the sled when the huskies suddenly darted off. There was rivalry between the two teams. Tabatiak's was some way ahead, and our team was eager to catch up. Tatigat was more agile than I, and in any case was more used to the dangers; he leapt aside and jumped on the moving sled. But I was left caught in the traces, which wound tight round my legs as some of the huskies pulled away to the right and the others to the left. I struggled in the snow, shouting with pain; my right leg felt as if it was being wrenched from my body. Tatigat managed to bring the team to a stop, and Pierre ran back to me. I was lying in the snow, the pain so sharp I thought I was going to faint. I was afraid to move, wondering if my leg was broken. Pierre lifted me up. "Are you badly hurt?" he asked anxiously. "Anything broken?"

"My gloves, Pierre. Quick, my gloves."

They had come off in the fall, and for some minutes I had been lying in the snow with naked hands. They were already white to the wrists.

Pierre found my gloves, but the snow and the cold had turned them into lumps of ice. I did not think I had broken a bone, though my right knee and hip hurt badly. I got to my feet, but my knee gave way.

"I'll be all right, Pierre. It's not much." I lifted myself on to the sled.

"How about your hands?" he asked.

"A touch of frostbite. I'll rub them."

We set off again across the icy wastes, still being swept by a blizzard. I kept moving my fingers and rubbing my hands, and the circulation gradually returned. The pain was excruciating, but I tried not to utter a sound. I was angry with myself for having cried out earlier. Keep smiling was the watchword.

Tatigat kept looking at me anxiously, and gestured to me to continue rubbing my hands. After an hour or so, the blood had returned to them, the danger was past. There remained the stabbing pain in my right leg, which had gone stiff.

We made tea in an abandoned igloo out in the middle of the strait. The Eskimos seemed in a hurry to get moving again. There was no improvement in the weather. The wind had increased in strength.

We passed close to a rocky island with a beacon. How many ships had sailed past it, I wondered, during the one month when the strait was open to navigation?

At about seven o'clock I had the impression that the sleds were moving with greater ease and that our speed had increased. There was still whiteness all around, but frozen banks of earth indicated that we were running along the shore. Then I caught sight of a pole with several thongs fluttering from it, high up on a beach, and surrounded by a litter of crates and empty barrels, even a boat with its sides staved in.

The huskies ran up on the beach and stopped in front of a great mound of snow, from which the top of a tent was showing, and sat down as though they had reached home.

There were two huge walrus tusks marking the entrance to an igloo; some harpoons and fishing-tackle lay scattered about in the snow. Giuseppi struggled up on the sled, his face feverish. "My father's summer camp," he managed to tell me. So that was why we had pressed on all day.

A gust of wind whipped at our faces, and Tatigat motioned to Pierre and me to crawl through the tunnel and into the igloo. It was obviously used as a store-room, and the smell of rotting meat turned my stomach. A low opening on the other side of the igloo brought us into the tent, a huge tent strengthened with planks, almost completely buried in the snow. A small window by the entrance let in some light. It was damp and ice-cold inside, but after the hours out in the blizzard, this gloomy cave-like shelter seemed a haven.

Tatigat and his family spent the summer here, hunting caribou on Melville Peninsula, trapping foxes, and especially hunting seal and walrus, which abound in the straits.

Giuseppi came crawling in and collapsed on to the sleeping-bench which took up the whole of the back of the tent, as in an igloo. He was coughing worse than ever.

Pierre and I went back to fetch our equipment. I found the greatest difficulty in crawling through the tunnel and the low openings, for my right leg had gone completely stiff.

We lit both primus-stoves, and dense steam spread across the tent. Tabatiak got an oil-lamp out of a crate, and this gave enough light for us to arrange ourselves and put the place in order. There was filth everywhere: the sleeping-bench was covered with mouldy skins, dirty, torn blankets and old sleeping-bags with their padding oozing out, while in a corner behind the oil-lamp was a smelly pile of seal-blubber. However, the Eskimos had the knack of making themselves comfortable, and in next to no time our caribou-skins and furs had been thrown over the filthy stuff to hide it. Tatigat went out to get some frozen snow from the top of a serac.

Soon the water started to boil, and Pierre got a meal ready. The two Eskimos had gone out to put the sleds and harness away safely. With their axes they chopped up the frozen carcass of a seal which had a putrid smell, and when they had enough pieces they went to feed the huskies. The blizzard was still blowing but there were signs that the wind might abate when the sun went down.

Tabatiak and Giuseppi were coughing continuously, although we kept giving them hot drinks. Tatigat lit the oil-lamp again, and as the primus was still burning, the temperature in the tent rose rapidly to three or four degrees below zero. This was real comfort.

Tatigat was the only one of the Eskimos still fit. His son was really ill, and Tabatiak had rolled up in a corner and was trying to get a little sleep between bouts of coughing.

My stiff leg kept me awake for some time, but I was happy to think that I had only torn a ligament. The consequences could have been far worse, and that would have meant a three-day journey through the blizzard. As it was, I should be handicapped during the rest of the expedition; but we could continue with it, and that was the important thing.

In the morning I was not surprised when Tatigat gave me to understand that his son was too ill to travel, and that we should stay where we were for a day longer. He was going to give Giuseppi some raw, rotting seal-meat to eat. My stock of aspirins had vanished in a couple of days.

It had stopped snowing, and although the cold increased as the morning wore on, the wind did not get up and we were able to move about and do various outside tasks. The snow had piled up at the entrance to the igloo during the night. This was cleared away and an ice-wall built as protection. Tatigat was delighted at finding things he had left lying about six months ago. He was happy to be back home. The huskies romped about in the snow, and Tabatiak repaired the damage done to his sled while crossing the pack-ice. He and Tatigat went and dug up a cache of seal-meat, a few hundred yards from the camp. There were about a dozen carcasses buried under a pile of big red stones. They had been skinned soon after being killed, and were now one enormous frozen chunk. The two Eskimos hacked at it with their axes, and when they had separated a few carcasses they put them on a sled and pulled it back to the camp. The carcasses were then chopped into small pieces and fed to the huskies, who devoured the lot.

Tabatiak was exhausted and in a feverish sweat after all this, and went into the tent and lay down. Giuseppi was still weak, and made

little reply when I spoke to him. Pierre and I were without an interpreter, but we managed quite well with sign-language. Tatigat made
some bannock, flat cakes of unleavened bread, over the oil-lamp
during the afternoon. He made it in the same way as the Indians, but
without any regard for cleanliness. The pan he made the bannock in
was used for all kinds of purposes. However, Pierre and I had become accustomed to the smells, and could now pass through the
igloo without our stomachs heaving at the stench of rotting meat.
But when Tatigat offered us a cut from a seal, we politely refused.

The wind dropped in the evening, and we went out to watch the
splendid spectacle of the sun setting over the ice-fields. Then a soft
light that seemed to pour like oil from between two banks of cloud
passed slowly across the distant slopes, finally touching the rounded
heights of Baffin Island on the other side of the strait.

On returning to the tent we found that Giuseppi was much
better. Could this be the result of eating rotten seal-meat? In any
case, he seemed almost well again. Tabatiak, however, was lying
silently in his corner, perspiring feverishly.

We sat up until late. Pierre and Tatigat played 'battleships'.
Eskimos seem to learn all kinds of games with surprising quickness.
I had found an English novel belonging to a Winnipeg library in
one of the crates lying about the tent, and reading it soothed my
mind.

Tatigat brought out an old box, after searching for a long time
among a pile of rubbish, and produced from it some yellowing,
tattered photographs which he proudly showed to Pierre and me.
His only experience of Western civilisation, apart from his stays at
Igloolik, was the hospital at Churchill. He had been flown there
after his sled had turned over on him while crossing some pack-ice;
it was feared that his back was broken. He had been kept in plaster
for six months. He now looked upon that period in hospital as the
most wonderful adventure of his life. He had been given every care,
and when he was well again he had had his photo taken with the
nurses who had looked after him. And there he was—a thin but

smiling youngster standing between two lovely girls. What age was he now, I wondered? His son Giuseppi was seventeen. Eskimos marry young, usually in their late teens. So Tatigat was the same age as Pierre. And Tabatiak, the king of the igloos of Prince Frederik Island, would be in his thirties. They would look like old men by the time they were forty.

The tent ceased to be comfortably warm once the oil-lamp was put out. Normally, in winter quarters, it would be kept burning all night; but Tatigat was economising with his small stock of seal-blubber. With the primus out and the oil-lamp no longer burning, the cold quickly spread into the tent.

The coughing and spitting of the two sick men made sleep difficult, and finally the extreme cold woke us all up very early. Pierre and Tatigat were the most courageous; it took me half an hour to recover the use of my right leg and to get outside. But the leg responded well, once I was on my feet. It was a glorious morning, very cold but with little wind.

The Eskimos seemed in no hurry to leave. Tabatiak was still dozing in the tent, indifferent to everything. Giuseppi, obviously much better, was rummaging about, looking for some of his child-hood belongings; he found a home-made toy, then discovered a picture-book hidden under the moulding blankets, and seemed delighted with it.

A few hours went by, and as no one was making a move I questioned Giuseppi: "Are we going?"

The lad glanced at his father, then at Tabatiak, as though seeking some indication. They said something in short, sharp sentences, and Giuseppi translated, or so I thought.

"You are the boss, you decide. If you say go, then we go."

I looked at the other two, but their smiling masks gave no hint of their opinion either way.

"Well, Giuseppi, we go," I said,

Pierre and I rolled up our sleeping-bags and started to pack our equipment. Tatigat, sitting on a heap of skins at the back of the tent, was staring at me. I was surprised to catch a hard glint in his eyes. He watched me for a while in silence, his look weighing on me like a reproach. Then he said: "You no good."

I gave a start. It was an accusation that hurt me deeply. Pierre and I had done all we could to be friendly with these Eskimos, living like them, sharing meals with them, and never complaining. I questioned Giuseppi, but he looked sullen and made no reply.

"What does your father mean?" I insisted. "Why did he say that? I want to know. When I asked you what we were going to do, you replied that I was the one to decide. So I said we'd go. But if there's some objection, then you ought to tell me."

Giuseppi looked away, embarrassed. "It was a joke," he muttered.

"No, Giuseppi, it was not a joke. Your father meant what he said. But what did you say to him?"

I suspected Giuseppe of having twisted my words. He translated only what he cared to, and whenever I had asked him about the route we were taking or put questions about the landscape, he had replied "I don't understand" or "I don't know". And now he refused to act as interpreter between myself and his father, which would have enabled me to remove the misunderstanding.

"Let it drop," said Pierre. "The kid's impossible. Yesterday he looked as if he were dying, and today he's throwing his weight about."

I felt I could not fully trust the Eskimos. Pierre still found favour in their eyes. I was the chief, the one who had to make the decisions, so he could not be blamed for anything.

I took all our luggage outside, with Pierre's help. Tabatiak was still in his sleeping-bag and showed no sign of budging. But Tatigat followed me out of the igloo.

It looked like a really fine day; the temperature had not gone below thirty, although the wind was stronger and was blowing the snow across the ice-fields so that thick smoke seemed to be sweeping into the distance. We ought to have covered twenty miles by this time on such a fine day.

Tatigat pointed to the west, at a far-off greyish bank of cloud.

"Storm," Tatigat said, and went back into the igloo.

No one came to harness the huskies. I crawled back into the tent. Tabatiak was rolled up in his sleeping-bag. Tatigat was sitting on a crate, looking uneasy; he suddenly made up his mind about something, and began to talk to Giuseppi. The lad condescended to translate his father's words.

"My father says that when aeroplanes do not leave, the huskies cannot leave either."

I did not see what he was driving at. What had planes to do with it?

Giuseppi tried again. "When there's a blizzard blowing, planes do not take off, my father says. He also says that when a blizzard is blowing over the pack-ice, huskies do not set off either."

"You mean he thinks a storm is coming up?"

"He told you so."

I thought for a moment, choosing my words carefully, to make sure that Tatigat understood properly.

"Listen," I said to Giuseppi. "If your father thinks a storm is coming up, then we ought to stay here. Another day won't make any difference."

"But you gave orders for us to leave."

"Look, Giuseppi, that's enough of that! When you said that I was the one to decide, I ruled that we'd set off. But you didn't tell me that your father feared bad weather was on the way. I may be the boss, but your father is the guide. He's the one who knows whether we ought to set off or stay here. He's familiar with the weather, the ice-fields and the winds. I know nothing of all that. Tell him from me that if he decides we ought to stay here, then we'll stay. Have you understood?"

"Yes, sir."

There was a long discussion between the two; I could catch the sense of it from their gestures and expressions. It seemed obvious that Giuseppi was explaining that he had twisted my words earlier.

Then suddenly everything was all right again. Tatigat smiled at me and gave a kindly look that seemed to say, *I understand it all now; we're agreed and you can trust me.*

He spoke to his son, who translated a little at a time: "This winter, my father set out from here to go to Agu Bay. The weather was as it is today. But a storm came up. Twenty miles out on the sea, the cold became unbearable because of the wind, and the huskies lay down in the snow. He had to return to the camp. The same thing would have happened today."

The incident was closed, and everyone became good-humoured again. Tabatiak went on sleeping, rolled up in his blankets.

I crawled out through the igloo and saw how right Tatigat had been; in less than an hour, the blizzard had come upon us. The wind knocked the breath out of me when I faced it. The cold was not so intense, but the blizzard was becoming stronger every minute. It would have been madness to set out. But why had they not said so straight away? Such is the mentality of the Eskimo, who considers it useless to try to make sense of the white man's way of thinking.

We all stayed snugly in the tent, not going out again except to dig up more frozen seal-meat for the huskies. We could hear the gale-force wind battering away outside and occasionally the dogs pattering across the roof. Tatigat kept the oil-lamp going, and it was nice and warm in the tent. Pierre and I huddled down in our sleeping-bags and dreamed the time away. Tatigat repaired a set of harness; Giuseppi ate and drank and slept; Tabatiak made a whip. The hours slipped past, time had lost all meaning.

The morning was fine. But neither Pierre nor I asked any questions. We left it to the Eskimos to decide whether or not to leave.

Tabatiak was feeling better, he had thrown off his fever. He read his Bible for more than an hour, sitting like a Buddha. Then he dressed himself completely, and Tatigat did the same, so Pierre and I knew that a start was to be made. However, we did not hasten them,

Chopping up frozen seal that had been buried,
to feed the huskies

A herd of musk-oxen in defensive formation

Eskimo woman with her baby in the hood of her parka

Tabatiak

Tatigat

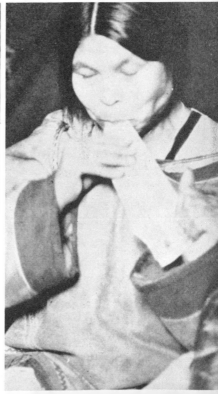

Inside the Kopak igloo. The
wife and the two children. Boot
soles are moulded to fit the foot
by the women who bite folds
into the skin

BELOW, LEFT: The Kopak boy at the
icy threshold of the family igloo

OVERLEAF: Polar bear at bay

Huskies attacking a polar bear

An Eskimo camp

Glazing the runners, after smearing them
with frozen mud

Winter igloos on Prince Frederik Island

Inouk, armed with harpoon and rifle,
waits for a seal to show itself

and waited until the last minute before rolling up our sleeping-bags and tying our luggage.

It was nine-thirty when the two teams, eager and fit after their rest, darted off and headed due west. For an hour or so we followed the southern shore of the strait, then turned north to cross to the other side. We were not far from the mouth of the strait, and the wind blowing in from the Gulf of Boothia became stronger the farther we got from the shore; fortunately, the cold was not too intense. As the mountainous outline of Melville Peninsula became blurred and faded from view, and the rounded, cloud-topped hills of Baffin Island gradually became larger, I could realise what our situation would have been if we had been caught by a blizzard out here in the open.

It took four hours to cross the strait and reach the shelter of Autridge Bay, which is about twenty miles long. Giuseppi, in a burst of confidence, had shown me our route on the map. There was a more direct way of reaching Prince Frederik Island, by keeping to the southern side of the strait and then heading straight across the gulf; but the pack-ice was very dangerous, with many breaks in it. So we were making a long detour to the north to reach the west coast of Baffin Island at the point nearest to Prince Frederik Island.

The Bay was sheltered from the winds, and the ice was as smooth as that on a lake, so our huskies were able to maintain a fast pace. I saw that the southern side of Autridge Bay is a long line of basalt rocks about five hundred feet high; as they face north, they were just one long, steep stretch of shining ice. The other shore, however, rises in a gradual slope towards high hills, whose more distant ranges reach an altitude of three thousand feet.

The morale of our little party was steadily improving, helped by the good travel conditions. Tabatiak kept urging on his team, but Tatigat dozed off and had a nap that lasted about three hours. The movement of our sled was smooth and regular. The head of the bay seemed quite near, but we took another couple of hours to reach it. Since leaving the camp, we had stopped only once to have some tea.

The huskies began to toil in the soft snow, and we halted to glaze the sled runners again.

Then we crossed the land, climbing a long slope, from the top of which we had a wide view over the Gulf of Boothia and could see our destination, Prince Frederik Island, in the distance. The other side dropped steeply down to Agu Bay. We sped over frozen grass and sheets of ice to a shore fringed by a chaotic mass of seracs and pack-ice. Tatigat found a way southward, but Tabatiak went off westward and we soon lost sight of his sled. It was more than an hour before we joined up with him and Pierre again, having been held up by numerous obstacles; Tabatiak had chosen the best route, but had made sure he did not reveal it to Tatigat.

We were about ten miles off the coast of Baffin Island, late in the evening. But apparently the Eskimos were not thinking of building an igloo for the night, a though there was some good thick hummock ice under the shadow of huge icebergs. Tabatiak and Tatigat were talking together; they looked at me and hesitated, then Giuseppi said: "Are you tired?"

We had been travelling for eleven hours, and I was beginning to feel numb all over. But the last thing I wanted was to go against the wishes of the Eskimos.

"No," I replied. "Why do you ask?"

"Tabatiak says that if we carry on we can reach the igloos on the island in four or five hours."

From where we were, it was just possible to make out the island, a low hump that indeed looked a long way off. Twilight was lingering over the frozen sea, and the red ball of the sun was touching the horizon without seeming to slip below it. The sun in fact would not set until ten o'clock, and during the short night it would give enough light to travel by.

We ran about on the ice to warm ourselves, while the huskies were given a short rest. The decision had been made to make for the island, and Tabatiak seemed very happy—in a few hours' time he would be back home.

The two teams wove their way through the pack-ice, but we were obliged to work around to the south and then head north to the island, at one point being about fifteen miles to the south of it.

I must have dozed off, for I suddenly found myself jerked to my senses and lying in a hollow filled with snow. I had been tipped off the sled as it crossed some jagged ice. This was just as well, for I needed to stay awake. However, Tabatiak was eading the way, sure of himself. For a moment, I thought I could see the island shore, a dark line against the ice on the sea. And was I really seeing three lights glimmering in the night, like three glowing windows?

Suddenly the huskies put on speed, streaked forward barking joyfully—and other barks came in reply. It was half an hour after midnight, but there was still enough light to make out the usual disorder of an Eskimo camp: the sleds turned upside-down and dogs running to meet our teams. Our sleds were pulled right up on the beach. Shadowy figures were gesticulating and calling to one another; some children were running about playing; a woman with her hair all loose and a baby in the hood of her parka came hurrying towards her lord and master. Tabatiak had returned to his domain.

Pierre and I stood waiting in the freezing night, half-dead with fatigue. Finally, Tabatiak came over to us and pointed towards one of the igloos.

"You sleep in there, with me," Giuseppi explained. "He says you ought to go in at once."

A small, low door made of planks, frozen to a snow wall, led into a sort of roofless alcove that protected the entrance to the igloo. Then I crawled through an even lower doorway and reached the store-igloo with its characteristic smells of rotting, frozen meat. On all fours, I found my way over harness and seal carcasses to yet another low opening cut out of fine bluish ice as hard as marble, and caught a glimpse of the feeble light from the oil-lamp in the main igloo. I crawled on, and came to an ice wall about eighteen inches high; this was the sleeping-bench, and squatting on it was a

woman—probably young, but with a wrinkled face—who wel-
comed me with a broad smile. She was alone. It was an odd way to
meet anyone for the first time, on all fours and craning one's head. I
extricated myself from the tunnel with some difficulty—igloos have
never been built to the size of white men—and was able to stand
up. It was a large igloo, about sixteen feet in diameter, with a
blackened canvas spread across the ceiling. Half the space was
taken up by the platform of ice on which the family sat and slept,
on old blankets and caribou-skins spread over large flat stones.

Pierre came crawling through, smiled at the woman, and un-
coiled his long body. Then Giuseppi appeared, and began at once
to take off some clothes. It was certainly nice and warm inside the
igloo. The woman kept the oil-lamp clean and burning well; behind
her was a heap of over-ripe meat giving off a putrid smell, and a
large tin containing stale urine. Some snow in a saucepan was
slowly melting. The living arrangements were the same as we had
seen in other igloos. Everything the woman needed was within
reach—the oil-lamp and its supply of blubber, the pots and pans,
her needles and bodkins and a large knife with a curved blade.
There was a rack above the lamp for gloves and footwear to be put
to dry. To the left of the entrance was another sleeping-bench, for
the use of a second family or guests; and this was to be ours for a
few days.

I was awkward in shifting about on the bench—a stiff leg is not
very practical for crawling through tunnels and squatting down—
and put a hand for support on a heap of furs, which then began to
wriggle. The head of a little girl emerged. She sat up and looked at
me with astonishment; her pretty round face had a low fringe of
dark hair that made a level line above large, black, slightly slanting
eyes. I was so surprised that I burst out laughing. The mother
laughed too, and this woke up another child—the head and shoulders
of a little boy aged about two popped up from the hood of her parka.

The ice cavern with its canvas canopy that had once been white
but was now blackened with soot and smoke suddenly felt like a

home filled with human warmth and tenderness. A child had smiled, and the ugliness of the place was forgotten—the ice floor stained with blood and filth, the smells and the dirt, the glimmering light from the oil-lamp. Of course, what was filthy and smelly to me was normal to any Eskimo. And it must be said that Eskimos keep their hands and faces clean; moreover, the cold acts as a steriliser, destroying bacteria and microbes, fleas and other parasites.

Tatigat's round smiling face appeared at the entrance, his plump body completely filling the arched opening. He handed up our packs and bedding, which he had dragged into the store-igloo, and we were soon properly installed. We lit our primus and made tea for everyone. Giuseppi said that his father would sleep in another igloo but that he would remain with us to be of assistance. Tabatiak, having distributed the four of us in two igloos, had vanished into the third, his own, and we were to see no more of him for a couple of days.

It was very late by the time Pierre and I got into our sleeping-bags and settled down for the night, or what remained of it. We could not bring ourselves to sleep with our heads to the centre of the igloo, as the others did. The truth of the matter was, I suppose, that we were sickened by the thought of our faces being close to the flat-nosed Eskimos all night while they were coughing and spitting. The most sensible position was undoubtedly with one's head towards the oil-lamp, the warmest place in the igloo; but we slept with our feet towards it and our heads near the ice wall, using our packs as pillows, and we slept comfortably. The spread of blackened canvas under the dome helped to keep out the cold. I was never so warm during the expedition as in this big winter igloo, where the temperature at night was between two and five below. The raised sleeping-bench kept one away from draughts coming through the entrance-tunnel. There was an air-vent, and a window, which was made from translucent seal or walrus membrane.

We were roused from sleep by a loud bellow of laughter; framed in the entrance was a hairy face looking up at us with a joyful expression. It was a thin, bony face, and the man's long, tangled hair was hanging over his forehead. His laugh revealed big teeth, though the incisors were worn down. He was obviously the husband, and apparently found nothing surprising in returning home at four in the morning to see three men sleeping in the igloo with his wife. He began to talk to her, punctuating his remarks with laughs and exclamations that we were becoming used to hearing. His wife started to laugh too; and then the two said nothing but "*Heeeh!*" and "*Hoooh!*" to each other for quite a time.

Later in the morning, Giuseppi told me what the couple had been discussing. It was a serious matter, a real tragedy for these poor people. The only boat possessed by the small colony had been left among the pack-ice, near a floe-edge; but the ice had broken up and the boat had been carried away by the freed waters. The Eskimos had searched for it all day and a good part of the night, without success. If they did not find it, they would be unable to go seal-hunting, for the ice was breaking up and there were channels and stretches of water everywhere. The colony was faced with disaster. Such was the tale that Kopak, our host, had been telling with frequent bursts of laughter. And Pierre and I had thought it was something amusing concerning ourselves.

When we crawled out of the igloo it was to find that a blizzard was sweeping across the Gulf of Boothia. Well, we had come here to live among this small colony of Eskimos, and now we had nothing to do but that. Our host, Michel Kopak, was a great seal-hunter. He did not understand a word of English and seemed a very primitive sort. Yet we at once felt on good terms with him. If only the same could have been said for Giuseppi! But he was again being difficult and unpleasant. We wanted to ask our host if he would allow us to take some photos inside the igloo, and so we needed Giuseppi's services as interpreter. But he spent most of his time sleeping, pretending to be ill, waking up at meal-times, however, and eating some of our food as well as gulping down large slices of raw fish or frozen seal.

"Giuseppi," I said, "ask Kopak if we can take some photos here in the igloo."

"Ask him yourself!"

"Translate what I say!"

"I don't understand."

"Where is Tabatiak?"

"I don't know."

"If the weather turns fine, shall we be able to film the seal-hunting?"

"I don't know."

That was all I could get out of this wretched offspring of our nice friend Tatigat: "I don't know, I don't understand." Fortunately, Tatigat himself came to see how we were getting on. He knew only a few words of English, but he had a lively intelligence and we made ourselves understood with the help of gestures. Tatigat approved of the idea, spoke about it to Kopak and his wife, and they agreed at once—in fact they seemed much amused by it.

But first, there was the difficult problem of light. Very little came in through the window, and frost nearly half an inch thick kept forming on it. Pierre lit our two kerosene lamps, and with the oil-lamp alight as well, he thought he could get results. The blackened canvas darkened the whole of the igloo, which did not help matters. Great precautions had to be taken against getting moisture on the lens; and there was not much space in which to operate. However, Kopak's wife was a great help; she took no notice of the camera, but went on with her daily tasks, sewing, biting folds into skins to make footwear, and seeing to her children. Kopak himself, tired out by two days of seal-hunting which had resulted in his returning with only one seal, was snoring away.

This photographing session took up much of our day. In the evening, everyone came into Kopak's igloo. Pierre and I were not the attraction; Kopak had a radio which he tuned in to the pro-gramme in Eskimo from the station at Frobisher Bay. The Eskimos liked listening to this friendly voice which spoke to them in their own language, issuing mysteriously from the luminous box. It gave the weather forecast, which interested them especially.

The whole population of the colony, gathered there in Kopak's igloo, consisted of three families totalling four men, six women and a dozen children. They were simple, friendly folk. The young wives were still pretty; the youngest of them could not have been more than sixteen, but I never knew which was Tabatiak's wife. He stayed only a minute or two, listening to the weather report, and said not a word to me. I had asked Tatigat to tell him that Pierre and I would like to be taken to the floe-edge, weather permitting, to film the seal-hunting. Tabatiak made no reply to this. Tatigat shook his head, and Giuseppi said, "We will see."

Pierre began to think that everything he had been told about the Eskimos was false. "Smiles, smiles, and more smiles. But the fact is that Tabatiak does what he likes with us. Ah, it was a lot better with the Indians!"

True enough. They were much easier to get along with. Yet we could hardly compare the Eskimos' way of life with that of the Indians. Here we were in contact with primitive man, in the fullest sense of the term; with prehistoric man, one might even say. We had no right to judge these people, but only to accept them as they were and take things as they came.

I told Pierre that we had to be patient.

"Yes, but we must have some shots of seal-hunting."

"We shall. For all we know, Tabatiak may be arranging it for us. We're in too much of a hurry. Eskimos sometimes put off leaving for ten days, even though their sleds are already loaded."

Tatigat came several times to spend an hour or two in Kopak's igloo. Water was always ready for boiling on the primus, and we all drank tea and smoked. Kopak and Tatigat held long conversations, and Pierre and I could tell from their gestures what was the subject under discussion: hunting, the missing boat, the bad weather. Nearly every sentence ended with a whining "*Heeeh!*" to which the other replied with a drawn-out "*Hoooh!*" By the end of our stay in the Arctic, Pierre and I could not exchange a few words without also giving a *"Heeeh!"* and a *"Hoooh!"*—to the great amusement of our Canadian friends, who told us, "You've become real Eskimos now!"

The blizzard began to blow again, so we all stayed in the igloo and played cards. Giuseppi was very quick at picking up the game. The two children amused themselves by climbing all over us. They were allowed to do just as they liked, slept when they pleased and ate when they wanted, whether it was midnight, two in the morning or three in the afternoon. The little boy's favourite toy was the carcass of a baby seal, frozen as hard as iron but still with its fine white fur intact. He would put a miniature set of harness—that his father had made for him—on the seal and play at driving it, as he had seen his father driving the huskies. Rosa, the little girl, was rather shy of me at first, but a few sweets won her over. She took me round the camp and to see her playmates; she did not seem to be afraid of the huskies that were roaming about freely. All the children were quite willing to let Pierre photograph them and did what we asked of them, running about, jumping and sliding, and generally giving a touch of life to this land of snow which stretched towards the ice-fields and their infinite horizons.

All the men went off to look for the boat again, and had still not found it when they came back late at night. I had again asked our Eskimos to take us to the floe-edge, but they refused, saying that their huskies were tired. But the teams had been well fed and had had twenty-four hours' rest. It was just an excuse, yet we would be patient.

The following morning was very cold, thirty-five below, and a blizzard was blowing, but the sky was beautiful. Pierre and I walked a little way across the island. It did not appear to rise much above sea-level, and was so ravaged by the winds that the slightest ridge was swept bare. The scene from a low hill was one of utter desolation. It was just possible to distinguish the white domes of the igloos and harness and traces hanging from poles. A few dark figures could be seen going about the daily tasks; children were playing, apparently indifferent to the cold. As we returned to the camp, women were raking the fresh snow from the roofs of the igloos, in case there was a thaw.

Tabatiak had still not put in an appearance. There was something disdainful in his attitude towards Pierre and me. He never came to see us, and as he had not invited us to visit his igloo we contented ourselves with Kopak's homely hospitality. Perhaps it was Tabatiak's way of underlining the differences between our race and his. He had brought us here only because he had been unable to refuse the request of the white men at Igloolik. He had been an excellent guide, and had always been correct in his behaviour. But we could never make a friend of Tabatiak.

Kopak, though, had become one. He readily complied with our requests, and his wife would go through the same action a dozen times to enable Pierre to find the best camera angle.

Towards midday there was a sudden burst of activity in the camp. Tatigat came to Kopak's igloo, or rather his head appeared in the entrance, and he gave an order to his son.

Giuseppi roused himself from his lethargy. "We go to the floe-edge," he said to me.

The hunters of the colony were getting their sleds ready and hitching their teams. There would be three in addition to our two; the barking of sixty excited huskies was at last breaking the deep silence of the icy wastes.

The wind had dropped. This was probably what the Eskimos had been waiting for. When each driver was ready, off he went. Kopak's wife, still carrying the youngest child in her hood, hitched his team to the sled for him; and the other wives helped their husbands too, bringing out a crate, a harpoon or a rifle. Tabatiak, again elegantly dressed in his green anorak and wearing a knitted woollen cap, was calmly and carefully glazing the runners of his sled. He signalled to Pierre to go with him, while I again joined Tatigat.

Our teams dashed down the beach and followed the tracks that wound through the pack-ice, keeping a brisk pace despite the many difficulties. We continued southward for about ten miles, then came up against a long wall of jagged ice some fifty feet high and which extended far to the west like a crenellated fortification.

Kopak was still with us, but the others had gone on. We halted in a sheltered spot between two enormous seracs. Tatigat climbed to the top of one, and I followed h'm. We had a wide view of a chaotic mass of pack-ice that was broken by sea-water. This was the floe-edge, and it was here that Kopak had lost his boat two days before. I could understand why the boat was so necessary; without it, long detours would have to be made in order to get across the stretches of open water. Kopak left us to continue his search for the boat.

Tabatiak and Tatigat, rifle in one hand, probing-stick in the other, carefully made their way towards an expanse of water with a covering of ice so thin that it broke with a sound of tinkling glass at the slightest blow. The difference in temperature between the water and the air was causing little clouds of steam to form above the surface here and there; they were signs that seals might be found.

Patience is the chief virtue of the Eskimo. I could not say how long Tatigat remained motionless, looking out over this calm expanse of water. I watched him from the shelter provided by two blocks of ice, away from the wind. It was twenty-five below, wonderfully mild. Pierre had set up the camera on its tripod and was becoming anxious that the long wait might cause the mechanism to freeze up; but if he was not ready he would miss the sudden surfacing of a seal.

Tatigat, who was kneeling on the ice, suddenly took aim and fired. I caught a glimpse of a black blob on the water, more than one hundred yards away. Tatigat had hit it. There was a stir on the water and then it sank.

"No fat," Giuseppi explained to me, meaning that the seal had sunk because there was not enough fat on the carcass to keep it afloat.

The two hunters fired at a dozen seals altogether, without success. I did not see how they could have reached a floating seal, since they still had no boat.

"It's a dead loss," said Pierre.

"Keep your spirits up. There'll be other seals."

I was quite happy. The hunt had taken place in glorious surroundings; there were massive grey icebergs wedged in the pack, forming an archipelago of islets among the broken, drifting ice. The sight of so much open water was comforting in itself. This was the first time in two months that I had seen water other than in a saucepan. Spring was on the way.

We had a fast run back to the island. The cold increased at twilight, and I was looking forward to the gentle warmth inside the big igloo which had become a home as well as a shelter to me. I imagined Rosa and her little brother playing with the frozen baby seal, and their mother chewing away at skins. Throughout the evening there would be talk of the hunters' exploits.

Our teams whisked us over the hillocks of ice at the foot of the beach and dashed up to the camp. It was dark enough for the windows of the igloos to stand out as dull reddish squares. The children came running to meet us, shouting joyfully and jumping on the sleds before we came to a stop. The wives crawled out of the igloos, eager to know whether the hunt had been a good one. But alas, there was not a single seal to show. Kopak and another hunter had not yet returned.

It was very late when the two arrived back, and Kopak woke us all up with his loud laughter. Giuseppi translated what he said to his wife. "They've found the boat."

Kopak was laughing as loudly as when he had announced that the boat was missing. He had probably gone a long way to find it, and by some miracle it was still intact. His wife was overjoyed, and Pierre and I joined in the chorus of "*Heeeh!*" and "*Hoooh!*"

We drank tea all night to celebrate this successful quest, which meant that the hunters could go after seal and that the colony was saved.

The day of our departure was near. Before leaving Igloolik I had informed the sergeant in charge of the Mounted Police post that Pierre and I would be away for a fortnight at most. If we were not back in time he would feel obliged to start search operations. Tabatiak knew of this, and he came to tell us: "We start back tomorrow."

Pierre was dissatisfied, doubtful of having succeeded in getting any of the briefly sighted seals "in the box." He made this understood to Tatigat, who replied, "We see."

Pierre and I started to prepare for the journey. When we checked the food supplies we found there was still a large amount of flour, sugar and tea. We kept enough for the return journey and gave the rest to Tabatiak to share among the colony. To our great surprise, he brought us a large frozen salmon in exchange and as a present from himself. What an enigmatic, silent person he was!

There was much coming and going between igloos and sleds on the morning of our departure: sled runners were being glazed, huskies being fed and harness repaired. I learned that all the men were going seal-hunting and would be accompanying us part of the way that day. Kopak had lashed his boat on to his sled, and I saw that he had indeed been fortunate for it not to have been crushed in the ice; it had very light plywood sides covered with skin. The real skin-boats of the Eskimos, the kayaks and umiaks, have largely disappeared from the Canadian Arctic. Umiaks, the larger boats which served to carry whole families when the time came to change camp, have in some cases been replaced by motor-launches. An ancient boat-building craft is thus vanishing.

I kissed the two Kopak children goodbye. It was their presence, their laughter and carefree ways that had made me understand how men could live in such wretched conditions in these icy wastes and create their own joys and pleasures. These two little children knew no other world but that of the igloo, the wind and the cold and the huskies. But they already took part in the festivities of the colony, and were present when hunting parties left or returned. The two ran behind our sleds as far as their little legs could take them, then slowly returned across the ice to their camp.

The five sleds followed the island shore westward this time. The pack-ice was much worse in this direction, but somewhere behind the interminable barrier of tall ice there was bound to be open water. We halted several times, and the Eskimos clambered to the top of an iceberg for a view of the ice-fields beyond. On one occasion they sighted a flight of wild ducks, the first birds we had seen; they were eiders, large arctic ducks with magnificent plumage. The Eskimos use the down in their pillows, but regard eiders more for their food value at this time of year when seals are scarce.

We halted again. Kopak quickly climbed the barrier of ice, then motioned to the others. I climbed up with them, and saw that away to the south the ice was broken; stretches of water were shining in the sun and giving off a thin vapour, looking like hot-springs. The Eskimos decided to try their luck, and we reached open water after making our way carefully across the ice on foot. Kopak managed to get over the barrier with his sled; he unloaded his boat and placed it near the water's edge. The sun seemed almost warm. We could not have had a better day. I caught sight here and there of the small black head of a seal coming up to breathe. The Eskimos went down on one knee to fire, the elbow resting on the other knee; this seems to be their favourite position. They are quite good shots. A seal's head at more than one hundred yards' range is not an easy target. But they do not look after their weapons, which are for the most part old Canadian army rifles, rusty and damaged. What a difference from the Indians, who took such great care of their rifles!

I had supplied the Eskimos with plenty of ammunition, and they fired away happily. A seal was hit; it floundered about for a moment, sank, then reappeared floating on the surface. One at last, and with enough fat to remain afloat. Kopak pushed his boat into the water.

But Pierre had run out of film. He made desperate signs to me, and I ran to him with the photographic equipment. But the spare film was in a different pack, on the sled. Pierre had to run two miles, there and back, fearing all the time that the Eskimos would have hauled the seal away or that it would have sunk. But no, Kopak and Tatigat had quite understood the trouble we were in, and they waited until Pierre was ready again. He was able to film Kopak paddling his frail boat out to the seal, harpooning it and towing it back to the water's edge. We had the shots that we lacked. Tabatiak was smiling.

The Eskimos shot and killed or wounded at least a dozen seals, but only one floated to the surface. However, the Eskimos now had two seals, including the one that Kopak had killed a few days previously; they thus had three or four days' food for the colony, and were very content.

Tabatiak gave the signal for our little party to set off again, at about four in the afternoon, and we left the others to continue their hunting. We said no farewells, nor shook hands with them, as apparently this is not the custom among these proud people. The colony had carried out its obligations of hospitality towards Pierre and me, and we only hoped that they had not been shocked or astonished by our behaviour. I felt that, with time, we should have been fully accepted. But we had only a few days available.

Tabatiak led the way across the pack-ice, and had to make several attempts to reach the ice-fields out in the gulf. At last he found the tracks we had made on the outward journey, and then we had but to follow them. The huskies were pulling strongly, and after four hours' travel we reached land, climbed the steep ridge and ran down to Autridge Bay, where we halted. The snow was not deep enough, and we went on for a few miles before the Eskimos found a good place to build an igloo. As usual, the cold rapidly increased. At eight o'clock it had been only twenty-five below; but by midnight, when the igloo was ready for occupation, the temperature had fallen to thirty-five below. Four hours had been spent looking for a site and building the igloo. However, it was the best igloo of our travels and I had a very good night.

It took four hours next morning to reach the mouth of the bay, passing the basalt cliffs that looked all alike, and then another six hours to cross the strait to the southern shore.

When we left Baffin Island and were out in the strait we began to feel the wind more, and the temperature dropped more than ten degrees in less than an hour. Tabatiak and Tatigat seemed bent on making a long day's run, to reach Igloolik as soon as possible. But the huskies were tiring; they had been working almost continuously for the past ten days, and were probably feeling the effects. A few refused to pull, their traces hanging slackly, and took refuge in the centre of the team, where it was difficult for the driver to single them out with his whip. We made only one short halt for tea, in the middle of the day.

About seven o'clock we were nearing the coast of Melville Peninsula and I could pick out Tatigat's summer camp. From there, we should be able to reach Igloolik in two days. We had taken three days to cover the distance on the outward journey, but that was at the beginning. We had had a blizzard nearly all the way, and then my accident had delayed us.

Tabatiak halted his team among the pack-ice when we were about half-an-hour's drive from the camp. What did this mean, I wondered? I suddenly felt a great longing for that smelly, damp, cavernous shelter where we had spent three days.

"We're going to stop at the camp, aren't we?" I said anxiously to Giuseppi.

"No. They want to go on farther."

"But why?"

"I don't know."

"That won't help us much," I said. "We can reach Igloolik from here in two stages. It's seven o'clock. The cold is increasing. We can't continue for much more than two hours."

These were logical arguments for a white man. But Eskimos are not logical; just the opposite, it seems. My two were probably thinking of continuing all through the night. I had noticed that although they never left their igloos before eight or nine in the morning, they appeared to think that night-time was ideal for talking and drinking tea—or for travelling.

We continued along the shore and were about to pass Tatigat's camp. I felt tired out. I couldn't face having to stick it out on the sled for another two hours, then wait two more while an igloo was built, when close at hand was a shelter all ready for us, with an oil-lamp. I had to show my authority. "Giuseppi," I said, "tell your father that I wish us to stop here for the night."

"Tabatiak wants to continue."

"I can see no sense whatever in going on to build an igloo two hours' journey from here, for that won't get us back a day earlier."

My reasoning must have seemed very poor—or else Giuseppi did not translate my words properly—for Tabatiak whipped furiously at his huskies and laughed uncontrollably, as though what I had said was the most ridiculous thing he had ever heard. Without a word, he urged his team towards the shore and up the beach to where the walrus tusks guarded the entrance to the igloo. Tatigat followed him. I crawled through to the tent, and hardly noticed the stench of rotten meat this time. Pierre and I carried all our packs in and arranged things in the tent, while the two guides did their usual tasks of seeing to the sleds and the huskies. Then they stretched out on the sleeping-bench and shared some frozen raw fish and seal-meat between them, following this by drinking tea and eating some soup with us. On the surface, there appeared to be no change in our relations, but I could feel the atmosphere of distrust that had existed at the beginning of the expedition. I was sure that Tabatiak had intended to get us back to Igloolik as quickly as possible and so be finished with a job that he looked upon as a bore. To do that, he was quite prepared to make the journey without stopping for the night.

That was how he had travelled from Agu Bay to Igloolik in three days—more precisely, in a seventy-two-hour sled journey.

Tatigat was not one to remain annoyed for long, however, and he was soon playing Battleships with Pierre. Giuseppi had gone to sleep. Tabatiak did some sewing, mending his spare clothes.

We should have a good night here, I was thinking, and by leaving early in the morning we ought to be at Igloolik the following afternoon. Pierre and I would be back in the well-heated Transit Cabin with its clean bunks and bathroom, and among friends. Igloolik, which had seemed the end of the earth when we first arrived, was now transformed into the centre of the universe, of life itself.

I had noticed during our journey that the temperature began to drop after seven in the evening and continued dropping until two or three in the morning, then started to rise again, sometimes by as much as fifteen degrees. So logically one ought to travel in the mornings and take shelter in the evenings. But the Eskimos do nothing of the kind, and for various reasons. In the first place, they do not feel the cold as we do—twenty below is warm to them. And the snow would not be as "fast" in the morning; the huskies would not pull so well. Tabatiak had wanted to continue probably in order to benefit from the better sledding conditions during the very cold hours of the night. His huskies were tiring; his team was not as swift as Tatigat's. I fell asleep while these thoughts were passing through my mind, and did not wake up until seven in the morning.

I went outside and found that the wind had dropped and that the temperature was only twenty below: a fine morning, ideal for Pierre and me. There was only one snag. Pierre told me that the batteries had given out and he could no longer use the cine-camera. However, we had taken the essentials and could complete the details later.

To our astonishment, there was no sign of movement inside the tent. The three Eskimos were sound asleep, or pretending to be; they had merely raised themselves on their stomachs to light the primus and make some tea, then huddled down again in their blankets.

"You wouldn't think they had ever been in such a hurry as they were last night, would you, Pierre?"

"They've gone on strike."

"I wonder what I've done to offend them. If they were still in a hurry, we could have been on the way two hours ago. But don't say anything to them, not a word."

When ten o'clock came and there was still no movement, Pierre lost patience and spoke to Giuseppi. "What's going on? What do they intend to do?"

"Ask them yourself," was Giuseppi's reply.

"Take it easy, Pierre," I said softly, in French. "We're in no hurry. No more than they are. I don't like the idea of spending two more nights in an igloo, when we could have avoided one of them; but if that helps to put things right, let them be. I'm going for a walk."

To show the Eskimos how little I cared, I wandered off inland, among the moraines and rocks. An hour and a half of walking soothed my mind. As I drew near the camp again I came upon a rusty iron chest and a number of cooking utensils, harpoons and broken crates scattered about. There had probably been a camp here before the present one. I opened the iron chest and found some school exercise-books inside. They were Giuseppi's, and the writing in them was very well formed, the drawings and maps clearly made. Giuseppi was evidently an intelligent pupil, but a lazy lad, just as Father Fournier had said. Throughout our expedition he had been a lamentable interpreter and a burden to us. I have always suspected him of twisting my words and being at the bottom of the mis-understandings with his father and Tabatiak.

When I reached the camp I saw that the Eskimos were busy preparing to leave. Tatigat and Tabatiak were glazing the runners and loading the sleds, and even Giuseppi was carrying bundles from the tent.

I made no comment. Pierre told me that the three had talked together for a long time when they realised that I had gone off. They had seemed puzzled. Perhaps they were expecting me to give a definite order. In any case, by copying them—not showing anger and putting on a carefree face—I had got my way. We set off without my giving the order they expected. The matter was closed.

It was midday when we began the journey eastward across the pack-ice along the shore of Melville Peninsula, where the strait is narrowest. On the outward journey a terrible blizzard had been blowing, but now we had only an intense cold to contend with, though the wind was threatening to get up. We passed the beacon perched on its rock out in the strait, and as I looked at the chaos of pack-ice I realised more fully what a desperate struggle it must have been on our way westward in those awful weather conditions.

We reached Amherst Island and began the long pull up the frozen slopes. The coast of Baffin Island could still be made out, while to the south and closer to us were the high rocky cliffs of Melville Peninsula, seeming to bar our way. I was thinking that it was time for the usual halt for tea, which would give me a chance to stretch my legs. The effort of jumping off the moving sled and trotting along for a bit was beyond me; a great weariness had set in. Yet I had not been making any physical effort, but remained huddled on the sled.

Our drivers were eager to get back to Igloolik, and kept going. We had crossed Amherst Island and were among the pack-ice again. I recognised, far ahead, the narrow pass that would take us over the mountains of Melville Peninsula. Then we should be more sheltered from the wind. On the outward journey we had built an igloo some-where among the pack-ice we were now crossing; I tried to discover the place again, but without success. The huskies were trotting on with their muzzles close to the snow, encouraged now and again by cries of *"Oe! Oe!"* The drivers sat at the fronts of their sleds and stared ahead towards the east, towards Igloolik. Giuseppi was lying on the bear-skin, sleeping peacefully. He was probably dreaming of the Eskimo girls at Igloolik and the wonderful things he would be able to buy at the trading-store.

I thought that Tabatiak would call a halt before starting the long steep climb to the pass. We had been travelling for two hours longer than usual without a break. But our two drivers did not even hesitate, urging their teams on with cries and cracks of the whip. Throughout the afternoon the temperature had never been more than twenty-five below, and the wind got up at about seven o'clock. Behind us, pink clouds were slowly rolling across the distant hills of Baffin Island.

Pierre had jumped off his sled and was trotting at the side of mine, and he reached the top of the pass without slackening pace. There we were among bare rocks shaped by the wild winds. Below us stretched the long, sunken inlet leading to the archipelago to the west of Igloolik. Still we did not halt. The two Eskimos seemed possessed by some demon, whipping the huskies to greater efforts, and only stopping when the entangled traces made it absolutely necessary.

We came to ice-fields again, gliding across a lake with a surface like a mirror. It was ten o'clock when our drivers suddenly turned towards the land, urged their teams up a snow-covered bank and came to a stop in a dip where a couple of collapsed igloos were half-buried in deep snow. We had been travelling for ten hours and had covered nearly sixty miles.

One of the igloos could have been made habitable in very little time, but I had noticed that Eskimos have an aversion to entering an igloo which has been previously lived in; so I just had to be patient for a couple of hours. I lay back on the sled to try to sleep.

Pierre came over to me. "You ought to walk about. It's thirty-five below."

"I can't. I haven't the strength."

He went down to the lake, and I saw him taking photographs.

There was still plenty of light. Tabatiak and Tatigat were laughing and chatting as they cut snow blocks and built our igloo, stopping to light a cigarette now and again. They were in no hurry to get out of the cold. Pierre was right—they didn't feel it as we did. They had taken off their parkas, and Tatigat was even in his shirt. They paused in their work to look up at the mountainous slopes to the north, where a small dark figure was climbing ever higher. It was Pierre, and when he returned two hours later he said that from the summit he had had an almost frightening view of wide empty expanses of snow and ice. He came down the slope neatly, steadying himself with his heels, to the great admiration of the Eskimos. I envied him.

It was midnight before we were able to light the primus inside the igloo. What comfort and ease! I was eating practically nothing; since the first day out I had taken nothing but a mug of tea and another of white coffee, with a little porridge, in the mornings, and some soup in the evenings. I did not feel hungry. It seemed to me that I was getting enough nourishment, but that was my great mistake.

In the morning, Tabatiak and Tatigat were up and about hours earlier than the previous morning, and we were on our way by eight o'clock. The temperature was still thirty-five to forty below. On the outward journey, the weather had been most favourable during this stage, but now the full fury of the Arctic descended on us. The wind howled across the heights and the lakes, and met us head on.

At one o'clock we came upon the first igloo built on the outward journey, so I knew there was still a full stage to cover before reaching Igloolik; but however late we arrived, there would be warmth and food and comfort at the end.

We made a long halt at the igloo, which was still as we had left it, apart from being half-filled with snow. The Eskimos were no longer in a hurry. Tabatiak dug up a large piece of walrus-meat from a cache; they cut slices from it and ate them. Giuseppi became active again. He started to climb the rocky slope, probably trying to emulate Pierre's feat, but was as clumsy and awkward as a bear. He managed to clamber up one hundred and fifty feet or so, then came down looking very pleased with himself. The other two were having a shooting-match. I was half-dead from the cold and wanted to get on. But Pierre was right—they were in their element, and what was to us the end of a journey was to them just an incident in their daily lives. Whether they were here or in an igloo, sledding across the ice-fields or back in the comfort of Igloolik, it mattered little to them.

Tatigat won the shooting-match, and Tabatiak accepted defeat with a laugh. We set off once more.

After some hours we reached the open sea, still frozen into one immense ice-field. Giuseppi had found his English again, and said to me, "When we reach that headland we shall see an island a long way off, and it will be Igloolik."

Another four hours passed before we reached the headland. Then I saw other sleds making for the same place as we were, coming from different points of the horizon and still a long way off. Never had an approach to land seemed so long! The coast of Melville Peninsula had become a distant blur, the sun was lingering on the horizon and its light reflected now and again on some solitary iceberg. We left the bay behind and slowly climbed the slope to the plateau; then the settlement appeared below, a few lights glimmering in the dusk.

A fortnight ago it had seemed a wretched, lonely place; now it looked a warm and populous haven, with its square dwellings rooted in the snow and ice. Our long journey to the ends of the earth finished here.

The huskies dashed down the final slope with joyful barks, and the whole adventure ended suddenly. Pierre and I stumbled awkwardly from our sleds, cramped and numbed by the sixteen-hour journey. Tatigat and his son put our packs on the steps leading up to the Transit Cabin, without saying a word. I wanted to thank them, to tell them how grateful I was, but all I could say was, "Okay, Tatigat."

He had already whipped up his team and was on the way to his own cabin.

Pierre and I were left alone in the cold night. At such a late hour, everyone was indoors. We found the Transit Cabin locked, so went to Jim Hennings' house. It was open, but he was not there. As we came out, feeling at a loss, we met Bartels. He took me for an Eskimo at first, in my parka of caribou-skin. Then he recognised us, and showed us the warmth of his friendship. He found the keys and went back with us to the Transit Cabin, made sure that the heating was on, then took us to his place and gave us a marvellous meal. I was utterly weary and could hardly say a word. Pierre, however, did full justice to the meal.

It was after midnight when we returned to our cabin, and I had a bath. When I saw how thin and gaunt I was, I realised just how much the journey had taken out of me. In fact I had lost more than thirty pounds in the fortnight. After my bath I had just strength enough to get into my bunk, where I slept the clock around. Pierre was too much on edge. He told me afterwards that he had unpacked his cameras, fiddled around, and not gone to bed until three o'clock, and even then had been unable to get to sleep.

Jim Hennings had been called to Frobisher for a few days, and Father Fournier was still absent. Fortunately there were the two charming school-teachers and Bartels, who did everything he could for us. They were much impressed by our expedition, for journeys to Agu Bay were usually made in summer. Moreover, the blizzard had hit Igloolik too, so they could well imagine the conditions that we had had to endure. Even the Eskimos appeared to have more respect for us; we no longer met with just the polite, smiling mask of their kind.

We examined the results of our journey. We were well documented on the life of the Eskimos, but our bag of game was very meagre—one seal. We ought to have some walruses and bears. Unfortunately, arctic animals are migrants; the walruses had not yet arrived, but we might still find some bears on Southampton Island, between Foxe Basin and Hudson Bay. We learned that there was a missionary who came from Saint Jean-de-Maurienne, in Savoy, at the Coral Harbour settlement; and at seven one evening we were able to talk to him over the radio. It was extraordinary to be having a conversation with a man more than a thousand miles away.

"Oh yes, there are plenty of bears on Southampton," he said. "The Canadians and the Americans organise real safaris on the island in the fall. But it's too late now. Southampton is much farther south and the thaw sets in earlier. The bears have left, for they travel over the ice to cover great distances. A hunting expedition would cost you a fortune and you'd be taking chances."

We were thinking of giving up all idea of hunting bears, when I received a wire from Montreal. Our friend Jacobsen advised us to go to Resolute. He had obtained permission for us to land at this Canadian base, which had previously been manned by Americans. He informed us that at Resolute we could charter a plane to take us to Eureka, where—so he had been notified—there were many musk-oxen. This was excellent news, and I wired back at once, agreeing to his suggestion. The next plane to Resolute would call at Hall Beach in a week's time, and we would take it. Resolute is on latitude 75, Eureka on latitude 80. The spirit of adventure made me forget my tiredness.

We went to see Pacôme, the manager of the Eskimos' Co-operative. We found him in the back room of the Mission, putting a price on the sculptures that had been brought to him by local craftsmen. The pieces were carved out of soapstone, which is fairly easy to work with. There were walruses, bears, caribou, and scenes of Eskimo life, made particularly for the southern white collectors.

Our visit, however, had a very different purpose. We wanted to go to the floe-edge not far from Igloolik where a great many walruses could sometimes be seen. Pacôme had been the best hunter among the Igloolik Eskimos, although he now preferred to manage the affairs of the settlement—which he did very well.

He tried to put us off. "The walruses only come when there's a south wind and fog, and it's too early for that. But I'll make enquiries, if you like."

We saw Giuseppi again. He was very lively and cheerful, and called "Hello." We asked him if his father would be our guide again for three days, but he gave an evasive reply. Tatigat had stayed in his cabin, telling visitors all about his journey.

Tabatiak was not to be seen either, and then one day he got his huskies, hitched them to his sled and at nightfall set off westward. He was eager to return to his wife and children on Prince Frederik Island. We never saw him again.

It was clear that Tatigat had no desire to set out again, so we had to find another guide. Bartels came to our rescue. He sent us Inouk, a young Eskimo who came to Igloolik occasionally but lived on Baffin Island. Apparently he was a skilled hunter and an intelligent young man; he understood English, though he spoke it badly. Inouk was very poor, and turned up with a team of only five huskies. He smiled apologetically and our hearts warmed to him at once. The previous summer he had taken a Danish scientist to Agu Bay. He knew that we had been to Tabatiak's igloos; and as he immediately agreed to go hunting at the floe-edge with us, our reputation could not have been so bad.

Bartels had described him to us in his German accent: "Inouk, very great hunter! But he lives on Baffin Island, he hunts all winter, all summer. He makes big stocks of meat. So when the Igloolik Eskimos go off to hunt caribou, they stop at his place and eat all his meat. They stop there again on the way back and gobble up his stocks. So poor Inouk has to start all over again, and that's how it goes on. Lazy, good-for-nothings, the Eskimos here. Only good for collecting their family allowances, instead of going hunting."

Bartels had unfortunately summed up the situation pretty accurately. In the region of Igloolik there were still a few small communities of hunters, but they were victims of the ancient customs of the Eskimos. Inouk could not refuse to give hospitality to callers, and so was eaten out of house and home while he looked on with a smile.

We put as little load as possible on Inouk's sled, but with only five huskies the pace was slow. We had to travel about fifteen miles to the east to reach the floe-edge, which extended roughly in a line northwards from Melville Peninsula to Jens Munk Island. The Eskimos went to it to hunt and to fish, and their sleds had made quite a track in the snow. The humidity due to the open waters made this very cold day even more unpleasant. On the way, Inouk picked up a light boat similar to Kopak's; he had obviously been told where to find it. We tied it on the sled and continued in a northerly direction. The patches of mist increased and the pack-ice became more broken; a hundred yards ahead of us was a vast stretch of open water, and the ice-field we were on seemed to be gradually sinking into it. There were many icebergs floating like white sails in the distance.

The ice had suddenly broken up when the north wind began to blow a few days previously. The walruses had all gone. They were probably far away to the east, drifting on this expanse of water. Thousands of wild ducks were floating on the calm surface; many of them suddenly flew up and circled wide, then came fluttering down again.

Inouk was carefully testing the ice. I ventured too near the water's edge, and the ice suddenly began swaying and dipping. I tottered about like a drunken man, alarmed by this unexpected motion, but managed to steady myself and returned slowly and carefully to my companions. Inouk made a warning gesture: "Ice. Danger!"

We travelled southward, following the floe-edge, and in the evening we caught sight of a seal. Inouk fired at it, but missed. Then we met a sled drawn by twenty-two splendid huskies and driven by an Eskimo from Igloolik, who was nonchalantly smoking a pipe. Inouk had a long conversation with him, then the man whipped up his huskies and turned back to Igloolik. Inouk managed to explain to us that the man was searching for two Eskimos who had been carried away on a drifting ice-floe somewhere in this area. At the time, the open water had been no more than fifty yards wide. The alarm had been given at Igloolik, and Inouk had said that we would keep a lookout for the missing men.

Inouk began to build an igloo for the night, not far from the coast of Melville Peninsula. It was hard work, as the snow was not very deep and he could not cut very thick blocks. The humidity made the bitter cold more intense. A coating of salt formed on our boots. I had become more susceptible to the cold, and Pierre and I could not stand it nearly so well as we had at the start of our expedition. We must have used up all our reserves. I knew that I had not been eating enough, which was a great mistake.

We spent a very pleasant evening talking with Inouk. He showed us his family photos and others taken on his trip with a Danish scientist. He kept a notebook in which people who had employed him wrote a few remarks, and they all praised him as guide and companion. This praise was well deserved; we got on better with Inouk than with any other Eskimo. He was cheerful, helpful, and intelligent, still a genuine Eskimo yet not scornful of the white man; in fact he appeared to take pleasure in our company.

It was thirty below in the morning, and there was a cruel north wind lashing at us. We headed southwards, still following the floe-edge, and came upon an igloo, one that had very likely been built by the missing men. We scanned the waters but could see no sign of them.

There appeared to be no point in going any farther, for we saw no signs of walruses. We shot a few ducks, and Inouk went out in his boat to pick them up; then we decided to return to Igloolik. I was very weary. The trip had lasted nine hours, for our small team was far from speedy.

We met some more Eskimos searching for their comrades. Rescue operations had been set in motion, and there were planes flying over the pack-ice.

Just before we reached Igloolik we were overtaken by the Co-operative's yellow snowmobile Bombardier, which had probably been to Hall Beach. It was bringing Father Vandervelde, who had been at Pelly Bay for twenty-five years. Before the DEW Line was built, Pelly Bay had been one of the most isolated Eskimo communities, for the sea there remains partially frozen all the year round. Nowadays, of course, living conditions are completely different.

Father Vandervelde was going to look after the Mission in Father Fournier's absence. He was a Belgian and very insistent upon his Flemish origin. His wide knowledge of the Eskimo world was to be of great benefit to me. However, for the moment he was concerned over the fate of the two missing fishermen. I told him of the abandoned igloo and our own search; but the two men were now being looked for on floes drifting to the east. The Eskimo community had chartered two aircraft which were systematically searching the area.

A little later, Pierre and I were sitting in the room at the Mission, and Father Vandervelde was showing us some of the finest Eskimo carvings I have ever seen, when the door burst open and a breathless Pacôme came in. The missing men had been found. They had drifted northward, but had managed to get back on firm ice at a point about seventy miles from Igloolik. They had met some hunters who had given them food, for one man was weak from hunger and in a bad way. They had been loaned a team of huskies and were on their way back. Pacôme finished his story amidst general rejoicing.

Father Vandervelde wanted us to drink to this happy ending, and he opened a bottle of the only supply he had—communion wine. "Not a word to Father Fournier!" he said as he filled our glasses.

We had booked two seats for Resolute on the plane that called at Hall Beach every Monday evening, and we spent the few days remaining to us at Igloolik in a round of visits. Jim Hennings had returned. How hospitable he was! He kept open house and entertained with great friendliness and simplicity, as though it was all the most natural thing in the world. We also saw a great deal of the two young school-teachers. They were looking forward to their fortnight's holiday, which they hoped to spend in Bermuda or Florida, "to get a bit sunburnt". But they would certainly be returning, for they liked their frontier life at Igloolik.

The work of these teachers did not finish when lessons were over for the day. Young mothers were always calling to see them. Eskimo girls marry at sixteen, the minimum age under Canadian law, and from then onward there is usually a baby in the hood of their parkas. A mother would walk into Miss Harper's room without knocking, sit down and wait—without saying a word. Miss Harper would give her a cup of coffee, the baby would be taken out of the hood and left to trot happily round the room, the mother making no attempt to control it. Miss Harper would enquire after the family, to be answered by a smile. After an exchange of "*Heeehs*" and "*Hooohs*", the mother would put the baby back in her hood and slip away, the visit over. A quarter of an hour or so later, another young woman would come in, dressed in her best parka and looking like an ivory penguin; she would sit down, have a cup of coffee, and the ritual would be repeated.

"But what do they come for, Miss Harper?" I said. "They don't ask for anything, do they?"

"They don't want anything. They just like to come and spend a little time in the home of a white person, to look at her household goods and furniture, and sometimes see strangers—like yourselves."

"But it can't be easy for you to do your own work."

"No, it isn't," she said with a laugh. "Especially as they call in at any time, at five in the evening or at midnight."

"They're very fond of their children, aren't they?"

"Oh yes, they adore them. But their feelings towards children are not like ours, you know. They can love another woman's child just as much as their own. It's not unusual for children to be exchanged, a boy for a girl. Sometimes it's quite a puzzle to sort out my new little pupils, to know which family each belongs to. It's even difficult to know whether a child is a boy or a girl, for when they're huddled in their fur clothes all you see of them is the same little round smiling face. And often they know only their Eskimo name, which can be given to either sex. Neither is it unusual to hear one Eskimo woman say to another, who has no son, 'If my next is a boy, I'll give him to you.' "

Thus does the white community live at Igloolik: the administrator, the school-teachers, the sergeant of the Mounted Police, the welfare officer, the missionaries, and the man who keeps everything in working order—the water-pumping stations and the electric generator, the snowploughs and the Eskimos' skidoos—Mr Bartels.

Pierre and I were sorry to be leaving this compact and friendly little community, when the snowmobile took us to Hall Beach on the evening of 2nd May.

After the sled, the Bombardier seemed to be flying over the ice. We crossed Igloolik Bay, then headed due south down the track to Hall Beach, which we reached in three hours.

The airport and DEW Line base are a few miles from the Eskimo settlement, which is strung out along the shore. We were disappointed to learn that the plane due at midnight was not expected before six in the morning. We spent the time going to and from the airport and settlement. Then we were fortunate enough to be able to stay in the Transit Cabin, which was heated, for in the end we had to wait twenty-four hours. The Constellation aircraft which should have taken us had developed engine trouble and had returned to Frobisher.

We were given seats on a DC-4 which arrived from Montreal in the middle of the night with a load of weary passengers, among whom was Father Fournier. He was returning from his conference quite saddened with the way things had gone. He said bitterly, "I just wonder whether the savages are in the north or the south." All he wanted was to get back to Igloolik and his dear Eskimos.

Father Fournier had lost all touch with modern industrial life. He was happy to remain an "Eskimo".

The night had almost ended when we took off from Hall Beach, and after flying for an hour we were again in sunshine. Below us was the Gulf of Boothia, and we tried to discover the route we had taken. Then we were over the northwest region of Baffin Island, a lunar landscape of grey and white, with barren summits, icy ridges and inlets frozen in their winter shroud. We flew over Prince Regent Inlet and cast our swiftly moving shadow over Somerset Island, then crossed Barrow Strait, the key to the Northwest Passage.

The plane began to descend. I could see the cliffs of Cornwallis Island, a long wall of ice reflecting the sun. Then, as we banked, Resolute base came into view: red hangars, towers, fuel reservoirs, domed roofs, and a long runway cutting across the small plateau standing three hundred feet above sea-level. The plane banked again, this time over the Eskimo settlement which was strung out along the shore, and then landed. There we were, on latitude 75. Despite the intense cold and the early hour—a quarter to three in the morning—there was great activity at the base. All our fellow passengers were employed at Resolute.

It was a most extraordinary sensation to find such comfort—luxury almost—in the way of accommodation. Thanks to Mr Jacobsen's wire, we were treated as VIPs and given rooms as comfortable as at any hotel in a large city. The building could serve more than two hundred people.

While we were waiting for our luggage to arrive, we saw the end of a movie. At four o'clock in the morning there were still men sitting about, smoking and reading or playing cards. Pierre and I were quite overcome by all this ultra-modern living. We had just flown a thousand miles nearer the Pole and there we were in the most splendid of barracks. Strict rules and regulations were pinned up everywhere, but much freedom was allowed too. Once we had seen our rooms we were free to wander anywhere. The restaurant was open; hot drinks were available at any time of the day or night.

We had to adjust ourselves to Polar time. Here there was no night; the height of the sun, which circled over the high hills without ever setting, showed how much farther north we had come. After our adventure in the land of the hunting Eskimos, we were about to embark on a new one, for there are few, if any, Eskimos living north of Resolute.

Outside, there was the bitter arctic cold. Inside, our rooms were as clean and warm as in New York or Montreal.

6

Resolute. Of Bears and Men

I T W A S quite impossible to sleep with the sun shining all the time.
Our comfortable bedrooms and all the activity around us did not
make us forget that we had come here to film the rare musk-oxen;
several herds of them were to be found five hundred miles to the
north, so we had been told. But the first thing was to meet the chief
administrator of the base, Mr Kingan.

He received us in his room at the end of a long corridor of
offices in which secretaries, accountants, technicians, meteorologists
and air crew were all busily employed. It was difficult to realise that
we were almost at the North Pole.

Mr Kingan already knew of our intentions. We told him about
our expedition to Prince Frederik Island and he at once became very
interested. All his working life had been spent in the Arctic; he
knew the Mackenzie District and the Beaufort Sea well, and had
gone on many sledding and hunting expeditions.

I told him briefly what we still lacked for our film. We were well
supplied with scenes of Eskimo life but had very few shots of
hunting—only seals. Even these were very ordinary. So we had
taken our friend Jacobsen's advice and come to Resolute en route to
Eureka to find musk-oxen.

"But why don't you film a bear-hunt?" he said with a broad
smile.

"Polar bears? We'd like to very much, but unfortunately they
wouldn't wait for us. The Southampton Island bears are making

their way north across the ice-fields before they break up. It's too late."

"Too late? Why, only last week the Eskimos here killed a dozen bears. And the best hunter, Idlout, is going off again this evening. If you like, I'll arrange for you to go with him."

Mr Kingan was extremely efficient. It was said that he was not just Kingan of Resolute but indeed King. And the facts seemed to bear this out. In any case, he proved to be the benefactor of our expedition. He picked up his telephone, and a French Canadian came to his office. This was Mr Saint-Jean, a shy, discreet man, one of the most helpful and capable of those we met.

"Saint-Jean, is it true that Idlout is going bear-hunting tonight?"

"Yes, sir."

"Right. Get a snowmobile and take these gentlemen down to the village, and arrange for him to take them with him."

"Very good, sir."

That was all, but it was enough.

The Eskimo settlement was six or seven miles from the base, on the frozen edge of a bay facing south. It was as new as the base. The Eskimos had all been brought from farther south to help build the base, some from as far afield as Coral Harbour on Southampton Island; others had come from Arctic Bay or Frobisher. There was still work for them, and the high wages had decided them to settle by this desolate shore. They spent their free time in hunting seals and bears, and arctic whales in summer. Idlout had arrived here by sled from Coral Harbour, a journey of hundreds of miles across frozen land and pack-ice. As he was the best hunter, he had become the head of the new Eskimo community. The only white people living there were the school-teacher, his wife and their two children.

It took fifteen minutes down a well-made track to get to the settlement, then Saint-Jean drove slowly along the line of cabins, most of which were buried in snow and ice, looking for Idlout. On nearly every roof a splendid bear-skin was stretched and being tanned by the sun.

"Seem to be some bears about," said Pierre.

Idlout was about fifty, with a thin, gaunt face and the gift of the gab. He was delighted to see us.

"So you want to go bear-hunting? Mr Kingan sent you to me? That's fine, then, come along. I'm setting off at nine tonight. My son's getting my skidoo ready."

I pulled a face. "We'd rather have gone on a sled."

"I'm going on a skidoo, but David will take you on his sled."

"Who's David?"

"Here he is now."

A youngster with a smiling but expressionless face came into the cabin. His name was David Windgot, and he looked no more than sixteen.

"David killed seven bears last week," was all Idlout said about him. That was quite enough introduction.

We discussed arrangements and the pay. But all that was of secondary importance.

"I'll take everything we need for camping," said Idlout. "Come back at eight o'clock. You can get your provisions at the base."

But Idlout would not let us leave without a drink. He produced a bottle of rum, which he proceeded to drink like lemonade. Half an hour later, the bottle was empty. Idlout talked a lot, and his English became very slurred. David had gone out as quietly as he had come in. One of Idlout's sons was repairing the skidoo outside the cabin. The weather was fine, very cold and windy.

We went back to the base, and found that Mr Kingan had taken care of everything. The head cook—a distinguished-looking Venetian who, despite his tall chef's hat, had the manner of a Papal Nuncio—had prepared for us such an enormous parcel of food that we were quite taken aback.

"Eskimos eat a lot, especially those who work at the base," he explained with a smile.

We just had time to get ready, to pack the films and check the batteries. After our recent experiences, we knew the right precautions to take. We had a meal in the restaurant at the first sitting of the evening, five o'clock. The self-service system was very well organised and two hundred people could be catered for in a few minutes. There was a good menu and the helpings were copious. The same rule applied as in all the bases we went to: "Take as much as you like, but eat all you take."

At eight o'clock Saint-Jean took us down to the settlement in the snowmobile. Idlout was not in his cabin; his son was still working on the skidoo. But David was down on the shore, hitching his huskies to the sled.

We found Idlout in his neighbour's cabin, a prefab similar to his own and with the same modern equipment: radio, washing-machine, oil-fuelled stove. Idlout was sitting at the table with a half-empty bottle of whisky in front of him. His friend was trying to reason with him. "Come, Idlout, that's enough." But Idlout went and fetched another bottle. He was soon completely drunk, and there seemed little chance of our going bear-hunting. I was wondering what would happen next.

At about ten o'clock Idlout managed to say, "My skidoo isn't ready yet. You go off with David and I'll catch up to you. His huskies only do ten miles an hour; the skidoo does forty."

We joined David, who had a fine team, and sledded eastward for an hour or so, following the coast of Cornwallis Island, then turned south to cross the frozen Barrow Strait. A lean black husky, a stray bitch, was accompanying the team; she had been patiently waiting for us to set off, and was now running along and yapping at the team, first on one side and then on the other. She was so thin that we thought she would turn back after an hour, but the plucky little animal stayed with us until we found our first bear.

Young David handled his huskies skilfully and gently; I never heard him shout at them, and when he spoke to them softly they understood at once. They were pulling well and seemed in excellent form.

I was rather surprised to see skidoo tracks well out on the ice-field, and learned later that the Resolute Eskimos often go bear-hunting on these motorised sleds, heedless of the risk of a mechanical breakdown. During the winter, one Eskimo had ridden his skidoo from Resolute to Grise Fjord, a distance of several hundred miles across difficult and uninhabited country. He could never have thought about what would have happened if the engine had failed.

The pack-ice increased as we journeyed south. To our right, the cliffs of Griffith Island stood out, seeming quite near. But for the three days we were zigzagging about the ice-fields, chasing bears, those cliffs always looked the same distance from us.

After midnight a mist began to form, indicating that there were many stretches of open water concealed among the pack-ice. The sun was low on the horizon, veiled by the mist, a red ball with a great halo. The hours seemed very long. Now and again David halted the sled and walked about to warm himself. There was still no sign of Idlout.

About three in the morning I felt very weak. My hands and feet were warm, but the rest of me was slowly freezing. This could be dangerous, I ought to walk, but I simply had not the strength. Some hot tea would have done me good, but unfortunately all our provisions were with Idlout, and he was missing. We had nothing to eat or drink; all we could do was to light the primus and melt a little snow. Pierre was worried about me, and thought we ought to turn back. But that would have meant losing the chance of finding bears, and I decided to stick it out until Idlout joined us. The temperature was twenty-eight below, but we had known much worse, and I wondered whether it was the dampness and mist that had affected me. I made a place to lie down on the sled, and dozed for a time.

It must have been about four in the morning when David saw tracks made by a bear. He halted the sled, and he and Pierre followed the tracks on foot. But David decided they were too old. We set off again. The thin black bitch was still with us, and she suddenly started barking madly and dashed off ahead of the team.

"Nanook! Nanook!" cried David.

About fifty yards away, a polar bear was scrambling over the pack-ice pursued by the plucky little bitch. Our team at once increased speed, dragging us with them in a wild race. David, crouching at the front of the sled, whipped them to greater efforts. He pulled his knife from its sheath and stuck it into the sled, at his side. We had almost lost sight of the bear, which was a long way ahead; it went straight over obstacles that we had to find a way around, and seemed likely to escape us. David bent forward and cut the traces of two huskies. They darted off, barking furiously. The others were stirred by this, and pulled with unusual strength. The sled tipped sideways in taking an icy ridge and some of the load spilled out; Pierre just managed to save the pack containing the cameras, which he always kept within reach.

For nearly an hour we chased after the bear among the icy chaos, and were beginning to think that it had got away. This seemed to be confirmed when two huskies, one of them the black bitch, came running back.

"They've lost the bear, then?" Pierre said to me.

Far from it. What followed was a proof of the high intelligence of these huskies. The bitch communicated with the team with yelps and furious barks. The others seemed to understand and dashed off again even more madly than before, jumping everything in their path, even ridges of ice three feet high. The bitch and the other husky were well out in front, and as we followed them around a snowbank we suddenly saw the bear, its back to a block of ice, holding off the dogs. The two had returned to let us know.

It was a young animal and almost out of breath. A strange and silent fight began, the bear against the circle of huskies. Pierre and I crept forward, cameras at the ready. David stood by to fire if necessary.

The huskies had their tactics; one attacked the bear from behind, and the powerful animal swung round with surprising agility and leapt at the husky, trying to strike with its left paw. But another husky attacked in turn, and the bear gave a leap which brought it within a yard of Pierre, who was filming away as calmly as though in his studio. The bear was intent on the huskies, but it was dangerous to be in the animal's path; with a swipe from its paw it could kill a man. Realising that it could not escape from the huskies, the bear started to dig frantically into the snow to try to find a break in the ice, under which it could take refuge; but the huskies gave it no respite, worrying it continually.

Finally, David decided that the bear had become too dangerous, and fired. It rolled towards us, then reared up. A second shot stretched it dead in the snow. The huskies hurled themselves at it, and David had to drive them off with the whip.

It was then about seven o'clock, still very cold, but the sun was dissolving the mist and distant shores were gradually coming into view. The day before we had given up all hope of bears, and now there was one stretched at our feet. All this activity had been very beneficial to me. I had forgotten my weariness, I was thoroughly roused from what might have become a dangerous lethargy.

"Are you satisfied, Pierre?" I asked when the bear had been skinned, the carcass cut up and loaded on the sled.

"The light wasn't very good, and the bear was not in the right position. We can do with another."

I made no comment. Pierre is always very particular about his work, and I could hardly blame him for that.

We retraced our winding route across the ice-field, recovering a lost crate here, a skin there, and a pack elsewhere.

There was still no sign of Idlout at midday. David, looking a fine sight in his frost-covered parka of caribou-skin, boiled up some water, lightly cooked several chunks of bearmeat and handed them round. Pierre ate a good two pounds. It was a pinkish meat and apparently very good, but I only chewed one piece and then spat it out; not just from a disinclination to eat anything, but also from fear of trichinosis. But I ought to have known that Eskimos can tell if a bear has this disease, and the fact that David was eating the meat meant that there was no danger.

We had to come to a decision. We were without camping equipment and had no food other than bear-meat, so David agreed that if Idlout did not turn up by two o'clock we would return to Resolute. Meanwhile, we got into our sleeping-bags and caught up a little on our sleep.

We were roused by a loud popping noise, and saw Idlout bounding towards us on his skidoo as though riding a horse at a gallop. He muttered some vague excuse about the repairs to his skidoo, but we had no doubt that he had been sleeping off his hangover. However, Idlout was a tough character. In next to no time he had lit his primus and made some tea and coffee and heated up some soup. He showed no signs of tiredness, but seemed a little annoyed to find that we had already killed a bear. So he allowed us only an hour before setting off again.

Idlout led us towards Somerset Island, at the southern end of Barrow Strait. I was now being carried on the small sled drawn by his skidoo, and was introduced to the pleasures and perils of a new form of sport. Imagine sitting astride a small sled being towed at twenty-five miles an hour across the ice-fields by a skidoo driven by an impetuous Eskimo like Idlout, and you get some idea of the exhilarating ride I was having. Idlout drove with the throttle full open and never looked back. The tow-rope broke, but he did not notice for a time. Then he did, and came back for me. Once the skidoo refused to start up again; Idlout got out the tool-kit and cleaned the plugs, unscrewed the fuel-pipe, screwed it up again, replaced the plugs, and we were off again. He had a two-gallon can of gasoline behind the seat, and there were ten gallons beside me on the sled.

Pierre was on David's sled. They were soon a long way behind and I lost sight of them. Idlout and I were roaring across the ice, taking incredible risks. It was lucky that the skidoo broke down now and again, allowing David to catch up. When he did, the two Eskimos had a discussion.

There were many tracks made by bears, all leading northward. This was the period of the year when the males, having wintered with a mate in an agloo—a cave dug in the snow—set off in search of a new companion; a period when they are hungry and dangerous, but also when hunters have the best chance of finding them. I had not expected that there would still be so many polar bears, but I was forgetting that we were very far north and that there are few Eskimos in the region. Moreover, it is not easy to have hunting expeditions for wealthy sportsmen organised in these parts, as in Spitzbergen, where bears are hunted in boats.

It was a real hunt that we were on. The first task was to discover tracks that had been made quite recently. Bears are great travellers and cover enormous distances across the ice. The Eskimos were expert at telling whether a track was fresh or a day or two old. David seemed to be as good at it as Idlout. The two frequently consulted together, though Idlout was obviously in command; he was now bursting with energy.

We found a track that looked fresh. Idlout brushed his hand lightly over a footprint to see if it had frozen. He could tell from the hardness whether the bear had passed two days ago, six hours or an hour ago. We followed several tracks that were relatively fresh, but without success. A bear can cover a considerable distance in a couple of hours. While following one set of tracks we discovered a cache of meat; the bear had killed a seal and hidden the remains of the carcass under a block of ice. The reddened snow was proof that the bear had had a good meal before continuing on his way. The behaviour of bears is oddly similar to that of Eskimos in some respects, and it is not surprising that they should consider the bear as a kind of brother. He winters in an igloo (agloo, in the bear's case) as they do; he, too, goes looking for a floe-edge to hunt for seal. But his terrifying paw with long black claws is more precise than a harpoon, as quick as lightning.

At about eight o'clock it was decided to make camp. Our travels had brought us within sight of the cliffs of Somerset Island, which stood out clearly to the south. There was no question of building an igloo. Idlout was a modern Eskimo. He earned good money at the base and his hunting was very profitable. He was equipped with an isothermal tent that he had bought from an American army surplus store, and he covered the floor of this with a fine black buffalo skin that had come from the same source. His primus worked well, but some of the tent-pegs were missing. This handicap was easily overcome by his cutting up a wooden support bar of the sled.

It was like being back in the Indians' tent. In a few minutes the heat and steam had become unbearable, and we were all in a sweat. But after a time the icy cold began to creep in. By that time we were snug in our sleeping-bags.

I must admit that my thoughts were very much on bears. There were certainly a lot of them about, for there to be so many tracks. One could easily come roaming round the tent during the night, thrust a paw underneath, pluck me out, and carry me off to its cache of meat. (Or so I erroneously imagined.) Then I told myself that the two Eskimos did not appear to be worried and that the huskies would give the alarm before any bear got near. So I could sleep in peace.

In the morning we came across many more tracks of bears and were led far to the west, close to Lawther Island. None of the tracks yielded any result; the bear had too long a lead.

Yet Pierre had not lost hope. "We need two more," he said to me. "One for the film and another for the book."

"Is that all?"

His laugh made me forget how cold and weary I was.

Early in the afternoon, Idlout stopped and asked me to transfer to David's sled. He had some plan, probably to do with the fresh tracks he had just found.

"Keep going due north," he said. "I'm going to run around for a bit, but I'll catch up to you and David later."

The sun was almost warm and the wind had dropped completely. David turned his team to the north and began to doze at the front of his sled. At least, so I thought, but in fact David's senses were fully alert. He had the amazing eagle eyesight of these outdoor people. What was to me just a little black spot, many yards away, he immediately identified as a lemming.

"Nanook! Nanook!" he suddenly cried.

Coming towards us, though still some way off, was Idlout on his skidoo, driving a polar bear in front of him. The bear was bounding along, stopping now and again as though fascinated by the strange enemy that was chasing him, by the noisy machine that moved faster than huskies. Idlout reminded me of a cowboy driving a steer back to the corral. It really was an incredible sight.

But the bear suddenly saw the huskies and his attitude changed. They were the terrible, known enemy. The bear went off at an angle. David at once cut the traces and his huskies dashed away in pursuit. The bear was intrigued by the skidoo, but he feared the huskies; it was a matter of life or death for him now, and he fled. But he was already tired out and kept stopping, flanks heaving as he gasped for breath; and the huskies snarled around him, yet kept their distance. The bear appeared to take no notice of them, then suddenly whipped round as quick as lightning. The huskies broke away and the bear trotted on again.

Idlout told us he had come upon the bear after following its tracks for two hours, and had then driven it towards us for five or six miles. It was not surprising that the bear was out of breath.

The hunt was on. David had gone running after the huskies. Pierre seized his camera and went hurrying after David, calling to me to bring the pack with the photographic equipment. So there was I, like a housewife weighed down by a full shopping-bag, but trotting behind a polar bear.

After several vain attempts to get away, the exhausted bear turned to face the huskies, its back to a wall of ice. We knew its end was near.

David reached the scene first, then Pierre. I was a long way behind, blowing like a seal in my heavy garments of caribou-skin as I lugged the pack along. But Idlout was not following at all; his skidoo had broken down again. I saw him in the distance doing some quick repairs, and after a few unsuccessful attempts he got the engine to start. He passed me, his rifle slung over his shoulder, and joined the other two.

By the time I reached them, the bear had become very dangerous. It looked little bigger than a husky when crouching down, but then made sudden bounds forward, sweeping at the dogs with its paw and thus clearing a space before moving back to the ice wall and bracing for another attack.

Pierre was calmly filming the scene and I was doing what I could to help.

"Hand me the filter. Now the camera with the colour film. Just a moment, I must reload."

Pierre crouched in the snow, less than twenty feet from the bear, reloaded his camera, then casually said, "Give me your handkerchief —there's something on the lens."

I was keeping a watchful eye on the cornered beast, for Pierre was looking into the view-finder, concentrating on his picture. Idlout was standing behind him, ready to fire. We both gave a warning shout.

"Look out, Pierre! It's too close. Stop now, you've got enough. It's too dangerous."

I motioned to Idlout, and he took aim. He was a good shot; the bullet hit the bear in the shoulder, penetrated the heart and lungs. But the fur was not spoilt, which was of great importance to the Eskimos. David skinned the bear in ten minutes; then Idlout cut out the fangs, with a view to the skin being stuffed at some later date. It was left to freeze for a few minutes before being rolled up and stowed on the sled.

The Eskimos did not eat any of the meat and they prevented the huskies from getting at the carcass. This bear had been suffering from trichinosis, and the signs of the dreaded worm parasite were pointed out to me.

It was then about three o'clock, and the weather was calm; Griffith Island could just be seen far to the north, and Lawther Island stood out on the western horizon. Idlout decided to hunt over this wide expanse of frozen sea, at the same time gradually heading back towards Resolute.

Every half-hour or so, Idlout stopped for David and Pierre to catch up; and nearly always the skidoo refused to start. By the time Idlout had cleaned the plugs, the huskies were a mile or two ahead; but we soon overtook them. There were many bear tracks to be seen, some quite fresh, and all were going north.

We stopped to make camp at about nine o'clock, pitching the tent in front of a high wall of ice. Facing us was a large flat ice-field stretching away to the south and bounded by a line of icebergs that looked like a range of snow-clad hills. We carried our bundles into the tent. David had not yet unhitched his team, and the tired huskies were stretched out in the snow or curled up with their muzzles tucked into their bellies. And it was then that David's keen eye caught sight of the bear.

"Nanook! Nanook!" he shouted.

About two hundred yards away, a very big polar bear was watching us. David's shout roused the huskies, and they leapt to their feet barking furiously. David ran to the sled, and Pierre and I hurried to get on it. Luckily, the pack containing the cameras had not been unloaded, and Pierre got them ready. Idlout had dashed for his skidoo, but could not get the engine to start. We left him to it. The bear had gone bounding off southward across the ice-field, and our huskies were being out-distanced despite their eagerness. One of them fell and got caught up by the sled. I tried to free him, and got out my knife to cut the trace, but just then David drew the team to a stop. Seeing that the bear was gaining ground, he released all the dogs and ran after them armed only with his knife. Pierre followed him, and I brought up the rear, carrying a pack in either hand. I had picked up all our equipment—cameras, batteries, accessories and spare film.

At one moment the bear was cornered by the huskies on a hillock of ice, but it charged twice and scattered its enemies, then bounded off. I was soon a long way behind, for the packs were heavy and the snow was uneven. I lost sight of the others. The bear must have travelled five or six miles, and I had covered only half the distance. I was hoping for Idlout to come along, and at last heard the noise of his engine. I signalled wildly to him, but he could not have seen me. He went speeding on towards the hunt.

When I at last got within sight of the bear it had taken refuge on an iceberg that gave it a clear space for manoeuvre. The huskies were keeping their distance. As I drew near, the bear lunged forward and sent a husky hurtling through the air, then made a break in my direction; but the dogs were harassing him, and he was forced to fall back.

It only now occurs to me what might have happened if the bear had broken through the circle of huskies. He was coming straight for me, and I should have been nicely caught, with my two heavy packs and only a pocket-knife for a weapon. But at the time we were all intent on the hunt and had no thought of danger. I had felt anxious about marauding bears when in the tent at night, but during the hunt I was too excited to be afraid.

The sun was still well above the horizon. The time was eleven at night, and the light was brilliant.

I reached the others, and then had a good view of the bear. He was huge, seemed ten feet tall. And he was in a very dangerous mood. Several huskies had withdrawn from the fray and were squatting in the snow, licking their wounds.

Once or twice the bear almost escaped. He bounded forward at a husky, which escaped by darting through Pierre's legs. The huskies were hardly barking at all, only to distract the bear's attention when they saw one of their number was in danger. The bear made no sound either. He was a magnificent animal, quick, supple, graceful.

Pierre was still filming. Idlout became anxious. The bear was increasingly aggressive. Idlout fired his rifle into the air, and the sound brought the bear up with a start. The huskies had recovered their courage. They had kept the bear cornered for at least half an hour, however, and could not go on much longer.

"Have you finished, Pierre?" said Idlout. "He is now very dangerous. He will escape."

"All right. Shoot him."

Idlout fired, and the huge animal fell dead on the snow.

The midnight sun lit up a strange scene. David tied a thong round the animal's jaws, hitched the few huskies that still had energy left, and hauled the long white carcass across the snow while the other huskies fastened their teeth into their enemy. By the time the bear had been skinned and the meat cut up, the sun was climbing higher in the sky.

We all went back to the tent and prepared to have a few hours' sleep. There was a joyful atmosphere, and the cold was forgotten. Three bears in less than three days was good hunting for the two Eskimos. Pierre was happy too. He had his three bears. "And you never thought I would, did you?" he teased me.

We started on the way back next morning, heading towards Griffith Island. To reach it, we had to make our way through a chaotic and dangerous mass of pack-ice. I was again astride the small sled towed by the skidoo. I have been told that I ride a horse well, but no cross-country event or jumping meet I ever took part in had anything to compare with this obstacle-race on ice that lasted from nine in the morning to five in the evening.

After the midday halt, Idlout went on ahead and we soon lost sight of David and Pierre, who were progressing placidly at the pace of the huskies. But as we drew near Griffith Island the pack-ice became worse and Idlout had great difficulty in finding a way through; there were huge, jagged blocks of ice all round us, frozen waves thirty feet high. The island looked quite close, but we seemed to be getting no nearer to it. Idlout was going backwards and forwards, and I was thrown from my seat more than once. Fortunately the skidoo was behaving itself and gave no mechanical trouble, but its track got wedged among the ice blocks and I had to help Idlout to free the sled and lift the skidoo clear. This became exhausting after a time, and finally Idlout said, pointing to the shore, "You walk, and wait for me there."

I quite enjoyed scrambling over the mass of pack-ice; I did not feel the cold, and the high hills of the island sheltered me from the north wind. However, I had to be careful, for some of the icy heaps were loose, and once I fell into a gap up to my waist, the soft snow covering it having given way under me. Now and again I heard the skidoo in the distance; Idlout was having to make a wide detour.

I reached the shore feeling all the better for the exercise, and was able to enjoy the fantastic scenery, the tumbled pack-ice filling the Barrow Strait, and the many islands poking up in the south and west, with the rectangular outline of Lawther Island just visible on the horizon.

Idlout joined me, and I took my seat again. He drove straight up the snow-covered hillside at its steepest point, demonstrating the power and versatility of his machine. The summit was bare of snow, and we skidded about on the frozen gravel. Idlout intended going directly across the island, but the descent was too dangerous and he tried going around the hillside. The sled kept slipping downward, pulling against the skidoo, and I was obliged to get off and run alongside, holding it in place. Finally, we dropped down into a valley with a frozen lake. During the run down I tried desperately to use my feet as a brake, but with little success. Idlout went at full speed to avoid being overtaken by the weighted sled.

We then went westward down the valley and reached the shore again by way of a cove. Far ahead of us was David's sled. Idlout was obviously annoyed at not being in the lead; he opened the throttle and roared away at forty miles an hour, taking no notice of my protests.

We passed the others, and I saw Pierre waving to me. David sat imperturbably watching his team trot along at a steady pace.

Idlout was driving along the shore as much as possible, and I noticed some traps placed among a stretch of moraine; one of them held a magnificent white fox, and I shouted to Idlout to stop, but with no more success than before. I made signs to Pierre, but he was too far away. It was the only white fox we ever saw.

When we reached the strait between Cornwallis and Griffith Island, we caught the blast of the north wind again, but Idlout continued at full speed. He suddenly stopped when we were out in the middle of the strait, took a white screen from a crate and unfolded it; then he picked up his rifle, motioned to me to remain silent and still, and went off. Many yards distant, a seal was asleep in the sun, probably by the side of its breathing-hole. Hidden by the screen, Idlout gradually drew nearer to the seal, making a semi-circular approach. Then the seal suddenly raised its head and plunged back into its hole.

Idlout returned, looking sheepish. "Bad wind," he explained.

Idlout set off again and never stopped until we reached journey's end, zigzagging across the pack-ice. There were many tracks of sleds and skidoos as we approached Resolute. We could see the radio towers, the dome of an observatory and the fuel tanks on the hill. It all seemed quite near, but was still a good way off.

We ran up the shore on the west side of Resolute Bay, climbed the slope to the plateau and came to a stop outside the big building where Pierre and I were staying. It was five in the evening. I was worn out, but the day's activities had done me a lot of good.

I was about to invite Idlout to have a meal, but he was off again before I had time. I took a bath and changed, then went down to the restaurant, and found Idlout tucking into a large helping. He hardly looked up to give me a fleeting smile. I took the opportunity to pay him, generously. He pocketed the bills without a word, and went on eating.

It was nine o'clock when Pierre and David arrived. I went down to the settlement to meet them. I had shaved, rested and eaten, so was all the more struck by the lines of fatigue on Pierre's reddened face. During the three days of almost continual hunting we had covered a distance of about 250 miles. Added to our journeys when based on Igloolik and Snowdrift, it made an imposing total: the equivalent of the distance from Paris to Bucharest.

All we needed, to complete our programme, was to find and film some musk-oxen. Mr Jacobsen had suggested the area around Eureka, and had advised me to approach Air Atlas about chartering a plane. This was a private company owning three or four aircraft, based on Resolute, and run by an experienced, elderly pilot named Phipps. He was employed by all the scientific missions which installed camps in the north of the Arctic Archipelago during the summer months. He and his Italian mechanic made a colourful pair; he was small and plump, the other was dark and thin. In their warm clothing, heavy boots and fur caps, they were ready to fly anywhere at any time, to land on an ice-field or a deserted island.

I went and saw Phipps and told him of my desire to go to Eureka, to fly over the glaciers of Axel Heiberg Island and to find a herd of musk-oxen.

"Why go all that far?" he said. "I can take you to Bathurst Island and back in a day, and you'll find many musk-oxen there. That wouldn't cost you nearly as much, for unfortunately my Stinson is being repaired and I've only an Otter available."

I gladly agreed to his suggestion. But man proposes and the blizzard disposes. The day we should have flown to Bathurst, all aircraft were grounded by a blizzard; and Phipps was not available for the rest of the week, his planes having been chartered by scientific missions.

Professor Fritz Muller, of McGill University, flew in with half-a-dozen students of glaciology, on the regular Monday plane from Montreal. They were going to set up their summer camp on Axel Heiberg Island again. Fritz Muller was an old acquaintance of mine. He had been a member of the second Swiss Everest expedition. We spent the evening together, talking about mutual friends and mountain climbing, and before we parted he gave me some very useful advice about musk-oxen.

"Be very wary of them," he said. "They are reputed to be timid and good-natured, but in my opinion they can be very dangerous animals, for you never know what they'll do next. I've never been so near death as on one day last summer when a friend and I went to take photos of musk-oxen. We came across one magnificent musk-ox alone on a hillock. Now we thought we knew all about these animals, especially their reactions. They try to break out when cornered, but they always charge up a slope, never down it. At least, so all the experts maintained.

"Well, we approached this musk-ox and were kneeling in the snow, photographing it from below, lower down the slope, when it suddenly charged down at us. We just had time to dive to one side, but the dog that was with us got hurled into the air by the animal's horns, was caught on a horn again as it came down and was ripped open. Neither I nor my friend would have been in any better condition, believe me."

I remembered Muller's advice. All the same, we had to photograph these musk-oxen. Phipps proposed a solution to our problems. He was flying the mail out to Greely Fjord, on latitude 82, between the weather stations of Eureka and Alert; and, if permission was given, he would take Pierre and me with him, for the plane had little cargo on board. This was a wonderful and unexpected offer. A radio message was sent to the station at Greely Fjord and a reply came to say that we should be very welcome, but if our main object was to find musk-oxen we should do better to go to Eureka, for the herds could be more easily reached from there.

"That's all right," said Phipps. "The plane's taking mail to Eureka as well. So if you change your mind on the way, you'll have only to tell the pilot."

The blizzard was blowing again at Resolute, but we were scarcely aware of it in this compact little world where some two hundred people live the whole year round. Unfortunately, strong dislikes sometimes develop between these men thrown together in the arctic solitudes, and then the regulations are enforced. Any man who makes trouble may have his contract terminated and be flown out.

I met about a hundred of the men employed, of all classes and conditions, while I was at Resolute; very few had come from a sense of adventure. Theirs was the routine life of technician, mechanic or electrician, doing what was required of them just as in a factory at New York or Montreal. There was one difference—the pay. A year at one of these bases is well worth it, financially. The men at Resolute made no secret of it, they had come to the Arctic to "make some dollars".

Phipps came to warn us that the Otter would be leaving for Greely Fjord in an hour. We just had time to get ready; we were taking the minimum of equipment. The sky was not very encouraging, however; the hills were shrouded in fog and there was an icy wind. But we should be able to land up north, it seemed, and that was the main thing. We were going to fly many miles farther north, where there was nothing but barren mountains, frozen islands, and inlets filled with pack-ice; where there were no Eskimos, no human life at all, except at the meteorological stations.

The Otter was a very safe but slow aircraft, and we took more than three hours to reach our destination. First we flew over Cornwallis Island and saw how very much snow there was; this explained the absence of musk-oxen, for in winter these grazing mammals seek windswept spaces where the frozen grass remains uncovered. Our pilot was in radio communication with Resolute and Eureka; he frequently consulted his map, and I could see the names of the places we were flying over—Belcher Channel, the Grinnell Peninsula, then Axel Heiberg Island, which is separated from Ellesmere Island by Eureka Sound. Now and again a gap in the clouds gave glimpses of glaciers, fjords and sparkling mountains. This Polar landscape is one of the most beautiful in the world. The mountains on Ellesmere Island and Axel Heiberg Island reach heights of ten thousand feet and are practically unknown. The bare earth appeared, a tortured, windswept landscape with ridges of naked rock and stretches of gravel; less snow was seen, the wind grew in strength, clouds brimmed over the hilltops, and here and there a sheet of ice gleamed on the frozen sea. And, to my surprise, I occasionally caught sight of an expanse of open water steaming like a hot spring.

The slow and uneventful flight had lasted several hours when our pilot flew low over a hill and there below us was a beautiful fjord as placid as a lake. On the northern shore could be seen several buildings, one with a high dome—an unexpected sight in these solitudes. Our pilot radioed our important question about musk-oxen, and the reply was that there were some quite near. The message ended with typical British humour: "French cameramen are welcome to Eureka, although we should have preferred French girls."

The landing-strip was no more than a few hundred feet of frozen earth on the edge of a mass of moraine, but our pilot showed his skill by bringing the heavy plane down neatly.

A tall, bearded young man came out in a jeep to greet us; he told us his name was Larry Petznick and that he was in charge of the Eureka Weather Station. We got into his jeep and five minutes later were making the acquaintance of his companions. There were twelve meteorologists in all, constantly observing and transmitting the weather conditions. Eureka is one of the most northerly of the weather stations covering the earth, being situated on the Fosheim Peninsula, in the northwest of Ellesmere Island, on latitude 80. Only one other station is nearer the North Pole—Alert, on latitude 83, on the north shore of Ellesmere Island, at the northern end of Robeson Channel.

The Eureka team work in shifts. I can hardly call them day and night shifts, for when I was there the sunshine and daylight were even more continuous than at Resolute. After a few days, it was impossible to keep to a normal timetable. The splendid human mechanism which responds to night and day, repose and action, is quite thrown out of gear. I would drop off to sleep at five in the morning, wake up at noon. Pierre went out to photograph the landscape at midnight, and we hunted white hares at three in the morning.

The scientists are very comfortably housed. The buildings are all close to one another; the largest is the domed one containing the recording apparatus. Weather balloons are sent up twice a day. Each carries a little box which is a technical marvel; it registers and sends back the temperature, atmospheric pressure and wind velocity.

The men at Eureka were just emerging from the long winter night, when temperatures had been down to seventy below. Their shortest term of duty is one year, but some of the men had been at Eureka for several years and seemed to like it. Their only regret was that they would never find wives if they remained there—hence the nostalgic element in the radio message we had received.

Our pilot had taken off again almost at once for Greely Fjord, an hour's flight to the north. He landed there just in time, for we heard by radio that Greely Fjord was being swept by a blizzard too. For two days after our arrival we were kept indoors most of the time by the bad weather, taking advantage of occasional lulls to photograph the spectacular scenery. The cloud formations were constantly changing; they sometimes gave one the impression of standing in a huge crater that was billowing smoke. Snowflakes were scurrying along the ice-covered Slidre Fjord, which still had many icebergs in its grip.

The weather improved and Pierre and I set out on a snowmobile driven by one of the radio-operators who was off duty. Another Canadian came with us, armed with a rifle in case of danger from the musk-oxen. We had been travelling eastward along the fjord for about an hour when one of the Canadians, who was scanning the hills of the Fosheim Peninsula through field-glasses, announced that he could see a herd of musk-oxen. There were about thirty, scattered like cows on an Alpine slope. We were still several miles away, and we proceeded cautiously, stopping every time we noticed an unusual movement among the herd. But they seemed quite peaceful, the calves frisking about and the bulls calmly grazing.

We were down-wind from the herd, so were able to hide our vehicle behind an iceberg without drawing attention. Then we continued on foot. Our aim was to surround the herd, so that it would form its usual, defensive ring. This is a sound defence against wolves, but unfortunately for the musk-ox has been very helpful to the hunter. The crews of whalers slaughtered whole herds during the nineteenth century, to obtain stocks of meat, and seriously depleted the species.

The musk-ox is now a protected animal; even Eskimos, who have the right to hunt game all over the Arctic, are forbidden to shoot it. The musk-ox has a short life in any case, and multiplies slowly. The cows commonly calve every other year.

We had flown over a herd of these splendid animals when crossing the Barren Lands, on our way from Snowdrift to Igloolik, and had been able to admire this ruminant with its thick coat drooping down to its hooves, giving it an appearance similar to the Tibetan yak.

The musk-ox is in fact an ovibos. It resembles a large, long-haired ram. Its horns are sharp and curve forward, growing out from a very strong frontal bone structure which in the male forms a kind of shield, as in the African buffalo. The very thick fur makes it look bigger than it really is. The finest bulls rarely weigh more than nine hundred pounds; the average is about seven hundred.

We approached the herd slowly and carefully, Pierre and I going straight towards it—he carrying the cine-camera on its tripod and I the pack containing the other cameras and spare film—while the two Canadians fanned out to left and right. The herd was still grazing on the hillside, passing from one windswept hummock to another, and Pierre was able to film it, using his telescopic lens. We began advancing slowly; whenever we saw a bull stop grazing and look up, we froze in our tracks. The herd was reassured, and we went on again. Our companions to the right and left were following the same tactics.

We had reached the foot of the hill when there was a sudden agitation among the herd; this time we had really been spotted. The bulls began galloping about, rounding up the cows and calves and assembling them on a hillock. We continued our slow and patient approach, making use of every bit of cover—like infantrymen in training.

One of the Canadians had worked his way unseen along a dip in the ground and reached the top of the hill; he showed himself to the herd, looking down upon it. The other man was advancing slowly along a bare ridge to the right. The bulls were anxiously circling the herd, rounding up the calves which, unaware of danger, tried to wander away.

Rather breathless after our long walk, Pierre and I finally arrived within a dozen yards of the compact herd. The musk-oxen glared at us, their phosphorescent eyes shining through their thick, dangling fur. We were able to admire them in detail—the white shield of the frontal bone structure, the horns as sharp as daggers, the folds of long tawny hair hanging down to their hooves, as though caparisoned for a ceremony. The shades ranged from dark red on the flanks to light gold under the belly.

Unfortunately, they did not care for our presence and galloped off to another hillock. We followed them, openly; the four of us deliberately showed ourselves so that they would realise they were surrounded and form a defensive circle. And this they did, presenting a solid mass of fur-clad bodies, a kind of thirty-headed hydra. Occasionally one or two enquiring little heads peeped out between the cows' legs, but were at once thrust back into the middle. There were three bulls, and they had taken positions from where they could watch all points of the compass. It was a solid defence.

Pierre was filming, and we were only about a dozen yards from the herd. A strong wind was blowing, sending the snow swirling between the animals' legs; the distant scene was blotted out by a mist of snow, but the ice in the fjord could be seen gleaming brightly. The bulls still had their winter coats, but were beginning to shed them. Little tufts of hair flew about in the wind.

The herd became more and more agitated. The bulls kept pawing the ground and lowering their heads; these were usually signs of a charge. Now and again one would step forward and try to induce the others to flee; but one of us had only to move towards the animal for it to retreat. We kept up this rather dangerous game for two hours, while Pierre filmed and photographed. The Canadians stood ready to fire if the animals charged, and I kept driving back any animal that showed initiative.

"I've finished," said Pierre. "They can go now. I've filmed everything that can be filmed. Let them go."

But our most difficult task was to persuade them to go, to make them break up their defensive formation and run.

We had first to leave a way free for them. The four of us gathered on one side, leaving the way clear to the east. But the herd hesitated, fearing a trap, although the formation was beginning to disintegrate. The anxious bulls went to and fro, sniffing and pawing the ground. I threw a few stones at them, and this decided matters. An old bull rushed down the slope, just as Fritz Muller had said; the herd followed, the bulls on the outside and hurrying to and fro, ushering the young calves that were getting left behind. Soon their stampede became more orderly, and resembled a fleeing herd of bison. The old bull led the way, the strongest animals on the outside of the triangular mass and the youngest carried along in the middle.

It was a magnificent spectacle, a vision from another age, as these wild animals rushed away in full freedom towards the mountains and disappeared among the Polar snows.

We were in high spirits as the snowmobile took us back over the ice, and that evening was one of the most enjoyable we spent. It was thanks to our new-found friends at Eureka that we had such success.

Our pilot was still at Greely Fjord, grounded by the bad weather, and once again we had to wait.

"Why don't you come and see our white hares?" said Larry.

So that night Pierre went out with his camera. Arctic hares abounded, large, pure white, and so tame that sometimes the only way to make them move was to throw a stone at them. It was like being in Wonderland. The midnight sun was shining, the hares gambolled about, leaping on their hind legs like kangaroos or drumming the ground with their tails, nibbling at dry grass, pricking up their ears and jumping towards us with their dainty little forepaws folded on their chests. They were little pets, and provided the only memory of gentleness and *joie de vivre* that I took away with me from the Polar regions. Long may they live in peace, without danger from any man or beast, except the white wolf.

The plane came for us next day. We felt rather sad as we again flew over those unknown lands, those unnamed glaciers and fjords that cut deep into Ellesmere and Axel Heiberg Island. Shortly after we left, the weather cleared and we saw the great straits in their eternal stillness, Grinnell and then snowbound Cornwallis, and finally the red clump that was Resolute.

The next few days were spent waiting for a plane to take us south. The Great Adventure was over. Looking through my diary, I see only a few more short entries: May 13: Resolute, rested. May 14, 15, 16: Resolute, waiting, very tired.

Pierre and I wandered about the base. We knew all the men by sight if not by name. In the evenings they gathered in groups in the bar and the hall where movies were shown. During the short time we stayed there we realised how hard this communal reclusion must be, with everyone having to put up with the others and the slightest cross word being likely to spark off a quarrel. Working hours are certainly the only ones that pass quickly at Resolute.

We found the waiting very long, despite all that was done for us and the pleasant hours spent with Mr Kingan and with Phipps. We took part in the weekly sweepstake, to which all the Eskimos were invited and in which they took a keen interest. I did not see Idlout again; he had flown on the first available plane to Frobisher, where he hoped to find another wife, having lost his first a year ago. David Windgot came to the base once, smiling and quiet as usual. We shook hands, and I had the impression that he quite liked me. But who can tell what an Eskimo is feeling?

I remember now that when I left Snowdrift, Henri Catholique came to see me and said shyly, "If ever you come back, I'd like to take a trip with you again."

No Eskimo ever said that to me; they are all too proud. And of course I do belong to the white race they scorn; for the Eskimos are Inuk, *the* men—the only ones who can live by their own resources in the arctic climate, probably the most terrible in the world.

The Constellation aircraft bound for Frobisher landed at Resolute at nine in the morning; it was well behind schedule, and had not been able to land at Hall Beach because of the spring fog. We were very surprised to see Jim Hennings on the plane; he was hoping to be able to land at Hall Beach on the return journey, to get back to Igloolik. We took off several hours late and flew above clouds which thickened as we progressed.

An attempt to land at Hall Beach almost ended in disaster. The pilot went down to 150 feet, then opened up and climbed again, for visibility on the ground was nil. He flew on to Frobisher, which he had left early in the morning with all the other passengers. Flights in the arctic regions are always subject to this uncertainty, which puts a great strain on both crews and aircraft. But no one complained. A delay of five or six days is accepted as normal. Jim Hennings was back again at Frobisher, after having flown hundreds of miles in the day and got no nearer home.

Frobisher, situated at the head of the bay of that name, is the largest centre in the eastern Arctic. A huge building constructed on piles, because of the permafrost, houses all the administrative offices and also serves as a hotel for people in transit.

The Eskimo settlement, with a population of about fifteen hundred, is housed in prefabs. But when a film company recently went there to shoot some exteriors, no more than three or four huskies could be found to make a team.

Frobisher Bay as I saw it reminded me of a Lapland fjord in springtime. The rock-face was showing on the weather-beaten mountains. The bay, which has an extensive coastline, was still frozen hard, but the thaw had set in on the hillsides. For the first time since our flight north, we saw tumbling water, and walked on spongy marsh moss. But our stay was short. We had hoped to fly over the Cumberland Mountains as far as Pangnirtung and Padloping, and the officer in charge of the Mounted Police post kindly offered to take us in his plane when he went on an inspection of the region. Unfortunately, in that season, Baffin Island is shrouded in fog for a month, due to the thawing of pack-ice. It was impossible for the plane to take off, and even more so to land on the narrow strips laid out on cliff-tops. So we had to give up the idea, and flew to Montreal.

The most impressive moment in the whole of our three-month expedition was just before the plane landed at Fort Chimo, in Quebec's Ungava Bay. The light had gradually faded over the vast frozen seas, and it was barely possible to make out the long black crevasses and stretches of water which showed where the ice was breaking up. Then the sunset reddened the sky; soon afterwards we plunged into darkness, and it was like entering a new world. After so many days with the sun circling above, to see it set at last brought us back into our own world. It was a strange feeling to sink into the peace of darkness, to know that the sun would rise again tomorrow and that nothing had changed.

A few hours later we saw the sun rising over Montreal. Beneath us, the thousands of lights of the great city were glimmering in orderly array. We were flying at a high altitude and could have proclaimed to the waking city that the sun was again shining on the earth. It was a sweet and soothing feeling.

The adventure we had just lived through seemed quite unbelievable—up north among the Inuk, and farther north still, in the icy wastes where the musk-oxen roam.

"We'll have to put a tie on now," said Pierre sadly.

"You mean a halter."